PROFESSING FEMINISM

PROFESSING FEMINISM

Cautionary Tales from the
Strange World of Women's Studies

DAPHNE PATAI
AND
NORETTA KOERTGE

A New Republic Book
BasicBooks
A Division of HarperCollins*Publishers*

Designed by Ellen Levine

LIBRARY OF CONGRESS CATALOGING-IN-PUBLICATION DATA

Patai, Daphne, 1943–
    Professing feminism : cautionary tales from the strange world of
women's studies / Daphne Patai and Noretta Koertge.
        p. cm.
    Includes index.
    ISBN 0–465–09821–5
    1. Women's studies—United States. I. Koertge, Noretta.
II. Title.
HQ1181.U5P37   1994
305.42'0973—dc20   94–18271
                                                                CIP

94 95 96 97 ❖/HC 9 8 7 6 5 4 3 2 1

For Gerald
—D. P.

For Deborah, Matthew, and Emma
—N. K.

Lying is done with words, and also with silence.
—ADRIENNE RICH

Every revolutionary ends by becoming either
an oppressor or a heretic.
—ALBERT CAMUS

CONTENTS

ACKNOWLEDGMENTS xi
PROLOGUE: ON AIRING DIRTY LINEN xiii

1 INTRODUCTION TO THE WORLD OF WOMEN'S STUDIES 1

2 CAUTIONARY TALES FROM WOMEN WHO WALKED AWAY 11
  Students Who Stomp in Seminars
  Political Purity and Hostile Colleagues
  "Women's Studies Can Be Harmful"
  "The Chickens Come Home to Roost"
  "Who Owns Women's Studies?"
  Scholarship in a Sea of Propaganda

3 IDEOLOGY AND IDENTITY: PLAYING THE OPPRESSION SWEEPSTAKES 44
  Unraveling the Web of Feminist Discontents
  IDPOL: Identity Politics and Ideological Policing
   The Amazon Laughed: "Tell Your Brothers"
   Sleeping with the Enemy
   Dismantling White Women's Studies
   Patriarchy and Pigs at the Trough
  The Price of Oppressive Privilege

4 PROSELYTIZING AND POLICING IN THE FEMINIST CLASSROOM 81
  Surviving Women's Studies: Students' Perspectives
  Training the Cadres
   Fulmination and Ferment
   Propaganda and Resistance

Confusion and Condemnation
Feeling Good versus Becoming Competent
Feminist Pedagogy: A Midterm Report

5   SEMANTIC SORCERY: RHETORIC OVERTAKES REALITY   115
Throwing Away the Master's Tools: Playing TOTAL REJ
WORDMAGIC and Other Language Games
Phony Philology
Metaphor Madness
Linguistic Litmus Tests
Accordion Concepts
The Power of Naming

6   BIODENIAL AND OTHER SUBVERSIVE STRATAGEMS   135
Socially Constructing the Birds and the Bees
Is the Mind the Only Sex Organ?
GENDERAGENDA: Cleansing the Curriculum of Phallic
Phantasms
How "Feminine" Tunes Are "Brutally Quashed"
"Logic . . . Is Insane"
Opposition to Exact Science

7   "MIRROR, MIRROR ON THE WALL": FEMINIST SELF-SCRUTINY   158
Assessing Women's Studies
"Women's Ways of Knowing"
The Mission of Women's Studies
Connected Knowing and the "Believing Game"
Critical Thinking, Feminist Style
"Quality Control": Big Sister Is Watching You

8   CULTS, COMMUNES, AND CLICKS   183
True Believers All
Problems in the Promised Land
Arrested Development
"For Fear of Finding Something Worse"

9   FROM DOGMA TO DIALOGUE: THE IMPORTANCE OF LIBERAL VALUES   207

POSTSCRIPT   216
NOTES   219
INDEX   227

ACKNOWLEDGMENTS

IN WRITING THIS BOOK, we have been aided by the contributions of a great many people. First, we wish to thank the dozens of feminists—mostly women, but a few men as well—who shared their experiences of Women's Studies with us, either in tape-recorded interviews or by letter and E-mail. It is customary to mention that some of the folks whose help one is acknowledging may not agree with parts of the book. In our case, given the critical message of this work, there are undoubtedly people to whom we are indebted who will disagree with practically everything we have written. So be it; still, we thank all of our fellow feminists, even those who think we are wrong-headed, for demonstrating what should be abundantly clear to all, that women can be just as brave and cowardly, generous and selfish, thoughtful and obtuse, insightful and insensitive as the other half of the human race. The failures of feminism are no different from the failures of all grand schemes that have set out to improve human society in one fell swoop, and they remind us of how important it is to have enlightened institutions and traditions that foster open discussion and critical debate.

We also wish to thank Peter Edidin, formerly of New Republic Books, who first encouraged us to write this book and then provided editorial advice. Special thanks go to Angela Ingram and

Edward Grant for their useful and detailed comments on the manuscript. We are grateful, as well, to Claudia Van der Heuvel for expert transcribing and research assistance, and to Teresa Anderson for turning barely legible scribbles into word-processed prose.

Daphne Patai   *Noretta Koertge*
Amherst, Massachusetts   *Bloomington, Indiana*

PROLOGUE

On Airing Dirty Linen

THIS BOOK began eight years ago, with a number of long conversations under the honey locust trees in the courtyard of The Runcible Spoon coffee shop in Bloomington, Indiana. Daphne, on leave from the University of Massachusetts at Amherst, was spending the year as a fellow at Indiana University's Institute for Advanced Study and offered to be a visiting speaker for Women's Studies classes. Noretta was teaching a seminar on Concepts of Gender and Sexuality at the time and invited Daphne to lecture about her research on sex role reversals in utopian fiction. As we became friends, our conversations meandered from the political commitments of novelists to the social responsibility of scientists, from complaints about lazy students to cynical remarks about university administrators—the standard chitchat of academics, except for the fact that almost everything we talked about was informed by, or at least flavored with, ideas and analyses that had developed within contemporary feminism.

But there was another thread that ran through those early conversations. As we got to know each other better and spoke more frankly, we began to discuss our concerns about the direction in which Women's Studies programs and feminism in general appeared to be heading. At first, we tended to view the unpleasant little anecdotes we reported to each other—irregularities in the way programs conducted their affairs or odd methodological turns in feminist research—as isolated excesses or local anomalies.

As the years passed and our conversations continued, usually long distance, first by post and then by electronic mail, it became increasingly clear to us that what we were really saying, if only we had the courage to admit it, was that many of the central tenets and favored practices of feminism within today's academy are seriously flawed. But it is one thing to convince yourself that the Empress has threadbare clothes and quite another to shout it in the streets, as the difficulties we experienced while we worked on this book demonstrated to us.

In many ways, ours was an unlikely collaboration. We were born on opposite sides of the globe; we have different computer preferences, sexual preferences, politico-economic philosophies, and disciplinary backgrounds, and, as we quickly discovered, quite different writing styles. But each of us in her own way has invested a great deal of intellectual and emotional energy in feminism and Women's Studies. We each identify strongly with the feminist movement. In criticizing certain aspects of feminism, we are therefore not only repudiating some of our own previous beliefs and practices but also jeopardizing friendships with many colleagues and allies. Even the people who basically agree with us often remarked during interviews how important it is not to criticize feminism in a way that would give legitimacy to the political and religious right. The old saying about not airing dirty linen in public kept popping up.

Nevertheless, in the end, we decided we should speak out about the troubling aspects of Women's Studies as we see them. Perhaps it was in part our feminist training that spurred us on. After all, does feminism itself not counsel women to refuse to be silenced by coercive ideological systems? Does feminism not tell us to criticize and dismantle traditions and institutions that harm women by impeding their development in all spheres, including—we would say, especially—the intellectual and moral? Does it not warn us about the costs of political expediency, and has it not encouraged women not to shy away from espousing positions that may be unpopular or misunderstood? And is it not feminism itself that teaches us how difficult and also dangerous it is to try to keep dirty linen within the household precisely because the boundary between private and public is so porous?

We believe that it is feminists, not their opponents, who must speak out about contemporary feminism's tendency to turn into a parody of itself. Where did things go wrong? And why? Answering these questions is hard enough; it is even more difficult to suggest solutions. But just as naming and examining the problem was an important accomplishment of the women's movement in its early days, so, we are confident, it matters today that attention be paid to the harm done to contemporary feminism by the ideological policing and intolerance going on in its own ranks.

From our personal experience we knew that some programs, in their fervor to use the academy as a staging ground for the liberation of women, were not doing a good job of educating them. But what we did not know was how widespread and deeply rooted these failures were, nor how serious their adverse effects. To find out, we began our research in typical feminist fashion—by asking a variety of women to talk about their own experience in Women's Studies.

When we told colleagues in Women's Studies that we were doing research about problems within contemporary feminism, some assumed we were referring to "the backlash"—a pejorative that is today slapped onto any and every criticism of feminism and whose main function seems to be to shut down discussion. Others thought we would write about lack of administrative support for Women's Studies. When we said, no, we were dealing with internal difficulties, our colleagues' conjectures turned either to racism and other diversity issues or to doctrinal conflicts over pornography, postmodernism, psychoanalysis, and the like. But as we began to speak of "ideological policing," "intolerance," "dogmatism," we evoked a different kind of response—knowing looks and sighs, a host of nonverbal admissions that things were not quite right after all. These gestures, however, were routinely and rapidly followed by expressions of concern about "horizontal hostility" (women criticizing other women), or about the possible appropriation by political enemies of any open critique of feminism.

It was only when we talked to some "exiles" from Women's Studies—colleagues who still considered themselves to be feminists and whose work and lives have been deeply marked by feminism, but who for one reason or another had withdrawn to other departments, or were contemplating such a move—that we found women who were prepared to admit the seriousness of the issues we were raising. Each of these women who has walked away, taken what we call "inner flight," or in other respects has become alienated from the enterprise of Women's Studies contributed a portion of the analysis we present here. Some complained to us of improper academic procedures or the tyranny of "consensus" in decision making; others were put off by personalistic and haphazard academic proceedings; still others resented the bullying tactics of militant students. Some felt that the pedagogy in many Women's Studies courses was thinly disguised indoctrination; others feared that the emphasis on "support" and "finding one's voice" threatened to turn Women's Studies classes into twelve-step programs or group therapy sessions. All expressed concern, disappointment, and unhappiness.

Academics are notorious complainers, and in every department and discipline one is apt to find faculty grousing about falling scholarly standards, undeserving colleagues, and students who are either too docile or too aggressive. But the tales we collected from women who had lost some or all of their confidence in Women's Studies stood out both qualitatively and quantitatively from the general background of academic grumbling. Furthermore, there was a pattern to the complaints that transcended local peculiarities and personality conflicts.

Again and again, women told us that they had long wanted to discuss their concerns but had felt isolated and hesitant to express opinions they knew could be dismissed as the experience of one disgruntled woman unable to thrive under the new feminist regime. Many of the women who were willing to talk with us were pained or distressed. No enemies of feminism lurked among them. Instead, we found sincere and thoughtful individuals, providing accounts of troubling experiences and disappointed hopes.

Our inquiry is concentrated on feminism as it is practiced in Women's Studies at colleges and universities. The reasons for this focus are self-evident to us. First of all, the academy is the scene we know best and care most about. More important, we recognize it as the setting that has provided a fascinating and—we think—revealing testing ground for feminist principles and claims.

Women's Studies programs have enjoyed the substantive protections afforded by the principle, and indeed the reality, of academic freedom. It is, in our view, the existence of the essentially liberal value of academic freedom that has allowed Women's Studies programs to develop in the diverse ways in which we observe them today. But our own experiences and those of many colleagues with whom we spoke have led us to conclude that some programs now deny the very values that allowed them to come into being. If Women's Studies does not promote, indeed does not stand for, open inquiry, critical exploration of multiple perspectives (even threatening ones), and scholarship not tethered to the political passions of the moment, what is there to be said for its presence in the academy?

Academe is in many respects a sheltered arena in which ideas and persuasions can be developed and thrashed out largely unconstrained by the world outside. But feminist academic behavior is not "academic." Feminism in the lecture hall, seminar, or committee room provides us with a virtual laboratory in which to study in microcosm the likely effects of social changes, were they to be set loose in the larger society. If even in the relatively protected world of the academy feminist endeavors, controlled by feminists themselves, too often run aground, should we expect them to do any better in the world at large?

The academy is also, as it turns out, a highly visible stage, upon which feminism's excesses have been plain to see for some time now. We are not claiming that every single Women's Studies program throughout the country displays the problems described in this book. But far too many do so for these matters to be buried or left unaired any longer. And this simple fact should be of major concern to feminists, wherever they are located. Important allies have already been lost. Too many among the first generation of feminists in the university, those who organized and fought for Women's Studies programs, are now profoundly alienated from these very programs and endeavors. More are on the verge of becoming disenchanted. Feminism cannot afford such a brain drain. Among women students—the next generation—"feminist" has already become a label many prefer to avoid. It is naive to imagine (or pretend) that this is all due to media malice and misrepresentation. Clearly, academic feminism must begin to acknowledge and address its considerable problems, or else shrink into an introverted and marginal sect.

A NOTE ON METHOD

Thirty women from around the country contributed their experiences and reflections to this work, in the form of lengthy and detailed taped interviews. Most of these women are or have been faculty members; some are or were students and staff members in Women's Studies programs. We have also utilized material offered to us from correspondence, memos, and journal entries, as well as communications from the International Electronic Forum for Women's Studies (WMST-List, run by Joan Korenman, the director of Women's Studies at the University of Maryland, Baltimore County), a rich source of information. While we have not conducted an exhaustive inventory of Women's Studies programs, everything we have learned convinces us that the voices heard in this book, and the problems discussed, are characteristic. Such a view is confirmed by the fact that many other women spoke to us of friends and acquaintances who had encountered similar situations, explaining why these individuals were not likely to be willing to talk to us.

In open-ended interviews (conducted between January and July,

1993) that lasted, on the average, three hours, we attempted to allow people to speak of their own experiences, their own hopes and expectations of feminism and Women's Studies programs, their own appraisals of the proper relation between educational and political commitments, their own pleasures and pains in the classroom and in their universities. Nearly every woman who figures in this book requested that her name, affiliation, and other identifying features be disguised. However alienated and disappointed these women (and we ourselves) felt, the desire not to embarrass colleagues and institutions continues to be strong, as is the reluctance to publicly acknowledge the failures of feminism in the academy.

We also note, with regret, that the desire for anonymity reflects some of the very problems this book aims to analyze: the tendency of feminism to stifle open debate and create an atmosphere in which disagreement is viewed as betrayal. We have honored all these requests and, for uniformity's sake, have incorporated many of our own accounts into the book in the same way.

1

Introduction to the World of Women's Studies

CHANGES IN THE STATUS OF WOMEN are undoubtedly among the most important social developments of the twentieth century. Each demand for equality has been contested; each step has made a vivid impression on the women who lived through it; each advance has become part of the birthright of the next generation. Despite the apparent lull in—and to some extent, even reversal of—women's gains during the 1950s, the contemporary feminist movement in the United States, now in its fourth decade, has carried the redefinition of women and their roles steadily forward.

In important ways, both intellectual and practical, this movement's agenda was shaped by the work of feminist scholars in the academy. The result of their efforts has been an enormous flowering of Women's Studies programs, feminist scholarship, and women's culture, as well as an increasing public awareness of job discrimination, domestic abuse, sexual assaults, and other impediments placed on women in the public and private spheres. Complementing all this attention, albeit on a more modest scale, have been political and economic gains for at least some women.

Women's Studies, which began in the late 1960s as individual courses typically offered through humanities departments, proliferated throughout the United States during the 1970s and 1980s. Now, after two and a half decades, there are more than six hundred undergraduate and several dozen graduate programs at colleges and universities. This success drove, and in turn was driven by, a spate of scholarly publications in various fields. During this time, too, the use of gender as a powerful conceptual tool and a key category of analysis in the humanities and social sciences transformed entire fields, of which feminist literary criticism was the first to attain national prominence and respectability.

Why, after these successes, have Women's Studies programs turned into such a combat zone? Some reasons are fairly ordinary. One is their anomalous position, which made them simultaneously contest and exploit established institutional structures. Another is frustration not only over the difficulty of getting more faculty positions but also over the slow pace of material change generally. Paradoxically, discontent and infighting also reflect the great achievement of Women's Studies. The study of gender is no longer news, and thus Women's Studies may seem to have lost some of its revolutionary appeal. Incoming students are no longer astonished to find Women's Studies programs in place; they take such programs for granted and are either attracted or hostile to them in advance.

Then, too, given the current economic and political climate, there is less optimism that the academic study of women and gender is itself an effective agent of change. Women's Studies programs also continue to experience conflicts over their acceptance in academe, and it is hard, over the long run, to sustain feminism's moral presuppositions and activist style unless new issues can be found around which to crusade.

But the deeper and far more disturbing reasons for the problems currently visible are, we believe, to be sought elsewhere: they are the direct result of self-destructive habits and assumptions that have grown up within Women's Studies itself. Long before the term "political correctness" gained currency in its present conservative/ironic sense, ideological policing was a common feature of Women's Studies programs. Women appraised one another; and, too frequently, found reason to judge others deficient, undeserving of the accolade "feminist."

Whereas feminists originally argued for a loosening of gender roles, now there is great pressure from within for conformity. Feminists used to urge women to explore their own sexuality freely, but now there is a figurative policing of the bedroom. At an early stage of second-wave feminism, consciousness-raising groups helped women work toward self-actualization and develop a nonstigmatized identity, but now women are pressured to conform to the microstereotypes of identity politics. In feminist pedagogy, the new valorization of women's modes of communication and interaction has led to the use of sentiment as a tool of coercion. Many feminist classrooms cultivate an insistence on "feeling," which, on examination, turns out to be the traditional split between intellect and emotion recycled, with the former still assigned to men and the latter to women. The characterizations of male and female have not changed; instead, the plus and minus signs associated with each gender have been reversed.

In yet another significant area of feminist endeavor, the early assumptions about women's "commonality" gave way to crucial realizations that not only gender but a variety of other important factors such as race, ethnicity, and sexual identity shape women's private and public selves and their life opportunities. In particular, "minority" women have increasingly entered feminist debates, which had too often neglected the problems these women face. But this valuable corrective now threatens to degenerate into a host of particularisms that could turn feminism into little more than a gathering of competing narrow "identities," each hotly promoted. Such wars have already been fought over sexual orientation, and we know how destructive they can be.

In each of these instances—as in many other aspects of contemporary feminism that we will explore in this book—we are witnessing the progressive deterioration of a vital movement. This has now reached the point that, today, distinctions between style and substance are blurred, escalation of rhetoric replaces real gains, and ostentatious posturing is taken for achievement. In the process, many women have come to feel marginalized by the coercive treatment received at the hands of some feminists and, as a result, are increasingly alienated from—and puzzled by—a movement they once embraced.

What troubled us most was that many of the aspects of Women's Studies that distanced, and in some cases drove away, women were the very features in which advocates took particular pride. The still-hopeful supporters of Women's Studies with whom we spoke often revealed, through their own accounts, the same landscape as that portrayed by the disillusioned. Where critics objected to emotional coercion in the classroom, advocates talked about the importance of transforming students' consciousness. Where dissenters saw feminist ideology distorting scholarship, advocates praised the virtues of research guided by political commitments. Where exiles complained about an atmosphere rife with hypocritical avoidance and shunning, advocates claimed to have found a sanctuary from patriarchal strife in groups based on the cultivation of women's "difference."

From the outset, Women's Studies occupied an unusual position in academe. It was not just multidisciplinary but had a dual agenda: educational (the study first of women and then of gender) and political (the correction of social injustice). As stated in the constitution of the National Women's Studies Association (NWSA):

> Women's Studies is the educational strategy of a breakthrough in consciousness and knowledge. The uniqueness of Women's Studies has been and remains its refusal to accept sterile divisions between the academy and community . . . between the individual and society. Women's Studies, then, is equipping women to transform the world to one that will be free of all oppression . . . [and is] a force which furthers the realization of feminist aims.[1]

Inevitable tensions have resulted from this grand, not to say grandiose, vision. As a brave new field that sprang up from grassroots efforts—first motivated by the student movement of the 1960s, and later spurred by the example of Black Studies programs—Women's Studies faced many obstacles within the university. The legitimation of any new academic field is a long process, but feminists believed that the challenges they faced were invariably manifestations of sexism. This sense of vulnerability contributed to the development of a siege mentality.

At the same time, Women's Studies was always allied with university reform: affirmative action, offices of women's affairs, and so on. Commitment to good causes meant that Women's Studies, in order to be effective, could not withdraw but had to play academic politics. This entailed a constant negotiation between feminist ideals (even assuming all feminist faculty agreed about what these were—which was hardly the case) and the pragmatics required to build a program in an academic setting. In the post-1960s atmosphere where in-your-face political activism was valorized above all else, feminist academics were often accused of being ivory-towered recluses, far removed from the barricades, and many academics accepted this characterization and felt guilty. Today, women "in the movement" are still leveling such charges against feminists in academe.

Confronting competing demands and pressures, Women's Studies adopted two self-defeating practices: academic separatism and a deference to political activism. These two strategies, as we shall see, are closely connected and reinforce each other.

Separatism has been a dominant theme since the inception of Women's Studies. The biblical injunction to "set yourself apart and be a separate people" describes a time-honored method for building group solidarity and is undoubtedly an effective way for a minority community to resist assimilation. But it cannot be a good long-term strategy for changing the ambient culture, and it is certainly incompatible with creative intellectual inquiry.

Today, separatism in Women's Studies is readily and graphically illustrated by the widespread exclusion of male authors from course syllabi, assigned reading lists, and citations in scholarly papers. In particular cases, there can, of course, be practical reasons for mentioning only female sources, and probably scholars in every field tend to overcite close colleagues and allies. But a systematic refusal to read or respond to male authors harms feminist scholarship in many ways. In addition, the separatist agenda has caused many Women's Studies programs not to seek collaboration with and support from male colleagues, as if mere association with men would contaminate feminist purity. Such moves are debilitating to the cause of feminism, and they may lure female students into the—obviously false—belief that all intellectual work produced by males is irrelevant to, or in conflict with, feminist projects.

Some feminists would argue that they were forced to set up their own programs, found their own journals, and form their own intellectual networks because the academic mainstream (or "malestream") would have nothing to do with them. This may well be so. But even if academic separatism was necessary in the past, it seems clearly counterproductive today, for gender analyses and the study of women have succeeded in making widely acknowledged contributions to the humanities and, increasingly, to the social sciences as well. In the hard sciences, feminist scholarship has been less influential, but the best way of gaining recognition there is by engaging in open dialogue with both male and nonfeminist female scholars. Separatism unavoidably discourages such dialogue. Instead, it favors dogmatic assertion, a standard tactic of ideologically inflamed movements, whether religious or political.

While academic feminism has tried to keep the rest of the university at bay, it has energetically fostered an intimate relationship with feminist political initiatives, both inside and outside the academy. Arguably, some forms of participation in these initiatives have been appropriate. For example, a professor might give her textbook order to the local feminist bookstore, thus offering financial support to a woman-owned business while also ensuring that her students are exposed to the novels, T-shirts, records, buttons, and periodicals of feminist popular culture.

But at other times academic feminism has made itself subservient to activist agendas. Consequently, in many programs, the appointment of faculty has hinged on the candidates' commitment to community organizing or other forms of feminist activism, rather than on the strength of their academic credentials. Some programs have adopted course and instructor evaluation forms that encourage students to judge the quality of their education in terms of its direct relevance to a rather narrowly defined and constantly shifting political agenda. It is not uncommon for students to be urged to engage in nonscholarly internships and practicums, for which they are able to earn academic credit. The degree of supervision of these internships, like the extent to which they include academic components (such as writing a final paper), varies enormously from program to program.

The American university accommodates many academic units that, like professional schools, provide intellectual service to various constituencies in the "real world." But these units typically maintain a certain critical distance from their practical objectives. Schools of education, for example, train teachers, but they also theorize about pedagogy and school policies. Forensic science departments offer courses of use to police officers and probation counselors, but they also scrutinize the operations of the criminal justice system. The ivory-tower model of inquiry has always been recognized as freeing the scholar from the need to demonstrate practical relevance, and the whole point of academic freedom and tenure is to protect the scholar from political pressure.

An unfortunate reversal of these tenets occurs when a program sees itself as a site of correct political action and therefore promotes not independent inquiry but adherence to a particular line of analysis and to the activities that follow from it. In such cases—as we find in some Women's Studies programs that attempt to minimize the difference between themselves and groups engaged in feminist activism outside the university—educational aims are made entirely subordinate to political goals.

Academic units that manage to balance these internal and external values do so by maintaining high intellectual standards while also using as texts some material selected for its political utility. Thus, a sociology department, for example, may have a Marxist orientation while insisting on excellent scholarship and publication records from its faculty and all-around competence in sociology from its majors and graduate students. Such a department sees its mission as providing a solid education shaped, but not outweighed, by a political commitment that many (but rarely all) faculty in the department share. But Women's Studies has never even acknowledged that achieving such a healthy balance is a worthwhile goal as well as an inherently difficult feat. Instead, both academics and activists have tended to repudiate the very desirability of such a balance and have agreed that "Women's Studies is the theory and activism the practice"—as if the relationship between the two were both comfortable and obvious. And because "activism" has had the brighter luster in feminist rhetoric, many Women's Studies programs have felt compelled to embrace and promote an activist stance.

The yearly NWSA conferences have always dramatically exhibited the uneasy mingling of academic and nonacademic concerns within Women's Studies—and this quite apart from the charges of racism that nearly destroyed the organization at its 1990 meeting in Akron, Ohio. Thus, the typical NWSA program includes not only symposia on Emily Dickinson or on the depiction of women in Hindu temple art, but also panels on how feminist organizations can get tax-exempt status or on how lesbian couples can practice do-it-yourself artificial insemination. Publishers' displays of academic books stand side by side with booths featuring crystals, drums, massage oils, and the other paraphernalia of "women's culture." Over time, the nonacademic components of the annual meetings have come to predominate, perhaps because activists outside the academy provide an important portion of the market for books in Women's Studies. Not surprisingly, many serious scholars stopped attending the annual NWSA meeting because (so they told us) they felt it was no longer a worthwhile professional endeavor. Here, too, people could, after all, vote with their feet—the "exit option," as some political scientists call it.

Activism as a legitimate goal of Women's Studies has certainly been communicated to students. When we put the question "What do you think Women's Studies is all about?" to approximately 150 undergraduates in Women's Studies courses at two contrasting institutions—one a large research university in the Northeast with a twenty-year-old, highly political program, the other a former teacher's college, now a university, in the Southwest, whose Women's Studies program is less than ten years old and quite unpoliticized—most answers touched only the practical side. Students wrote: To "raise women's self-esteem," "create a less patriarchal society," "break down sexism," "empower women," "lessen discrimination against women," "help women find a career centering on improving women's lives," and so on. When we asked "What do you think *other* students at your school think Women's Studies is all about?" the vast majority of the respondents answered with some form of the notion of "male bashing"; and a few added "a touchy-feely class," "militant," and "raging militant feminists." This negative image, too, should be of concern to those responsible for Women's Studies.

The twin tendencies toward academic separatism and deference to activism have developed in concert. Academic feminists who either felt rebuffed by the established disciplines or wanted to develop a radically different approach often turned to the welcoming audience of cultural feminists and activists. As they elaborated their writings in response to the concerns of this largely nonacademic audience (an important market even for university press books), much of their research tended to become both less accessible and less acceptable to colleagues in the mainstream disciplines. Traditional academics, moreover, could readily be denounced for their "elitism" and narrowly academic concerns. As a result, those Women's Studies faculty whose own research remained connected to the conventional disciplines have come under increasing pressure from activist students to base their courses on more radical or less scholarly texts.

In such an atmosphere, scholarship itself becomes suspect as faculty members feel constant pressure not to betray the cause. One result is the rhetorical assertion that scholarship *is* politics, an insistence that only signals the devaluation that scholarship has already undergone. A feminist professor who says, "My scholarly work is my form of activism," or even, "Teaching is my form of activism," is thus inevitably affirming that "activism" is indeed the correct measure of all aspects of Women's Studies.

Women's Studies, in its early phases, had a choice. Its justified critique of much traditional knowledge as biased and limited (if not overtly misogynist), and therefore ultimately erroneous, could have led it to claim the high ground by insisting on broader, more balanced, less biased curricula and research. But this is not the choice many programs and Women's Studies faculty made. Instead, at every juncture at which feminist bias emerged, it was justified by reference to the prior bias of men—as if emulation of the thing being rejected had, unconsciously, become the feminist agenda. Such inconsistencies are unworthy of a feminism that hopes to have a future. By capitulating to them, Women's Studies has become the defender of the faith within the academy's walls. In the chapters that follow, we explore the ideology constituting that faith and see why it has become impossible for some feminists to adhere to it.

2

Cautionary Tales from Women Who Walked Away

WHEN WE BEGAN conducting our interviews for this book, we expected to elicit strong opinions from our subjects, for Women's Studies is not a field that attracts the dispassionate or the impassive. We were not disappointed. The stories we collected from faculty, students, and staff members in Women's Studies programs are vigorous, concrete, and often eloquent. The experiences recounted in them—many happy, many painful—were vividly recollected and proved highly informative. Most of all, we were struck by the sharply contrasting judgments we heard. Some students had "found their voice" and gained self-confidence from feminist classes; others felt they had been "silenced" and ostracized. We heard from professional and clerical staff with intense personal commitments and loyalty to the programs they worked in, and from others who found their allegiance sapped by selfish or hypocritical faculty and students.

But it was the interviews with faculty members that proved most revealing—and most disturbing. Even the most enthusiastic among these women acknowledged serious tensions. We encountered tenured members of Women's Studies programs so dissatisfied that they had quietly withdrawn or taken inner flight: they continued to teach their courses, though estranged from the whole Women's Studies enterprise. Others had taken the next step and actually resigned from their programs, choosing to work, instead, in more traditional departments. Not surprisingly, it was those who had initially given their best to Women's Studies and had then become disillusioned who offered the keenest insights into the problems we were trying to analyze.

Among our informants, three women told stories that seemed to us emblematic of the dissatisfactions now besetting Women's Studies. All three define themselves as feminists and are still engaged in research that is informed by feminist perspectives. All were enthusiastic participants in and supporters of Women's Studies programs earlier in their careers. All of them have now given up their official involvement in Women's Studies and have returned to their respective discipline-based departments.

Jeanne, as we will call her, is a well-known and widely respected historian in her early forties. She began her present position, at a large state university, with a joint appointment in Women's Studies and history, which provided her with a perspective from which to evaluate the operations of two very different programs. She considers leaving Women's Studies the "most difficult thing" she has done in her professional life of nearly fifteen years.

Anna, a prolific and highly visible scholar in one of the social sciences, has been involved with feminism throughout her professional life of more than twenty years. She first joined a Women's Studies program in the fall of 1973, "full of excitement." But after consistently unpleasant experiences in feminist programs on a number of campuses, she is thoroughly fed up. "Sooner or later people are going to have to face up to this crap," she says.

Margaret, now a professor in a humanities department, directed a Women's Studies program for over a decade and was also very active in the National Women's Studies Association. She describes the rupture with her former associates this way: "I experienced it as a divorce; that was my metaphor for it. And, obviously, if you get divorced, the marriage wasn't happy. It was a very isolating experience. I was such a true believer, and I worked so hard for so many years."

There are important and interesting differences among the stories these three women have to tell and in their present attitudes toward Women's Studies programs. But what they told us is marked by so many points of agreement that we have not found it difficult to assemble, from their narratives, a coherent picture of the unhealthy conditions and self-destructive tendencies that appear to be intrinsic to many Women's Studies programs.

STUDENTS WHO STOMP IN SEMINARS

When asked about the circumstances that led them eventually to abandon Women's Studies programs, all three women said they had found it increasingly difficult to do intellectual work in a hostile and intolerant environment. Each of them attributed a large share of the blame for creating an inhospitable atmosphere to militant feminist students, and each described how such students tried in various ways to impede open class discussion of ideas that did not conform to these students' politics.

In Anna's case, such students seem early on to have decided that she was not "the right kind of feminist":

> I began to get some bad vibes, as we used to say in those days, when I started teaching a feminist theory class which became a standard offering for the Women's Studies curriculum. And what I did there was to rehearse the different feminist positions: radical feminist, liberal, Marxist. The psychoanalytic feminists were just beginning to make an impact. And, of course, I would come into class and offer what I thought were balanced views of these different texts. Some of my comments were very critical, because I thought the texts were philosophically incoherent and politically disastrous—not to put too fine a point on it. I mean, they weren't scholarly texts—books like Shulamith Firestone's *The Dialectic of Sex*—they were really polemics. But that was the feminist literature of the time, it had that character, and I thought it was important for students to

work through them and to hone their critical skills on them, to be able to separate some of the texts from one another and to be able to ask themselves, "Now, what kind of world would we live in if this person got her way? Is it a world that would be more just, more equitable, or is it a world in which you'd sort of change one class of oppressors for another?"

And that started to get me into trouble. Some students were tremendously irate, and would run and tell tales out of class. You weren't supposed to criticize the feminist text. One of them said to me that she was shocked and horrified, and it was very upsetting to her that I was criticizing the historical accuracy, for example, of parts of Firestone's account, where I said, "The scholarly literature does not support these claims." So there were students who were being perturbed by this, and I thought: Well, that's okay; they need to learn how to deal with this.

Then, at the request of the Women's Studies people, I signed on to do a senior seminar. As it turned out, this was a ghastly experience, one of the worst I've ever had in my life. I was doing a topic on mothers and daughters, which is probably like a red flag to a bull in a bullring. And there was a group of really tough students—they called themselves "dykes," actually—who, in the first class meeting, just launched an all-out assault on me for having men on my reading list.

They came prepared with all this animus. One group sat in the back and actually stomped their feet and kind of hooted sometimes when they heard things they didn't like. And, by the way, this particular group, at the end of the semester when I was passing out teaching evaluations—you just pass out a stack and they grab one—they all took two apiece, and they were marking the lowest category for everything. They were sort of trying to stuff the ballot box with bad teacher evaluations. I caught them at it.

I was told later, by a graduate student who felt guilty about the whole thing, that she in fact had sat in on a strategy session where specific plans were made—and she swore to this—to disrupt my classes and those of another professor, because we were not doing the right thing. And this was confirmed later, that this meeting had in fact taken place. Now, whether there were faculty instigating any of this, I don't know. But it happened. Needless to say, experiences like this start to sour you.

It is worth pointing out that Anna can hardly be considered an ineffective teacher. She is, in fact, the recipient of a distinguished teaching award for her work in her social science department.

Margaret recalled similar difficulties in the early days of Women's Studies, caused, in her case, by students who identified themselves as "radical lesbian separatists":

I remember the atmosphere then. I remember feeling afraid in the classroom. One time when I was teaching an advanced seminar, the class was totally polarized, literally. The lesbians sat on one side, the straights on the other, and I was constantly terrified that they would attack each other physically, hate each other, hate me, that the class would completely break down. In this particular class the heterosexual women were intimidated. And this was often the case. They would feel intimidated, silenced, and later they would come and cry and tell me that they just couldn't go on this way. Yes, I'm sure they assumed I was heterosexual myself. I don't think I declared myself. I remember really not liking to feel that I had to do that, and resisting that.

This particular course was on literature and gender representation. It was really about women's writing, and, like everything else, the locus of debate, or the terms of debate, came to be whether or not the books were offering positive images of women—that was part of the theoretical discourse of the time. And the activist issue was right there. The lesbian students wanted to look only at works that were in some way able to help women. That was their idea of what women's writing should be. They had no interest in any aesthetic questions, in any structural questions. They were not even interested in reading against the grain, let's say, or reading works that one could see were, in spite of themselves, "subverting the patriarchal discourse."

Jeanne, too, expressed much dissatisfaction with the behavior of Women's Studies students, and she wonders what they were taught in their other Women's Studies courses to produce the attitudes they brought to her classes:

You have to know something in order to think critically. Now, if your project is to deconstruct, you have to know what it is that was constructed to begin with. For example, I teach Freud, and I understand the feminist critique of Freud, but he's not someone you can just dismiss out of hand. And I remember starting out one of my classes, the one where we were going to be taking up Freud, and I asked students to write on a piece of paper: "Free associate. When I say the word *Freud*, what do you think?" And these students would come up with statements such as: "He's like Hitler" and "He's the most damaging person to women in modern history." These were the undergraduate Women's Studies students. Now among the other students [those not in Women's Studies], some just had very simplistic notions, and others said, "Well, I really don't know very much about him and I'd like to know something"—you know, they had an openness.

You need to read Freud, you need to read Marx, you need to read Adam Smith. I mean, you need to read all of these figures if you are going to develop a feminist critique. And where do they ever read them? What I hear from the Women's Studies students is a kind of automatic rejection of people who have made enormously important theoretical contributions because they are "patriarchal," or, even worse, simply because they are "male." It's just an utterly knee-jerk, "dead-white-male" kind of thing.

My teaching evaluations are hilarious. I always know which are from the Women's Studies majors because they'll also write comments like, "This was not really a Women's Studies course," "There's not enough radical feminism in this course." That's what I'll hear. They want a course that is more explicitly political. I think what I do *is* political. But what they're looking for is something more programmatic, that results in an agenda.

You know, the argument for complexity is a very hard case to make to people who are eighteen, nineteen, twenty years old, especially students here who, I think, are uncomfortable with intellectual work. They don't come out of an environment in which they're comfortable arguing about ideas. So it's difficult, because there's a certain kind of true-believer desire among many Women's Studies students, and that's not what I can give them.

POLITICAL PURITY AND
HOSTILE COLLEAGUES

Even more disturbing to these professors than the troublemakers in their classrooms was the realization that they could not discuss their concerns about this belligerent anti-intellectualism with other faculty members in Women's Studies. In part, this was because they suspected that some of these colleagues were, by their teaching, reinforcing the students' tendency toward disruptive behavior. Anna reports hearing strange stories about one of her colleagues:

She started to do some really bizarre things in her courses. For instance, she put reserved reading in brown paper bags in the reserve room, and instructed the students in that class to not even permit a man to peek at it. Seriously, I have this on good authority. Students in her classes were to keep the material in these bags, and they weren't to let a man look at it, because some of it was really hot stuff, like information about women's bodies that the male medical establishment had tried to keep hidden.

I also, by the way, had two students, who were taking a class, who came to me complaining that they were being treated unfairly because they were heterosexual women. They and the other heterosexuals had been asked to identify themselves at the beginning, with the suggestion that by the end of the term, if the course were successful, there would be no heterosexuals left. One of them had been asked to do extra papers. I actually went to the ombudsman about this, because a married woman with kids was being asked to do extra work as a kind of punishment, because she'd been stubborn about her sexual orientation.

Jeanne recalls that the constant emphasis on political purity, coming, as it did, from both students and professors, early on created an atmosphere in which it was impossible to have an open discussion aimed at the resolution of conflicts:

Before there was a name for it, I certainly experienced what we now call political correctness in Women's Studies, in the sense of not being able to speak freely. I think there's a lot of fear about being publicly denounced. There's so little margin for error, for saying anything that's even experimental. People are so ready to pounce.

And that came from all kinds of different people. It wasn't one single political line. So I think it was happening very early in Women's Studies, but there was no language for naming it, and then, of course, the right picked up this terminology and painted all of us with that brush.

Part of the problem is the lack of—for want of a better

term—professionalism. Professionalism is seen as something bad. It's seen as something masculine or patriarchal. But to me that is the way you function in an institution. It allows you to have a disagreement and yet be able to work with one another. And what seems to have happened in this program is that everything is deeply personalized, and people hold these grudges for decades. It's really interesting to me to hear how people are always referring to history, the historical precedent, and frequently these precedents are figments of somebody's imagination, or very partial recollections of what actually happened. But it speaks to a way in which there's all this personal conflict exerting a hold over the program.

In my other department, we'll have a conflict, we'll vote on it, people will say, "Okay, I lost," and then we move on. I think the problems in Women's Studies have to do with the specific temperaments of this group of people, which is, I think, an unusual cast of characters, and the kind of political purity that many people are committed to. I have studied left-wing politics, and this kind of factionalizing and purity and rigidity is very much present in leftist movements.

Margaret, too, commented on the inability of Women's Studies faculty to resolve differences amicably. As director of the program in her university, she was especially aware of the tendency of members of her program always to assume the worst about one another:

At one point my colleagues decided they wanted to hire [a well-known African-American woman], and I was supposed to do something to make this happen. But I had to wait for the Afro-Am department to write me a memo about it. They never got me the memo, and I was blamed for this not working out. I was in effect accused of being a racist. . . .

There was a lot of appearance of solidarity, but not a lot of exploration of difference. There was certainly awareness of difference, and the disciplines were dividing lines, as well. I think people really did have a hard time dealing with conflict. And a lot of conflict was suppressed. But sweeping problems under the rug was part of the rhetoric of the women's movement, which was "sisterhood," and that meant no conflict, which was ridiculous—anybody who has a sister laughs when you say that.

Increasingly, Margaret found herself dreading going to her office:

I felt lonely. I would walk into the office, and I could feel real antagonism from the staff and not very much connection to the other faculty. I felt I was lacking real colleagues, and I very much needed and wanted to have them, in order to develop in my own work and just to be able to have some fun. The program was getting bogged down with the race issue and the sexual preference issue—there was just so much argument and so much antagonism and self-interrogation and daily confrontation.

It wasn't clear to me what was feminist about any of this. I came to feel that it was just pathology, that it was just individual and group pathology. I thought that too much behavior, bad behavior, was somehow rationalized in terms of feminism and that there had to be other categories for me, or I just couldn't go on.

One of the things that became boring to me was this inward-looking mentality—people so convinced of their superiority and acting like a club. I never liked the clubby atmosphere. To me, it just didn't belong in a university.

As time went on, Margaret began to "think longingly of traditional academic departments as a haven and a refuge." The irony of this nostalgia was not lost on her:

This program, this very entity that we had created supposedly because we were all being oppressed in our so-called traditional departments, seemed even worse than most departments, and people started talking about that privately. The more I got out of the program, the more I presented papers, the more I was in the world, at conferences that were not Women's Studies conferences primarily, the more I thought: This is really nuts! Because the people I was with outside of Women's Studies were interested in what I had to say and what other people had to say. There is a genuine discourse of feminism which can critique the disciplines and is not done in a hostile way, where you're not made to feel like shit.

"WOMEN'S STUDIES CAN BE HARMFUL"

The excesses of Women's Studies affected not just faculty, but, even more so, students. And the deepest outrage of our three informants was directed at the miseducation suffered by the students they had left behind.

Anna, the social scientist, says flatly, "Students are being cheated":

Over the long run, the students are the ones who suffer, and that's the sad part to me. I mean, what kind of mentoring is it, for God's sake, where a whole range of issues is just not to be discussed? And if they are discussed, it's only to denounce those who raise certain questions. This really does not serve students well. Once they leave the university, the world is an ambiguous place, it's filled with ambiguity, it's filled with irony, and not to be able to handle that does not serve them very well. The world is filled with disagreement among people who are people of goodwill. The students, poor things—I feel really bad for them, because they're not being given an education. And, you know, once they're in Women's Studies, it's like the

Stepford Wives! Women's Studies turns them into ideologically inflamed Stepford Wives!

I was always able to recognize them, these kids who come in, kind of zombified, who start uttering stock phrases. And you say, "Well, so-and-so certainly put her bootprint on these kids." Because it's obvious they're terrified of a thought, because if they ever had a serious thought, they might start reflecting on this stuff they're taught to repeat. I don't want to make it that clear-cut, but the ones who identified themselves as Women's Studies students were the worst. It was just a relentless dogmatism: "We will not talk about this!" Any criticism is because you're homophobic, or you're a patriarchalist in disguise, or you're this or you're that!—whether the criticism came from me or from other students. Politics is driving out their ability to think!

You see, what "feminist process" in the classroom winds up being is a push toward conformism and toward silencing dissent. It's all done under the rubric of being nice and open, and not being an authoritarian, old-fashioned type of teacher. But this winds up being tremendously more coercive. Because with authoritarian teachers you *know* they're being authoritarian, and you can resist. You know who's doing what to you. But this other way is manipulation, which is far worse than straight coercion, because students are being led someplace without any clarity as to who's accountable for what and who's leading them there. And since it's all supposed to be for *your own good,* you see, there's this terrible paternalism, or should we call it maternalism? "It's all for your own good." And I think that's *far* more dangerous than a more old-fashioned, straightforward authoritarianism, because it's harder to resist that kind of maternalism than it is the other, and to be clear about what's going on.

Jeanne had similar criticisms. She told a story of a very bright student who was "jerked around intellectually" by her Women's Studies professors, and she commented on the emotional stress to which all students in such classes are subjected:

> I can't speak in terms of numbers, but what I can say is that I've had some really fantastic students who I think have been ruined by this program, intellectually and, in some ways, emotionally. There's one in particular who studied with me when she was a sophomore, really smart, really creative, very committed to both intellectual work and political action. She took a course with one of my colleagues and sort of went off the deep end into a kind of radical feminist mode for a while, then came back to take another course with me, and we had a lot of conflict. I felt that her reading of the pornography debate was completely wrongheaded. She was unable to listen to any contrary evidence. I thought, Well, maybe she'll grow out of this. And she was very much involved in the campus women's center, where they have this violence-against-women training—it doesn't problematize the relationship between pornography and violence against women; it just says they're essentially identical. And she was very much involved in this.
>
> And then I went on leave, and I saw her when I came back, at graduation. I asked how she was doing, what she was doing. And she said, "Well, I'm really glad to be out of this program. I'm going to work for a little while. Maybe I'll go to graduate school, but I will *never* do anything in Women's Studies."
>
> She had taken a course with a black colleague, in womanist theory—yes, this student was white, and Jewish—and she told me about this experience, in that course. She had raised certain questions about anti-Semitism, and had been viciously attacked for her views by students in the class, with the support of the professor.
>
> She said to me, "You know, they didn't have to agree with me, but no one would even listen." She was shouted down. She was doing a presentation and she was shouted down. It's unconscionable. She was really shattered by this experience.

And she was one of the smartest students I ever had. I think she was jerked around intellectually. That's my reading of it. You know, she goes into one course and becomes a true believer in the radical feminist position. Then she goes into another course and it's something else.

That was the worst case, partly because the student had so much promise. But I've had other good students as well who just couldn't figure out what was going on. They're in this classroom in which things are exploding, in which they are made to feel guilty because they're white or because they're heterosexual or whatever, and they just don't know how to even begin to think about it. If a student feels that there's no space for her in a classroom to make a response unless it is the response expected of her, I don't think it's very healthy.

These are young people who are not only trying to figure out what they believe intellectually, but are also emotionally fragile. It's a period, you know, of youth typically questioning their own identity, sexual issues, all of it. And it's dangerous. Women's Studies can be harmful.

Margaret, as a longtime program director and a founder of the NWSA, speaks of having grown "embarrassed to be representing" the later developments within Women's Studies:

By the time the eighties came around, it just didn't seem that there was much new being developed within the program, and some of the really exciting developments, in the country and in the world, weren't finding their way into the program. And there evolved a kind of language, which was almost like a "committeespeak," of how each course was described, and they all started to sound the same: "issues to be addressed will include:" and then the list—pornography, rape, abortion, those things. I think there's a leveling there, for want of a better term, that I found boring. It was not challenging.

She believes the insularity of Women's Studies was in large part responsible for the paucity of students entering the program:

> I think lots of young people were afraid, felt intimidated, felt unwanted. I had lots of students who told me so—because I taught big courses—who felt that they themselves were not radical enough, or that they would be rejected because they were with men. Men felt that they would be rejected because they weren't women. We have all heard stories about that. The insistence on "women" as opposed to "gender" had something to do with it, though gender came to be used more frequently over time. But in my particular program there was a solid commitment to being on the side of women's issues, and not so much the study of gender, which would have to include men, male experience and male sexuality.

In speaking of the general intimidating atmosphere within Women's Studies, Margaret concludes:

> I'm really opposed to it, totally opposed. How can that be an education, a liberal education? No, I don't think it's retrograde to believe in a liberal education. I think we have real struggles now to make sure that things don't go completely over into thought police. I see it in other areas of the university, too, but nothing like in Women's Studies.

"THE CHICKENS COME HOME TO ROOST"

The women who withdrew from organized Women's Studies programs have spent much energy trying to gain some understanding of what went wrong. All agreed that Women's Studies programs had from the very beginning been impaired by deep internal flaws, and that the programs they knew best could not pretend to be academically respectable.

But our narrators expressed very divergent views when asked to explain just what they thought had gone wrong. Their diagnoses range from psychoanalytic conjectures to suspicions of personal nest feathering.

Anna notes a line of continuity between the political ethos of Women's Studies and the protest movements of the sixties:

> Some of the people who have written about this, Roger Kimball and others, their books are certainly very exaggerated. But they are on to something, which is that the academy has become a sort of redoubt for 1960s radical politics. When you're not getting very far with the working class, the academy becomes an outlet for all your energy. As it turns out, the academy is a rather fragile place, and more easily manipulatable as well, and a lot of people went into it for this reason.
>
> I think a lot of it has to do with having as much power as you can get in a particular local situation, and the last thing you want is a debate. The politics of the 1960s was not very generous in its approach to disagreement, and I think that the kind of moralistic fervor—where you're absolutely convinced of the rightness of your own position—carried over, and the idea that people could actually disagree was simply not considered appropriate. Plus, of course, you could also draw on a theoretical position, or a quasi- or pseudo-intellectual position, which says that, basically, there's no truth anyway, and everything is just a matter of someone arbitrarily imposing something on somebody else. So it's our turn to impose now, and you can't come in and make an argument based upon truth or historical accuracy or any of those old-fashioned values, because we know that all of those things are just constructions and have no absolute validity in any case.
>
> It took me about a year to realize that a lot of what was

going on had to do not with intellectual issues at all, but with a political strategy. The question really concerned the big philosophic difference over: Is Women's Studies primarily about scholarship? Is it an intellectual enterprise? Or is it primarily about pushing an agenda, turning gender into one of those major categories, like race, where special interests are involved and special needs have to be met, and you have a very close tie to the campus women's center?

The intellectual orientation women brought to their programs also affected their ability to handle conflict. Anna continues:

You know, having thought about this for a while, I decided that one of the problems from the very beginning was that the Women's Studies faculty was overloaded with people from literature, people who didn't have any training in the social sciences. And so, because we were raising certain kinds of questions that were foreign to them, they just decided our way of approaching problems was somehow masculine. For us, gender couldn't be the all-determinative category, because we knew that there were other issues that divide people.

Where there are separate Women's Studies programs, there has been a tremendous animus against the social sciences. Philosophy can be more loosey-goosey too, like literature, but in the social sciences, every now and then you really do have to deal with the *facts*. There *are* facts in the world; there are phenomena; there's real evidence out there that's intractable; there's real *data* about what people are thinking about a certain thing, or how they voted, or what's happening with education and income levels. You can't just wish all that away, and I think this determination to, sort of, wish away the real world is easier to accomplish if you're not compelled to deal with it as part of your professional work.

A friend of mine in economics was describing to me some

things that were going on in a faculty seminar set up by Women's Studies people. One time, she was tremendously upset because she had been accused by one of the Women's Studies people of exhibiting "masculinist categories of thought," simply because she was an economist. I said, "Quit going. Don't put yourself through this crap. It's just not worth it." But she hung in there for a while.

Anna suspects that if Women's Studies faculty were all housed in regular departments, some of the problems of factionalism and policing would decrease. Such a change might also lessen the hostility stemming from professional jealousy, which she and other feminist scholars have encountered. There were always those in Women's Studies, she says,

who did have both scholarly and political passions, who really were determined to do good work and be good historians, good sociologists, good whatever, and to do this under the rubric of Women's Studies. But there were also others who, it seems very clear to me, were very weak in a scholarly sense, whose work was almost entirely a form of special pleading or polemic, and the only way they were going to make it in the academy was by validating this as a legitimate academic activity.

I think that, with something like six hundred Women's Studies programs throughout the country, we now have a situation in which there is a lot of animus against women who do well in scholarship and are succeeding in it. And this comes from people who could not pass rigorous muster in a department of history, for example, and who are holed up in Women's Studies and carp from the sidelines at the women who are doing good work, by charging that somehow they've sold out or they're male-identified or they're all the other labels. We can all point to really terrific scholars in the field of Women's Studies, so you know I'm not making a blanket indictment, but there's absolutely no doubt in my mind that that carping was part of it.

Anna believes that a major problem with Women's Studies programs that continues to this day is what she calls a "rush to a kind of groupthink" and an unwillingness of many participants to engage in, or even to allow, self-critical inquiry into the aims and practices of their procedures:

> Absolutely nothing! There was no such inquiry. And just to let you know how hard it is for people to even think about that: I did a presentation at a conference at another university, at which I talked about feminist studies and feminist rhetoric. I talked about the strategy of women as the universal victim, and how this approach did not exactly yield the best scholarship in the world. And even at that late date—and this was probably toward the mid-eighties—there were women jumping up and having fits. And the irony for me was that I had gone over these different strategies and resoundingly endorsed one that I thought yielded a tremendous amount of important and interesting scholarship. And I talked about that scholarship, and talked about the fact that there *is* bound to be a relationship between feminism as a political enterprise and Women's Studies, but that you *can't* collapse the two, because then everything Women's Studies people do is judged by some political result, and then it's not scholarship anymore, it's something else. And it was just amazing, the ire of the people in the audience, the women jumping up, and one of them was so angry her voice was quivering. There was to be no criticism! Just no criticism!

Anna comments on the current allegations that Women's Studies programs are dominated by the agenda of white bourgeois women:

> It just reminds me of all those strands of Marxist revisionism and deviation—where a position that lasted for twenty years then gets accused of hopeless deviationism and it's all trash and you move on. I mean, it's the same kind of sectarian battle,

you know. The idea that the program [at this university] was somehow racist seems to me ridiculous. For example, if one teaches Western political thought, the fact that the great masters of the canon, to anyone's knowledge, were not black, should not surprise anyone, for heaven's sake. There you're dealing with historical issues where you can't invent people who didn't exist. That's just not taking account of the very historic contingencies that they say determine everything.

To make those charges is part of the ongoing need, I think, to set up a Manichaean universe, where you've got these horrible people who used to do horrible things, and now it's going to be wonderful and pure and virtuous. But, trust me, ten years from now the people doing all of this denouncing will themselves be denounced for some crime or other. They're going to be denounced, because this *is* like Communist politics.

Jeanne, who is the youngest of these three women and whose experience with Women's Studies dates back only fifteen years, gives the least pessimistic analysis of the causes of the malaise in the particular program that she left:

I assume it all has something to do with the origins of Women's Studies in a specific political movement. Clearly, Women's Studies needed that political movement to even develop, but at this point in time, when it's institutionally entrenched—I mean, this program is not going to disappear unless we cause it to, unless we destroy it—the conflict between being in an academic program and part of a political movement helps to generate what happens in the classroom.

But she also offers a different kind of explanation:

I hate to reduce things to the psychological dimension zone. It's not my usual mode of interpretation, but in this case I think there just are some temperaments that are really troubled. I think we act like a dysfunctional family. The Women's Studies faculty is locked in a set of dynamics that it cannot escape from. And I think that to have a program that would bring in all, or as many as possible, of the faculty at the university who are working in feminist scholarship in some way—and there are *huge* numbers whom we never see, who never cross the threshold of our program—that would diffuse the conflicts that we have as this small group. It's not that they would disappear, but they would be diffused by just the sheer numbers. So if there's a way to solve the problems of Women's Studies, I think it is to change the structure to a true program, with people housed in regular departments, and not have faculty lines in Women's Studies.

Jeanne comments on what she calls the current "challenges of women of color," and she describes the effects on Women's Studies programs:

I feel compelled by the challenge of women of color, whoever they are, however you want to define that—African-American women, Hispanic women, Asian women, et cetera—to change my courses. I mean, race has always been central in my courses, but it was always a biracial analysis—black women and white women. And now I'm feeling much more compelled to try to think about ways to really talk about the diversity in American women in a way that's not just a salad bowl—"we'll spend this day on Asian women"; that's totally unsatisfying to me. So finding some analytic tools for an historian to convey what this might mean historically, how these dynamics played out in significant ways historically—I am compelled to do that.

But I also think there's a gigantic amount of static around these legitimate issues that has to do with local politics, individual self-aggrandizement, motives that are not highly intellectual. It's hard to separate out these moves. But trying to position yourself so that you are really engaged in what needs to be addressed and what needs to be changed and at the same time saying there's a lot of bullshit going on here—that is the difficult thing to do. Right now there's a privileging of racial categories. This is not legitimate, and it ought to be resisted. And how to be as a white person is also a very difficult question, now, because when you know that what you say is going to be discredited, well then, do you say it anyway? It's not made easy for you in a situation in which deviation gets labeled racism, you know, because it's so hard to take that label, to be called a racist.

I think it would help the program if it acted as though it were an academic program, rather than one in which political purity was a requirement. I think it would help all of us. But the program hasn't changed; it was always political. I mean, ways of behaving that were there from the day I set foot in the program have continued, and they've just reached the breaking point. And a lot of this does have to do with racial politics, which were not as palpable in the mid-eighties, although there were racial politics going on. I think it's all just reached the point of explosion over the last year or so. But this was already there; the seeds of this were already in the program when I came. I think the chickens have finally come home to roost.

"WHO OWNS WOMEN'S STUDIES?"

Given her extensive administrative experience, Margaret not surprisingly offers a diagnosis that centers on institutional aspects of Women's Studies. She speaks in particular of the nonacademic goals that many programs adopt, their reliance on professional staff who lack academic credentials, and feminist antipathy for traditional governance procedures:

I think that the program was always confused about its identity and its purpose institutionally. And having started as a kind of adjunct to the campus women's center was a really strong part of that. For a long time our office was adjoining the women's center, and there was an absolute confusion of who did what. I remember even resentment on the part of some of the staff of the women's center that we were getting a little too academic. You know: "Isn't Women's Studies really The Women's Movement?" Well, no, not exactly. And that was in the origins of the program—this confusion between academic and activist goals.

We were supposed to be the public institution where we could be down and dirty, so to speak, and real politicos, real hard-line politicos and not afraid of struggle and storming barricades and demonstrations.

As director, I felt a very strong sense of mission—that it was *my job* to help all women on campus who wanted and needed support. This was the rhetoric of the program. But I always felt that you can't do everything and do it with a high quality.

I thought I was being hired to be an academic. But I saw, of course, that it was a very complicated organization. There were seats on the program's executive board for staff, for the women's center, for the community, for this, for that. And during the first years of the program not too many people were involved who were really academics. That's where, I think, some of the conflict arose about who were "the faculty," who was "the program." The faculty, who had appointments in other departments, had tremendous power, because they *were* faculty; and almost everyone else was not faculty, including me, because I hadn't yet completed my Ph.D.

There was always a kind of two-tiered system. There was "the faculty"; and "we" all know that they're prima donnas, and we have to do all the dirty work, while they just do what they want to do. And then there's "us," the staff, and we're the *real core* of the program. It was a matter of loyalty, as that was

enacted at the time. And there was also the question of owner-
ship—who owns Women's Studies? These were the old arguments, but I think they originated way back there.

Because staff people participated in the program's governance—
in accordance with the feminist principle of operating as a collec-
tivity, regardless of rank or position—they were able to impose
their views:

> The way this program started, the whole business of having
> professional staff as opposed to faculty—I still insist that this is
> at the core of the whole conflict. I was very slow and stupid. I
> didn't understand *for years*, because I *was* a true believer—and
> I'm not saying that there was nothing good in there, because
> obviously there was—but I did not understand how much self-
> promotion was involved, how strategies and courses and struc-
> tures and ideas were being rationalized to serve a particular
> agenda that was at once personal aggrandizement or security,
> job security, as well as a particular ideological agenda.
>
> Some of the staff didn't think that Women's Studies ought
> to be academic at all, because they either couldn't make it
> themselves in a regular academic context, or they so despised it
> and were envious of it at the same time, while wanting all the
> perks. They really wanted to have it both ways. I think they
> wanted it to be pretty much what it ended up being—a pro-
> gram that had people working for it who were legitimate
> enough in the eyes of the rest of the university to get the
> resources and the institutionalization that it needed, and then a
> privileged existence in a separate realm that was unassailable,
> so that they would have the same status as Afro-Am, where
> people would say, "You can't touch them."
>
> People were threatened by the accomplished women on the
> faculty, those who had achieved what seemed unattainable to
> others. Probably the unconscious fear was that if we were to
> hand the program over to them, then people like "us"—the

ones who started the program—wouldn't be acceptable. I think any woman who was really accomplished in a scholarly way was suspect to some. Such women were criticized for a number of things, but people saw that we were going to need to be able to demonstrate scholarly qualifications if they were going to get tenure; and if they didn't get tenure, there wasn't going to be much in the way of clout for the program. But I don't think there was genuine respect for scholarship. I never felt there was much interest in people's scholarship. There wasn't at that time an environment that could promote it.

I think what was so distressing was that everything seemed to become exacerbated. It's hard to know whether that was a function of working so closely with people who were, in some sense, not my peers—the staff. Much of my time was spent in doing what I thought was pacification. I had to hide my own ideas and abilities to some extent, because of this notion of "leveling"—that we are all the same.

This effort at "leveling," also noted by other Women's Studies faculty, has led some to observe, ironically, that the feminist notion of "empowerment" seems to result above all in the equal disempowerment of each by all. Margaret remembers having to fight for control of the budget. Some of her colleagues in Women's Studies wanted every single budgetary decision to be submitted to the plenary group, which met once a month. The idea was dropped only after Margaret's unrelenting insistence that such a restriction would make it impossible for the program to function at all, since she had to make decisions about money on an almost daily basis. Nor was this Margaret's only experience of staff members' resistance to allowing distinctions among program participants:

I remember there was a big hassle about whether I should even have a vote on anything. There was a huge fight about even using the word *director*. For many, many years I was called "coordinator," and people on the staff certainly did not want that to change, because they thought that the name *director* carried too much power. They didn't want anyone to have any power in that position; they didn't want "stars."

It was all about having to know your place! And this was the rhetoric from the very beginning. It seemed to me that there was a strong desire to have staff people who would "do the work," as they called it, and not necessarily new faculty. There was always some resistance to getting new faculty in the program, because that threatened the position of the professional staff.

The things that I heard, the kind of bad-mouthing of faculty on the basis of their so-called politics or their personality or their research or hearsay about their teaching—this was done in an absolutely unchecked way for the whole time I was there! And the power of the staff to determine how faculty were seen by students, and also their egging on of the students—that was the locus of what I'd call politics at the time. The students were being encouraged to rise up, to find the program wanting, to attack us. The staff was doing this, in their clubby atmosphere. I overheard many things that were deeply shocking to me.

Like Jeanne, Margaret is in some measure attracted to psychological explanations for the problems in Women's Studies:

I think you have to ask what kind of personalities and temperaments and psyches are attracted to Women's Studies, as opposed to those who aren't. I mean, is there a psychological profile that can be discerned? The tendency—which I've always thought of as, in psychoanalytic terms, a borderline personality disorder—to always take an either/or, an us/them, an all-good/all-bad approach, this tendency very much characterized Women's Studies. And I always wondered about that. Is there something about those of us—including me, of course— who were attracted to this? I'm not sure.

But certainly there seemed to be, as time went on, an increasingly almost violent acting out against one another. There was a certain process of Othering, which is not too different from what you see in the rise of nationalism. It's almost like the Balkans. I found this also among some of the European feminists, not just the Americans. I remember European conferences where there was screaming and yelling and accusations directed at other women. But I also remember Monique Wittig, whom I very much admire, telling everybody, "C'est un scandale!" that women are acting this way toward each other.

For all the anger that was acted out, there was, it seems to me, a deep fear of confrontation. This was couched in terms not unlike what is done in the black community where you're not supposed to accuse in public or in front of the Other. But even privately there was no openness. I mean, our retreats didn't really get at what was going on. People spoke in politicized terms, arguing over how we define ourselves as a program. But I found myself increasingly coming to think in almost pathological terms about our problems, because it was a pathological situation in Women's Studies.

Does she attribute this deplorable environment to a lack of respect that women display toward one another?

I wouldn't want to generalize from that experience, to assume that women generally don't respect each other—I'm not sure that's true. But there was certainly envy that was not dealt with; there was competitiveness; there was anger—I mean, the whole range of traits that academics have in common, or the problems they share, which have to do with a general feeling of being undervalued or insufficiently appreciated or not rewarded tangibly.

I also think there are just tremendous feelings of inadequacy and insecurity in Women's Studies, vis-à-vis other disciplines. It's the flip side of "We are better, more important, more radical." The other side of that is: "Are we as good?" It's what I would call "splitting," in that it makes for a very uneasy sense of self, individually and collectively. It isn't just taken for granted and then you go on. It's always reproblematized, somehow, every day. Every day the territory has to be conquered again, somehow. I really hate some of the thought-police stuff that's going on now in universities, and it was going on earlier in Women's Studies than elsewhere. Absolutely, I think it was. I think there was silencing of people, there was exclusion, and certainly there was shunning.

SCHOLARSHIP IN A
SEA OF PROPAGANDA

Despite their negative conclusions and outlook, our narrators are convinced that much research inspired by feminist commitments has been eminently worthwhile. They expressed serious misgivings, however, about whether Women's Studies programs, in light of their history, could reliably serve as sites for such research.

Jeanne, the historian, speaks enthusiastically about the many contributions feminist scholarship has made to her field:

> For one thing, just on a very fundamental level, a compensatory level, we now have all this history of women's activities—whether they be public contributions or household labor, mothering, and so on—which was completely ignored in past historical scholarship. Increasingly, there is now a turn to analyzing gender as it affects power relationships that may not have anything to do specifically with the relations between men and women—for example, the gendering of the welfare state. And all of these ideas about how social life, institutions, ideologies are structured in certain ways by gender—that gives us a wholly new way of looking at history. So the questions that

historians ask have changed. What historians used to see as significant in history has been contested by feminist scholars, and pretty effectively.

She also welcomes research that is inspired by feminist politics, as long as the work conforms to disciplinary standards:

You know, there are historians who work "on women" who are clearly not feminist. I think there is a distinction, and I would say the work I do is "feminist," even when I'm disagreeing with a lot of feminist scholarship. I place myself within a feminist discourse, definitely.

If it is to be feminist research, there has to be, at some basic, common-denominator level, a belief that women have, in the past, been oppressed or repressed, and that we are looking for ways to emancipate women, to give them greater freedom and justice. And I think that you bring that perspective to your work.

In its fine points and its details, this can mean many different things. But it's more than simply working on the subject of "women." I have no problem with work coming out of a political impulse. But when this impulse takes over the work, then I think it becomes a problem. You know, what I tell my graduate students is that the questions they ask *can* be informed by their politics—and inevitably will be—and the more conscious they are of that, the better. But when they're devising ways to find answers, they have to adhere to the methods of our discipline, because it *checks* them against their assumptions and their biases, and in some ways their politics.

There are historians who err by putting ideological considerations before scholarly ones. But history is a field in which you don't see that happening very often, because of the way the discipline works, because of the empirical standards to which we subscribe. The advantage that history has—and, again, it depends on the individual historian—is that there are definite standards for what constitutes a good historical study.

And it's not just that there is evidence, for example, but that you actively seek out evidence that, if it existed, would contravene your assumptions. There is an understanding of what the proper relationship should be between evidence and claims. These methods help to mitigate some of the political thrust you bring to your work. Because we hold to these standards, we are more likely to acknowledge the truth claims of other people if they can back them up, if they can substantiate them.

Anna, too, readily recognizes the important contributions made by feminist scholarship:

> I could point quite happily to all sorts of important work that's come out, that's made a big contribution to knowledge. The most important ones to me are actually not from my own field; they're from history. The new social history has been looking at the whole issue of women's work historically, at women and the family, at relationships between women and how these relationships had political and social implications that have not previously been examined, at women's labor unions, at women as political actors, at women as resistance fighters. I think the scholarship in social history has been tremendously important.
>
> Also the anthropological work that has specifically looked, or looked again, at some societies and asked: Were some things missed about the power and authority that women in fact have? Maybe they weren't the powerful ones juridically, but they do have evident power—let's examine it. I think that's a tremendous contribution. Some of the new work which gives a more complex account of the history of Western political thought also is a contribution. And economics—well, isn't the household a part of economics? So I think there's been a lot of interesting work. And in literature, too, though I must say I'm tired of the trendy lit-crit stuff. I think the women and moral reasoning issues raised by Carol Gilligan and others, those are

interesting and important debates and contributions. So all of that has been valuable.

Then there are the feminist commentaries on the fieldwork of people like Jane Goodall, her work with the chimpanzees, and Dian Fossey's work with the mountain gorillas, and Cynthia Moss's work with elephants. It's interesting that a lot of this pioneering work in watching animals in the field has come from women. It's not explicitly a critique of science, but it stands as a critique of the laboratory versions of trying to figure out what these creatures are about. So all of it I find very interesting.

One question I have, and I don't know how to answer it, is: Would all this have happened without Women's Studies? But this might be the entry point for a more basic question, which is: Has Women's Studies served a purpose? To the extent that it has supported and sustained these scholarly efforts, and given people an academic place, a toehold, so to speak, and helped to legitimize these scholarly efforts, of course it's been worthwhile. But to the extent that Women's Studies has become a refuge for a kind of overpoliticization that pushes certain dogmas, it's done a real disservice. So I would say my report on it is mixed, and I would say, also, that my evaluation of it would in itself be a historically contingent one, which is: Did Women's Studies serve an important function at one point that it no longer serves?

But, of course, as soon as you say that, people are going to ring your home and do voodoo chants, because that's where their jobs are, that's where they've got a vested interest.

As to the future of Women's Studies as an academic enterprise, Anna is very blunt:

Sooner or later people are going to have to face up to this crap. There are too many nasty things going on out there.

I think the change will come from generations of young scholars, black and Hispanic and women and so on, who really want to go out into the world and be the best historians they can be, and the best economists they can be, and who may in fact come to see being defined exclusively by programs like Women's Studies and Afro-Am as itself a marginalizing thing. I don't know how soon this is going to happen, but that is one possibility.

Another sign of hope is that a lot of parents are getting fed up with paying for education that doesn't seem very much like education, and I think there's a little bit of reaction setting in. Sometimes this can take forms that are not particularly attractive—that kind of parental ire. But I think some people feel that their kids are getting a little bit cheated on the intellectual content of the education they're receiving, and that's coming to the attention of college administrators.

And after all, money does talk. It may even talk louder. And if they say, "Well, gosh, what are the stories I've been hearing about this place? Is my kid going to get caught up in all this?"—that might lead people to think twice about some of the virulence and aggressivity they are displaying, and about the tremendously bad impact and chilling effect, as they used to say in the old days, it's having on free speech.

Let's face it, however, a lot of the people we've been talking about are tenured, and they're going to be around forever, and they can't *do* anything else. I mean, it's not as if they could be integrated into other departments. They don't have the qualifications in many cases to say, "Well, I've had it with this program; I'm going to go have the sociology department take me in." That's kind of a built-in problem.

Margaret, who feels that Women's Studies has never developed a clear view of itself as an academic discipline, concludes:

I personally am not interested now in being active in Women's Studies on an institutional basis. I'm entirely involved with what I'm doing in my own department. But within my work there, there *is* women's studies. I encourage that in every way I can, with individual students, with my own courses, with my research. I was a feminist before I came to Women's Studies, and I still consider myself to be one.

3

Ideology and Identity:

Playing the Oppression Sweepstakes

THE STORIES in the preceding chapter stand on their own as poignant recitals of great expectations reduced to bitter disappointments. But they also touch on all of the issues that any critical discussion of feminism in the academy must engage. This is why we have singled them out. From these stories, and from others that appear in later chapters, emerges a portrait of the problems besetting Women's Studies today: saddening accounts of shunning, personal betrayal, and unkind practices—all perpetrated amidst avowals of sisterhood; but even more evident are the shocking instances of unprofessional behavior and subversion of normal academic standards and procedures—all carried on in the name of feminism.

Perhaps most disturbing were the tales of feminist pedagogy that too often looked like indoctrination and harassment in the classroom. As we listened and read, we slowly began to realize that some of the things we heard about not only were affecting the lives of Women's Studies faculty (a relatively small group) and their students (a much larger group), but also were having significant repercussions outside the narrow circle of Women's Studies. Ideas central to Women's Studies were being taken up by secondary and even elementary school educators and policy makers. If, as we suspected, these ideas were not, in fact, working well within Women's Studies but no one was saying so, did feminists not have an obligation to address these problems frankly before the rot spread any further? But to do so, we had to go beyond "speaking bitterness" and attempt to understand the underlying issues.

UNRAVELING THE WEB OF FEMINIST DISCONTENTS

Reviewing the trajectory that goes from hope to despair is a melancholy business. Like all those we interviewed, we had started out excited and energized by Women's Studies and its challenges. What had soured the stew? An assortment of superficial and partial rationalizations were offered to us by women we interviewed. Just as feminist discontents are part of the folklore of feminism, so there are many folkloric explanations of why feminists have trouble organizing themselves and getting along with one another. As with the attempts to understand a suicide, probably there is a little truth in each explanation; at one time or another we entertained all of them ourselves. But we now think they fail to go to the heart of the matter. In brief, our narrators offered the following analyses and rationalizations, which we used as a springboard in formulating our own hypotheses.

A few of our informants felt that the problems in Women's Studies are only growing pains and will disappear as the field gains definition and acceptance. A greater number tended to blame patriarchy for all these problems and held that men and male institutions gain by keeping Women's Studies weak, isolated, and marginalized. Small wonder, then, that the bonds of sisterhood get strained and people lash out at one another in frustration over their inability to make headway against the system.

In a more ambitious try at explanation, some of the people we spoke to pointed out that because of previous oppression, both faculty and students bring a lifetime of experience in dysfunctional nuclear families to Women's Studies programs. All academic departments have internal problems, but women's oppression in patriarchal society makes Women's Studies faculty and students play out their tensions in particular ways. Too much is expected from women; thus, blame is cast more fiercely and hurt is more deeply felt when things do not go well. We have not recovered from our resentment against our mothers. We cannot accept Women's Studies as a "good enough mother" (to use the famous phrase of the British psychoanalyst D. W. Winnicott).

Moreover, according to this attempt at analysis, we have internalized some of the gynephobic elements of the patriarchy, and we harbor a lot of "horizontal hostility" because patriarchy has taught women to distrust each other and look only to men for leadership. As Adrienne Rich writes in "Women and Honor: Some Notes on Lying," under patriarchy women can only survive by lies and manipulation; we then carry these weapons into relationships even with those who do not have power over us—other women.[1] Rich exhorts us to learn to deal openly and honestly with each other.

From well before adolescence, this line of argument continues, we have been socialized to form cliques, to be gatekeepers, and to engage in what might well be called "social sorting." We protect our own status and limited possibilities by discrediting other women, just as proper Victorian wives would open their homes to a male adulterer in their social circle, but not to his mistress. Not surprisingly, then, what we see in Women's Studies is an intellectual and personal preoccupation with the tasks once assigned to Victorian women: to keep the language pure, to act as guardians of morality (feminist morality, now), and to spread tales about those who do not measure up to the prevailing norms (whether it be questions of etiquette or political correctness). From this point of view, Women's Studies as theory reflects the traditional location of women in domestic arrangements, while Women's Studies as practice derives from the sort of tribal/consensus/shaming strategies that work best in family-sized groups.

Still others blamed the media representations of feminism: Because feminist gender analyses have been so distorted by enemies of feminism, many people are resistant to the new perspectives that Women's Studies offers. Other feminist scholars, however, suggested that the very success of feminism may also be responsible for students' alienation (a point alluded to in chapter 1). Though social problems and inequality persist, they said, gender is no longer news. Incoming students no longer find the feminist analyses presented in Women's Studies programs novel and original. Women's Studies, unless it can continually find new issues around which to crusade, may seem to have lost some of its raison d'être.

Moreover, some of our narrators noted that, in the current economic and political climate, the academic study of women (and gender) seems less promising as an effective agent of change than it had once appeared to be. Social transformation turns out to be a long and arduous process. Nevertheless, some activists criticize and even disdain Women's Studies as "merely" academic. Whether voiced or not, such a perspective hangs like a menacing cloud over many Women's Studies programs today. In fact, the more established and successful such programs become, the more vulnerable they are to this sort of accusation. In other words, Women's Studies programs cannot fail to be subjected to a kind of undermining from within. Most other academic programs are immune to this sort of attack: Their self-definition as "academic and educational" does not invite such assaults from within or without, and neither "backlash" nor complacency haunts them.

Other women we interviewed offered more particularistic explanations. Some activists felt that Women's Studies has become too immersed in arcane theory; others blamed "white privilege." And one feminist, now a dean, insisted that Women's Studies had no greater internal difficulties and bad vibes than other academic departments. Women, she said, get "demonized" when they behave the way men do.

Even those feminists deeply distressed by the internal problems faced by Women's Studies tended to blame them on outside forces and suggested that they would wither away "after the revolution." Sadly, we cannot agree.

Although we see some truth in most of the preceding arguments, we find that, upon reflection, all are insufficient to a greater or lesser extent. And so we opt for a different approach, one that looks more closely at Women's Studies programs as an outgrowth and embodiment of a specifically feminist ideology. It is not the personal or institutional relations, in other words, that deserve scrutiny, but rather the explicit premises and practices on which Women's Studies was built. Such a perspective gives quite a different meaning to the oft-cited definition of Women's Studies as "the academic arm of feminism." Responsibility for the difficulties faced by Women's Studies lies, in our view, not primarily with malevolent patriarchy and its effects but with the ideological variant of feminism that has been embraced by and incorporated into the academy.

We are aware of an immediate skeptical response that may be raised against our endeavor to understand Women's Studies as an expression of feminist ideology. Does it make sense to talk about a "feminist ideology" when every student in a feminist theory class has learned to differentiate and contrast the various "feminisms"? There are socialist feminism and Marxist feminism, psychoanalytic feminism and postmodernist feminism. There are radical lesbian and womanist approaches, and others as well.

We acknowledge the existence of this proliferation of feminist positions, and we know that this very pluralism of views makes for interesting debate. But we also hold that the feminist academic community embraces a particular cluster of elemental precepts and patterns of response to social and educational issues, and that it is these basic precepts and patterns that are responsible for the sorry situation in Women's Studies. We use the word *ideology* in the common sense of a set of general ideas people have about the world (more specifically, about human society), which influence what they believe, what they find important and valuable, and how they think people ought to act. For our purposes, we prefer this term to *worldview* or *philosophy of life*, because *ideology* connotes that some of the ideas people hold are unarticulated and unacknowledged. Furthermore, in certain of its usages, *ideology* conveys the suspicion that the basic beliefs in question may be distorted and self-serving. Thus, one speaks of "analyzing" a philosophy of life but of "disclosing" or "unmasking" an ideology—the implication being that the person who subscribes to an ideology will be either reluctant to own up to it or unable to examine it critically.

The identification of someone's allegiance to an ideology normally rests on indirect or circumstantial evidence. One looks for recurring patterns of behavior and characteristic locutions as well as explicit formulations. What the investigator in effect says is: "You are comporting yourself as if you were acting on the ideology I have attributed to you." The investigator cannot prove that her interpretation is accurate. She can only show that, if correct, it will explain behavior that would otherwise appear strange, or even bizarre.

People usually adopt ideological stances unknowingly and rarely subject them to systematic scrutiny. Their beliefs tend, therefore, to be not only vague and incomplete but also often inconsistent. Since this is certainly true of feminist ideology, we do not attempt to offer a set of propositions with the pretense that these define the feminist ideological canon. Instead, in the next few chapters, we describe and analyze a series of maneuvers that we have found popular in contemporary academic feminism. We call these maneuvers "games," partly in an allusion to the concepts of "language games" and "forms of life," as developed by Ludwig Wittgenstein. But primarily we wish to emphasize the fact that these patterns of behavior incorporate conventional rules that the participants could, if they wished, agree to change. We definitely do not mean to suggest that these games are frivolous or recreational. Those involved in them take them very seriously, and—as we show later—the games have consequences for real people in real life. In the long run, the players can only come out as losers.

Despite the underlying seriousness of these games, we have not attempted to suppress the satirical tone that has often crept into our descriptions of the games feminists play. Once these ideology-based maneuvers are exposed, it is difficult not to treat them in a deprecating manner. We hope that other feminists, too, will see the absurdity of these games and acknowledge their self-defeating nature. That is surely the first step toward a turn to good sense and professionalism.

IDPOL: IDENTITY POLITICS AND
IDEOLOGICAL POLICING

We begin with the most popular game of all: identity politics, or what we call IDPOL. (We note with satisfaction that it could also stand for ideological policing, an enduring feature of feminist politics.) The central mission of feminist activism is to put the needs of women first. Its single criterion for appraising a political initiative is: Will it help women? Such a focus may be entirely appropriate for rallying support around particular issues. But we need to examine the consequences of allowing such a mission to be embraced by an academic program. What happens when the activist notion of basing politics on identity is allowed to shape the ethos of Women's Studies?

Social scientists use the term *identity politics* in a neutral way to describe the various methods that social movements employ to "alter the self-conceptions and societal conceptions of their participants."[2] But in recent years, identity politics has come to mean something quite different. IDPOL now stands for the attempt by a particular group to gain a political advantage from whatever makes it identifiable *as* a group. Its practitioners wield IDPOL as an instrument for disadvantaged or oppressed groups to seize their rightful share of power in the world.

Seeking favors for one's own group is as old a practice as politics itself. But while lobbyists for special interests rarely own up to their quest for disproportionate benefits, feminist players of IDPOL proudly demand preferential treatment, claiming that their history of oppression entitles women to special consideration. Much can be said for what Aristotle calls "rectificatory justice," but it immediately raises two very complicated questions: Who should decide what is just compensation for past inequities, and who should pay the retribution?

By and large, feminists offer a simple answer to these questions: Oppressed people are uniquely situated to say what they should get, and the oppressors are morally obligated to acknowledge their claims.

According to feminist epistemology, the knowledge produced by those in power (typically, white European males) inevitably reflects their partisan interests and is prejudicial to all those not in power. The knowledge needed for liberation must, therefore, be generated by the oppressed themselves. In addition, feminists often claim that the morality and value systems of oppressed groups are inherently superior to those of the oppressors, whose long history of exploitative behavior has demonstrated their moral bankruptcy. Last but not least, it is assumed that the only way for an oppressed group to remedy its unsatisfactory situation is by single-mindedly pursuing the needs of its own members.

As long as gender was the key variable in defining identity, it was men and a few "male-identified" women who were seen as oppressors, while most women occupied the status of victims. In time, however, other stigmatized identities emerged, and soon nearly everyone could lay claim to some need for special treatment. The result has been a degrading struggle among members of identity groups for the recognition of each group's oppression, generating an atmosphere of condemnation directed at anyone who could be labeled a member of a more privileged group. Comparing types and degrees of oppression is a tough business, and, not surprisingly, it has led to much hostility as one group elbows another for pride of place in the contest for "most oppressed" status. Rather than contributing to an atmosphere of collegiality, self-pity and allegations of guilt lead to suspicion and mutual recriminations. As played today, IDPOL is more than the ugly spawn of old-fashioned special-interest jockeying and ethnic politics. In recent times, this offspring has been further crossed with oppression analyses coming out of the left to create a virulently personalized form of IDPOL that is perhaps the single most destructive aspect of Women's Studies programs today.

Certainly, feminists neither invented IDPOL nor monopolize its use today. But many feminists have found it a thoroughly congenial tool. In turn, they have often seen it aimed at themselves. After all, no one has an unassailable identity. To recognize this simple fact is the beginning of humane fellow feeling. If seriously played, the game of IDPOL would leave only corpses on the field. It divides allies from one another as it feeds its appetite for ever-new targets to attack. Formerly devalued, now highly prized; formerly on top, now at bottom; the cast of characters changes, but in the game of IDPOL the clock never runs down.

The Amazon Laughed: "Tell Your Brothers"

When we talked to people about difficulties in Women's Studies, a recurring theme was the "problematic" presence of men in Women's Studies classes. Some said male students interrupt women, talk too much, question the authority of the female professor, are defensive when the topics of rape or wife battering come up, and in general "just don't get it." Others, however, were appalled at how rudely the more radical women students treated any males who strayed into "their" classes. And although some feminists have said that male undergraduates should be forced to take at least one Women's Studies class in order to confront their own sexism (and, indeed, some colleges now have compulsory sensitivity training sessions or require all students to take a course on gender and diversity issues), there was wide agreement that Women's Studies classes go more smoothly when men are not around.

Men who have strong sympathies with feminism are frequently surprised and hurt when they find they are not welcome in feminist circles. In an unpublished novel called "The Amazon's Brother: Testimony of a Committed Coed Feminist," Allan Hunter, then an undergraduate, wrote allegorically of his disappointment:

> He was sternly informed that [joining his sister to live with the Amazons] was out of the question, and was told of all the terrible man-crimes and man-ways that made male presence in their land intolerable. Said he, "I am not like that; try me for any such crimes, and if your court finds me innocent of [them], allow me to pass."

The Amazon sentinel laughed and told him that they had far more important things to do than evaluate each individual man who claimed to be different from the rest, saying, "I have yet to meet a man who did not think himself to be the single exception."

The young man protested. "I agree with your way of thinking about many things, and I want to share your lifestyle as an equal, for you are like unto neither the women nor the men in the maleworld, as you call it, and life there is intolerable."

Again the sentinel laughed and said, "Tell your brothers."[3]

Writing ten years later of his experience in a feminist theory class, Hunter, now a graduate student in sociology and Women's Studies at the State University of New York at Stony Brook, says that his attempts to debate theoretical issues in this class invariably led to "the constant question of 'Who asked you? Why should any of us give a damn if YOU don't like the direction that feminist theory is taking? It's our stuff, not your stuff.'" He finally concluded that it is conceptually problematic for any male to be a full-scale committed participant in the political effort to transform patriarchy.[4]

Nor is Hunter alone in having reached this conclusion. One consequence of a strict interpretation of gender IDPOL is that only women can be fully engaged in women's liberation. If Women's Studies is conceived of as an academy for training young feminists, it makes no sense to devote energy to male students, and males will not be welcome in Women's Studies classrooms. But this attitude cannot coexist with the broader feminist goal of educating everyone about gender issues. From the beginning, therefore, IDPOL was destructive to feminism's long-term aims.

Some feminist faculty recall their own discomfort with the way in which gender IDPOL was being played out in their programs. Linda, a white woman in her fifties, is a historian at a large research university. She has been involved with her school's Women's Studies program from its inception, more than two decades ago. Deeply committed to the ideal of community, she has reflected extensively on the causes of the lack of civility and the absence of tolerance among feminists:

> I have felt this all along, since the early seventies. This is nothing new. Lack of tolerance for high levels of diversity has been endemic to the program from the beginning. I would trace it to the inability to deal with a fundamental difference—and that is men. Once you've defined the world as a world of women, and you have decided that men cannot be assimilated into the way in which you develop your theory and methodology, and the way you interact socially, then you've already placed yourself in a curious contradiction to the whole concept of diversity. This feeling I've had has, I think, affected my social relationships with members of Women's Studies.
>
> I don't really want to sound as conservative as I'm going to sound right now. Let me just lay out this position for a second and then take it back, or qualify it. I do believe in divorce, but I think the ease with which people's intimate relationships are dissolved—whether they're married or nonmarried—because they can't get on with one another, because they are incompatible in some fundamental way, and the degree to which our culture has fostered the notion of not struggling together to work on differences and accept conflict, is also a reflection of what I call the separatist tradition of American society.
>
> That goes back to the Puritans separating from the Church of England in order to set up their ideal City on the Hill. We have had a profoundly separatist mentality in which denominations separate from one another, political groups separate from one another, rather than struggle together to work on their differences, to find modes of accommodation and pluralistic solutions. That separatist mentality was there in a very powerful way by the sixties in marital relationships and ultimately in women *needing* to separate from men. . . .
>
> There's no question in my mind that women *had* to separate

from men, that most of those partnerships were probably hope-less. But that became a way of not facing that there might be lots of situations where that was not the best solution, where working with men and learning how to deal with profound dif-ferences might have been a better way of handling things.

Because Linda believes that the organization of Women's Studies as a separate department generally exacerbates intolerance and the playing of IDPOL, she does not favor such a structure:

> I think one reason for the difficulties at my university is that Women's Studies has to make political appointments. We have to hire people *in* Women's Studies. My theory is that we were *much* better off before we were a department. When you do those things—hires, fires, reappointments, tenure, all this per-sonnel decision making—power enters. Not only does power enter, but also the question of, Who do you want to work closely with? Do you want a clone? Or do you want someone very different from yourself? And on the whole, I think that women—and it may well be because they've had enormous difficulty dealing with the otherness of men—want clones. Maybe they wouldn't say they want clones exactly, but they want people with whom they would feel a high level of rapport ideologically and personally.

There is an alternative to polarization and separatism, one that Linda much prefers, but she did not see this alternative model devel-oping within Women's Studies:

> It would have been an inclusive model. Before you get to the point of adding issues of race and ethnicity and religion and sexual preference and the disabled and all these other cate-gories of difference, there has to be a respect for other people's decisions to live certain kinds of lives, whether it's to have chil-

dren or not to have children, to be married to men or not to be married to men. These choices can't be seen as excluding someone from being a thoroughgoing feminist in theory or in practice. And I think there was this problem of exclusion from the beginning.

Having embraced exclusiveness and hostility toward those identified as outsiders, women, perhaps inevitably, soon turned on one another once the category "women" began to fragment along identity lines.

Sleeping with the Enemy

If, at first, women in the feminist movement considered gender the source of their primary identity, it quickly became apparent that this classification was no guarantee of internal unity. Many activists also identified themselves as lesbian. But since, according to the logic of IDPOL, one can only trust the perceptions and values of people who share one's identity, it is not surprising that conflicts arose, especially as the process of "coming out" and positively affirming a gay identity had been such a significant feature of lesbian existence.

The idea that the definition of one's identity incorporates political commitments is a central tenet of gay liberation analysis. As long as being homosexual was defined by traditional religion or by psychoanalysis, it was very difficult for gay people to view themselves as anything other than sinful, sick, or freaks of nature. By redefining themselves instead as gay (in both senses of the word), people of a same-sex orientation could begin to shed their stigmatized identities, to use the phrasing of Erving Goffman.[5]

But lesbian feminists then proposed a different and more radical definitional shift, one that led to political realignments. Feeling that it made better political sense to separate lesbians from the gay male liberation movement and wanting to form stronger alliances with nonlesbian feminists, they suggested that *lesbian* be redefined as "woman-identified woman." This change, they said, would remove sexual preference as the defining criterion of lesbian identity, and thereby would create potential common ground among lesbian feminists and other women interested in liberating women from male domination.

There were lesbian and heterosexual activists who argued that they should be able to work together, since both lesbian identity and feminist identity hinged on commitment to women. The liberation of women envisioned by feminists would automatically liberate lesbians, so the argument went. Instead of talking simply about patriarchy, these groups spoke of "heteropatriarchy," and in a famous often-anthologized essay called "Compulsory Heterosexuality and Lesbian Existence," Adrienne Rich contended that any woman who questioned male privilege and put emotional energy into women was part of the "lesbian continuum" of women-identified women.[6] Sexual preference was only one aspect of the feminist project of concentrating on women's needs and potentialities.

However, these attempts by theoreticians to build bridges between heterosexual and lesbian feminists were not very successful. Lesbians never forgot that Betty Friedan and other founders of NOW had called them the "lavender menace,"[7] while heterosexual women resented being told that they were "sleeping with the enemy." Furthermore, lesbians often felt that they were putting more than their fair share of energy into the new feminist institutions, such as battered women's shelters and Women's Studies programs, and that straight women did not appreciate their contributions. As one woman, Silvia, told us bitterly: "We worked our asses off, but we were told to be invisible because it would be bad for the big picture if the movement was cast as a bunch of radical dykes. The idea was to work for the rights of all women with the belief that the gains would trickle down to us. It simply never happened." Nonlesbians, on the other hand, noted that lesbians now seemed to be trying to turn *feminist* into a codeword for *lesbian* and were thereby using feminist organizations as a kind of cover to deflect stigma.

The logic of sexual identity politics also played itself out in the classroom. Just as radical feminists had argued that works by men had no place in the syllabus, radical lesbian feminists now demanded that the syllabus include *their* people. And Rich's concept of the lesbian continuum, which some had hoped would forge bonds between feminists of different persuasions, was used instead as a yardstick to determine the depth of one's commitment to feminism. Not surprisingly, Women's Studies students who talked about boyfriends or whose dress seemed intended to attract male attention did not measure up very well on the lesbian continuum.

Quite different tensions developed when feminists who had previously identified themselves as heterosexual decided that it would be politically preferable to sleep with women. These so-called political lesbians, unaccustomed to the courtship patterns in the lesbian subculture, were often accused by "born lesbians" of exploiting the latter's erotic energy. And although many political lesbians aggressively displayed their newfound sexual preference publicly as a badge of their feminist commitment, when springtime came they frequently found themselves falling in love with men again. When the failure of the feminist attempt to redefine sexuality in terms of polymorphous sensual sisterhood became apparent, lesbians then felt that it was they who had been tricked into sleeping with the enemy. Resentment of bisexual women increased dramatically as the AIDS epidemic worsened.

Silvia, the lesbian cited earlier, reserved her deepest criticism for the doctrinaire attitudes that developed within feminism itself as these conflicts were played out:

> I do what I interpret is precisely the main feminist message: to be independent, to think for myself, to question assumptions and stereotypes, and to claim an empowered life outside the realm of tradition in which a woman had to be "completed" by a man. When I heard those messages, I was excited, overwhelmed with enthusiasm, and thus naively believed what was

said. I set out to be independent, to think for myself, to question things, et cetera. However, when I entered into the realm of the "movement," I found that this wasn't what feminism was "about" at all. My experience has been that feminism has been just as conformist and stifling of creative thought as the most right-wing religious groups.

It seems that many in the feminist and lesbian subcultures require that you meet all of their criteria and address their agendas before they are willing to listen to what you have to say. We—women, feminists, lesbians, whatever—so often make statements or wear buttons proclaiming "Question Authority" or "Question Everything." However, we rarely, if ever, question feminism. Is it justifiable for women to trash or embarrass a male in a Women's Studies class on the grounds that men have done the same to women for ages? Questioning the authority of feminism or the heavyweights within the movement is akin to heresy, and is basically treated as such.

I have watched with great interest (and sometimes sadness) as the feminist and lesbian subcultures evolve. My latest barrage of criticism came when I made the statement that we lesbians have treated our bisexual sisters much the same as heterosexual society has treated us, and that we should be ashamed of ourselves because we should know better.

As we have seen, feminists had argued that women must isolate themselves from men. By the same logic, faults quickly appeared within feminism along lines of sexual preference. Many other fissures were to open in a chain reaction that, eventually, would threaten to leave feminism splintered.

Dismantling White Women's Studies

In 1977 a group called the Combahee River Collective issued a "Black Feminist Statement":

We believe that the most profound and potentially the most radical politics come directly out of our own identity, as opposed to working to end somebody else's oppression.... We realize that the only people who care enough about us to work consistently for our liberation is us. Our politics evolve from a healthy love for ourselves, our sisters, and our community which allows us to continue our struggle and work.[8]

This manifesto became an important statement of the growing belief among African-American women that "white feminism" was in many respects ill-suited to their political needs. One vivid example arose in connection with the feminist stance on rape. Whereas the official feminist analysis held that there is a very strong presumption that any female who alleges rape is telling the truth, black women remembered too many cases in which black men had been lynched as rapists simply on the say-so of a white woman. In their version of identity-based epistemology, then, race was sometimes a better guide than gender. And there were many other grounds on which they felt uncomfortable with the feminist agenda. Abortion on demand, for example, was not a good issue around which to organize grassroots support in the black community. And all the energy that early white middle-class feminists had devoted to liberating themselves from the "feminine mystique" seemed pretty silly to black women who had grown up with hardworking mothers who were outspoken and strong-willed.

Black women activists were faced with a confusing array of identity niches. Some joined African-American studies programs, but others found those arenas too male-dominated and turned to Women's Studies. Black lesbians had even more decisions to make. For example, when they attended a NWSA meeting, should they work through the black caucus or the lesbian caucus? Or should they form a black lesbian caucus?

Similar decisions faced the well-meaning feminist instructor who wished to design a syllabus that reflected all the major identity groups. If she devoted only one assignment to the concerns of, say, black lesbians, she was likely to be accused of "tokenism." Some students even went so far as to argue that a course should not be offered until the requisite number of works by authors of "proper identities" were available. As one professor reported: "That is exactly what a white Women's Studies student last fall commented on my course, in a tone of high censoriousness. She wrote that if I didn't know of more than one work by a black writer that fit into my rather specialized course, I damn well shouldn't be offering the course until I'd researched the subject thoroughly."

Such dilemmas arose in connection with scholarly publishing, too. Black feminists complained that they were invisible or, at the very least, underrepresented in feminist journals and anthologies. White feminists countered that for a variety of reasons, some of them demographic and others having to do with the history of racism, there was a dearth of material written by black women. But the perspectives of black women were taken to heart, and it quickly became a standard trope of feminist criticism to claim that any work of feminist scholarship that does not explicitly focus on race is seriously defective. A white woman professor told us that when a book she had edited got blasted in a feminist journal for not containing a sufficient number of articles by and about women of color, a concerned friend informed her that she was "dead" as a scholar because of the imputation of racism.

On the other hand, it is usually considered inappropriate for white women to do too much research on minority women. After all, how can they pretend to have genuine insight into another identity? Are they not simply usurping the voices of women of color—engaging in ventriloquism? And it has also become very difficult for white women to reflect critically on anything written by a woman of color. A white professor reports:

> In one of my classes a student made a criticism of a metaphor utilized in a novel by a black writer. One of the Women's Studies majors sniffily observed that it was not up to us, as white women, to criticize a black writer's metaphors. A rather shy student in the same class, who was also a Women's Studies

major, confessed in paper after paper her guilt over her "white-skin privilege" and her status as "oppressor." And why not? I have repeatedly heard a black colleague of mine declare: "There are two kinds of people in the world: oppressors and oppressed—and these correspond to white and nonwhite."

IDPOL can also readily lead to disputes about grades when teachers and students belong to different identity groups. Another Women's Studies professor wrote to us:

There is a professor of history here who teaches the course Women in History (a core component of the program), who is being raked over the coals for not including [in her syllabus] all women of all countries. . . . At the last meeting at which this problem was discussed, a student who is a woman of color said that she got a 78 percent on her paper—which she considered to be a poor mark—because the faculty member involved, not being black, did not understand her. The whole issue has become very scary to me, and the instances of people either losing their jobs or leaving voluntarily are increasing.

What most bothers me personally is the way people measure their words in order not to offend. Let's face it: people can be offended over virtually anything, and if we spend our lives worrying about it, we really will not have too much to say. As Susan Sontag says, we must be against censorship and self-censorship and for the right to offend. It is frustrating to me to be told that I cannot respond or speak a certain way because I am of a certain skin color. I thought we were supposed to have gone beyond all that. There are racists and there are sexists. I am not one of them, and I do not like being accused of being one simply by virtue of my appearance.

Silvia, the lesbian critic of feminist orthodoxies whom we quoted earlier, also protested against what she called "this double standard stuff":

What could possibly be more racist and/or condescending than to expect less of an individual, to allow an individual to present positions (and even praise them) that are riddled with inconsistencies, or to hold another individual to higher standards of rigor, based upon their ethnicity or race? Sometimes I am ashamed to call myself a feminist, and I often feel that I have to add so many qualifiers that it is hardly worth it.

IDPOL has also frequently led to charges of racism concerning administrative decisions. This was the experience of one of the authors of this book when she served briefly as program director. A particularly nasty blow-up occurred when new funds could not be located for an elective course proposed by two minority graduate students, who were to be the instructors. At about the same time, the director had used the last of the existing budget to hire the most experienced graduate student (who was white) to teach a required course for which no faculty member was available. The minority students protested and accused the director of being racist:

> At a large meeting of our governing board, I attempted to explain how the two, quite unrelated, decisions regarding courses and teaching assistants had been made. A young black colleague said (as I had heard her say on other occasions) that when a woman of color states that she has been the victim of racism, *she* is the authority on that experience and cannot be challenged. I replied that this assertion made examining any problem impossible. That comment only made things worse. No one supported me in trying to move our discussion to a different ground. More accusations followed: I was said to be guilty of racism personally, while the program was tagged as pervaded by "structural racism." The white graduate student announced that she could not, in good conscience, teach the course for which she had been hired.
>
> By now I have learned that the only acceptable response in feminist circles when accusations of racism surface is, "Mea

culpa." It was also clear, even to me after a while, that a power
play was going on. Accusations of racism gained for the accuser
points of some sort. Keeping others on the defensive seemed to
have become a strategy no one was willing to challenge.

But I believed that the issue of the truth or falsity of particular accusations needed to be addressed. Knowing the "identity" of accuser and accused simply was not enough to resolve
a grievance. I denied the charges—which only brought a storm
upon my head. The result was that I found myself increasingly
isolated as memos flew about, accusing me of one thing and
another, while my "friends"—senior, tenured faculty in Wom-
en's Studies, who were in perfectly secure positions—tried fee-
bly to support me behind the scenes but were unwilling to say
anything in public.

Evidence of my "racism" was produced, such as a memo I
had written to a Women's Studies committee urging us to
attempt to work together without casting blame or attaching
labels to one another. My suggestion that it did not help matters
to bandy about terms such as "Eurocentric" and "racist"—
which by then had become virtual synonyms and were repeated
by our students—was itself cited as a further mark of my
"racism." Long afterwards—small comfort—one of my former
friends, who had remained publicly silent throughout this
depleting episode, said to me: "You did nothing wrong, and race
had nothing to do with it." That was one of the few times reference was ever made to what had happened. None of the princi-
pal belligerents said a word to me later about their accusations.

In such a climate, professional decorum, concepts of collegiality,
and proper academic procedures are quick to fall:

A colleague of mine, I later found out, allowed two of her students that semester to do an "analysis" of racism in the program which highlighted that same memo of mine—a confiden-
tial memo addressed to a Women's Studies committee.

Toward the end of that semester, a group of graduate students proposed that, during the following term, they team-teach a course on indigenous women. My colleagues accepted the sketchy proposal without asking any questions about it, over my protests that we needed time to consider the proposal calmly. One voiced the predominant view: "We can't afford to turn it down"—this, despite the fact that there was no detailed course proposal on the table before us, merely a couple of lines followed by a listing of half a dozen North and South American "identities," which would presumably serve as the subjects of the course.

These episodes cost me any lingering faith I had in our program as a place where serious academic work—not to mention normal collegial relations—could exist.

Denunciations of homophobia and racism can, of course, just as easily be made by heterosexuals or whites as by actual members of oppressed groups, and some of the most bizarre situations arise when it is white women who are accusing one another of racism in situations where no women of color are directly involved. Often the allegations seem to be serving primarily as ammunition in personal struggles for power.

What is the atmosphere like in a program that has gone through such battles? One professor wrote as follows:

I have no doubt that in our Women's Studies program, each of us felt that we were working in an extremely hostile environment, surrounded by women who for the most part had no respect or liking for one another. One day, after a particularly tense meeting, I imagined how the scene might look to a being from another planet. Such a creature's account might go like this:

"I descended to earth one afternoon and found myself in a room filled with beings colorfully dressed. From their discussion I understood these were, or were acting on behalf of, a group called "women"—a category apparently suffering some sort of disadvantage in relation to another category named "men" who did not seem to be present. These women, if such they were, were of a variety of colors—some pale ivory, some dark brown, some beige, some pinkish. Though to my senses they looked very much alike—all had two eyes, a protrusion centrally placed on the face and serving I know not what purpose, a pink-colored opening from which sound emerged, and shell-shaped appendages on either side of the face from which pieces of stone and glittery metal sometimes dangled— it was clear that they saw themselves as very different from one another, and made much of these differences. Foremost among the distinctions was the hue of the skin—all used the phrase "women of color" repeatedly—and I sensed that some of the darker-complexioned among them harbored a particular grievance against the others that was often on the verge of exploding but equally often was expressed in innuendo and gesture. The lighter-skinned, by contrast, were nervous, poised as if prepared to receive a blow and, judging by their expressions, awash in feelings of conflict and guilt ill concealed by their apparent acceptance of angry words from the others. Fear was evident in all these beings, mingled with hostility and resentment, over I knew not what."

IDPOL based on race can, of course, also lead to animosities among women of color. A black Latina woman speaking at a conference session that one of us attended told of participating in the first Latin American meeting of women who identified themselves as black (many Latin American women do not, either because they have no African ancestry or because they downplay it). The speaker reported that the organizers had decided not to admit lighter-skinned women of African descent to the meeting. She personally had seen a light-skinned, straight-haired woman challenged at the conference door with, "What are you doing here?" In recounting the episode, the speaker seemed to applaud this procedure. She reported that when she conducted interviews, she made it a point to challenge light-skinned women who spoke to her about their "black grandmother." While many in the audience squirmed uncomfortably, noting that the speaker herself had far lighter skin than many blacks, she declared in tones of moral righteousness that she would not let such interviewees "get away with denying their light-skin privilege."

Many of the white Women's Studies professors we interviewed seemed genuinely puzzled over what could be done about the allegations of racism they had encountered, and the ritualistic denunciations and confessions of "white-skin privilege." These accusations seemed especially troublesome to them in light of the frequent and rather desperate searches for "affirmative action" candidates to fill "special opportunities" positions within their departments. Moreover, many white women teaching in Women's Studies programs had never been guilty of "ignoring" women of color in their courses, a common charge. Linda, the history professor cited earlier in this chapter, who has been very active in her university's Women's Studies program for the past twenty years, analyzed the situation this way:

> There is a tendency to mythologize the seventies as being unaware of the issues of race and ethnicity. Quite honestly, I was then teaching my women's history course very little differently, in terms of its race component, than I do now. That is, I always taught a lot about women under slavery, I taught a lot about ethnic and immigrant cultures. I think the major change is that I deal much more now with indigenous American women, Native American women. But my course was always pluralistic. So it's not like this became a sudden new agenda in the late eighties. It was there all along, it just took on a much greater urgency and intensity in the mid-eighties.

The most common response to the angry allegations of racism has been to elevate this issue to the theoretical level, where calls for an "integrated analysis" of race, gender, class, sexuality, ethnicity, and so on, are recited "like a mantra" (as several of the professors we interviewed put it). In practice, this means that, whether discussing a novel or a social problem, one must always focus on race, gender, class, sexuality, and so on, and demonstrate how these factors interact. Proponents of "integrated analysis" always claim that the forces that create oppression (and the privilege that is its counterpart) are systemically related and that unless all are removed, no real or lasting progress will have been made. Mysteriously, the central force or forces that this integrated analysis purports to expose are never specified, beyond rounding up the usual suspects: hierarchy, heteropatriarchy, contempt for the Other, phallocentrism, multinational capitalism, imperialism, hegemonic nationalism, worship of "power over" instead of empowerment, and on and on.

Black women, on the other hand, have grown increasingly angry at what they view as the refusal of white feminists to admit their own racism. They favor the term *structural racism* to refer to institutional arrangements dependent on both the heritage of racism generally and the subtle complicity they allege exists between white women's self-definition and the white American male's assumption of an identity constructed on the oppression of African Americans.

This sweeping charge was spelled out in detail for us by Marilyn, a black professor in a social science department who is also active in her university's Women's Studies program. She identifies herself as a "womanist," using a term popularized by the writer Alice Walker to refer to nonseparatist black women who see their struggle as one on behalf of black women *and* men.[9] "*Feminist*," Marilyn says, "for me, is too narrowly associated with white women. And most women of color who have issues and are active around them are not feminist, do not define themselves as feminist." Women's Studies, in Marilyn's view, is *white* Women's Studies:

> I would like to be able to see students of color who are attending predominantly white institutions be able to study them-

selves in relationship to whites and other women of color, and to get their degree doing it. Right now, in order to get their degree, they still have to predominantly study whites, and I think that's inappropriate. But that's the only Women's Studies there is. We don't have a nonwhite Women's Studies; we have white Women's Studies. Everybody else kind of plugs into it.

I happen to be at this school, but there are plenty of schools where there's *no* people like me. So, therefore, I'm saying that the mass of the curriculum that's available for anybody who's doing Women's Studies is a white curriculum. When I teach a course, I'm plugging my little bitty course into this big white curriculum. It's a fly in a glass of milk. So I don't see that as change.

What would it take for real change to occur? Marilyn outlines her vision:

I think it's going to take white women dealing with their complicity with white men, and I don't think they will do that. I don't think that they want to look at that. You know, white women, on the one hand, are willing to acknowledge the way the whole women's movement itself really caught fire on the coattails of the black movement. People will give lip service to that in an intellectual form. People don't want to think about the pragmatic, practical implications of that, in terms of what this program should be looking like. If the black movement gave birth to the women's movement, why aren't black people central in the women's movement? Racism, that's why.

What I'm saying is that if it's ever going to change, that change has to be an internal one, in those women who currently hold power in Women's Studies. What needs to happen is for those women to be able to *acknowledge* the way in which their efforts to include themselves in a particular group of power has exclusionary tendencies. Even when people of color are invited by them, there are ways in which people of color who have been invited in are constrained in their opportunities to articulate *their* vision of what the program ought to look like. That constraint is specifically designed to make the people who are the *core* of the program—i.e., the white women—feel safe. And so, until white women who are the core of these programs are willing to look at that, and to give up some sense of that safety, and to take more risk, I don't think we're going to see a change, no matter how many creative courses people of color create.

Marilyn explains what she means by the "power" that white women exercise in Women's Studies:

These women have white privilege—that's their power. I'm not saying that they run the university. I'm not saying that they have the power to make their Women's Studies program or department whatever they wanted it to be. But I am saying that they collude with the university in the maintenance of white power—white privilege. And even their subordination is part of their collusion—in the same way that the subordination of white women to white men made white male supremacy possible. That's exactly what I'm saying.

I'm saying that white women as a class of people had to allow themselves to be subordinated by white males in order to reify this notion of white supremacy. So white supremacy in a general sense applies to all white people, but in a very specific, analytical sense it mainly refers to white male supremacy. And white women have always known this. They have generally raised their sons to be white male supremacists. I think that the interest of a woman in doing that is that she will have a dominant white male son who is able to gain greater access to the available resources than most other people on earth.

To a question about whether some of Women's Studies difficulties might be due to lack of respect or civility among colleagues without this having anything to do with race, Marilyn responded emphatically:

> Well, this is one of the places where you and I probably differ, and I know this is very much because I was born in a black body and you weren't. But in my opinion, it's completely ludicrous for me to hear you say that those particular kinds of problems that you just described don't have anything to do with race. White women don't know who they themselves are in isolation from women of color, and white women don't know who they themselves are independently of the construction of male power. So it makes sense to me, since vertical oppression—that is, oppression by males against white women—always produces horizontal oppression—that is, people fighting among themselves. So I see that as a racial phenomenon. It doesn't bother me that you don't, but I think that until you *can*, we won't ever solve the problem. I don't know why you're not willing. I suspect it's fear, fear of what could happen with the relinquishment of authority.

"Definitely one of the disappointments of my adult life," says Marilyn, "[is] that I fail to see more emphasis on people of color in most Women's Studies programs." Although their complaints differed widely, everyone we talked to was disappointed at the way Women's Studies programs had negotiated issues of race. Whatever their take on the nature of racism and what should be done about it, our narrators had all expected Women's Studies to be a strategic site for making some progress on these problems.

We submit, however, that IDPOL, which has been the main strategy for addressing the problem of race (as well as gender), does more harm than good to this cause. According to the logic of IDPOL, one must always act in one's own group's interest as long as that group is oppressed. Oppressors are assumed to be doing the same for their side, but they should be castigated for doing so. Thus, a man who does not support a feminist cause is automatically a sexist; a white person who disagrees with a black person's position is a racist. The reverse, however, is not the case. Consequently, those defined as oppressed place a high premium on keeping that identity.

Patriarchy and Pigs at the Trough

The logical result of extreme identity-based politics is tribalism or balkanization, the partitioning of a complex system into small ethnically and culturally distinct units of homogeneous identities, none of which seeks coalitions with any other unit (not unlike the situation that has been occurring in the former Yugoslavia).

The expanding intricacies of IDPOL have led to the creation of entirely new categories of oppression. At many feminist public events there are now special scent-free seating areas for the "environmentally disadvantaged" who cannot tolerate the smell of deodorants or hairspray. Feminist institutions, not surprisingly, have become notorious for their factionalism. The large annual Michigan Women's Music Festival has even introduced segregated seating, drawn on identity lines, for its concerts and camping grounds. Feminists are proud of their abilities to accommodate the needs of diverse women, but they also joke uneasily about this multiplication of "identities" and realize that it is apt to lead to a splintering and trivializing of the feminist movement, so that it loses its potential for genuine political action.

A recent college graduate reported to us on how the focus of concern in the "Take Back the Night" marches in which she participates gradually changed from dealing with college jocks who harassed the marchers from the sidewalks to trying to maintain harmony among different groups of feminists:

Being on Internet gave me an opportunity to meet people and receive information—like a twelve-page list of activities, meetings, conferences, and receptions to be held prior to the march [sponsored by] Catholics, Jewish women, lesbians, bisexuals, polysexuals, African-American women, women of Spanish descent, Greek women-loving women, reformed Catholic lesbian women loving Greek women with tattoos. The list just went on and on. There seemed to be a little subgroup for every single person who categorized herself as "oppressed"—or maybe just a special interest.

Yes, I fit into more than one of the above categories, and I understand the ideas behind separatism. But what do we have now? We have a women's movement made up of all these little tiny groups, because each one wants special attention. There's no solidarity, because we're all so interested in making sure the world knows that people are diverse. We don't come together often enough anymore. It's becoming too segregated. And there's no utopia for people who want different things, unless those different things balance each other out. But they can't balance, because one thing they want is the same: recognition and respect. If ALL the groups have that, no group is "special" anymore.

Contrast this with the hopes of the early days of Women's Studies. A historian who, in the late 1960s, taught one of the first women's history courses left this field because of her unpleasant experiences at the hands of other feminists. She expresses the sense of loss that, years later, still overtakes her as she recalls her original expectations:

> I'll tell you the kinds of ideas I used to spout, back in 1969 and '70 and '71. I would say things like, "We're all women—what does it matter that this one is a lesbian and I happen to be married and this one has chosen to do this or that? Isn't the umbrella big enough to shelter all of us?" I really did believe once upon a time that all women could be sisters.

I think that's where the rage in me comes from: that there

are so many powerful things that should be binding us, that we should be able to acknowledge, to create a forum where we really could share these things and talk about our pain and help heal one another and really be together, and, if we wanted to change the world and make it more in our image, to truly stand shoulder to shoulder to do that.

It makes me feel terrible to have lost that part of what I believed could be so. . . . [sobbing] Part of me wanted to believe that could be possible for us. And to see us more divided and less able to deal with the things that are really important, and less able to give young women like my daughter the tools that she needs to go out and lead her life. . . . —it not only feels sad to me, but it feels like such a missed historical opportunity.

I don't blame us; I don't think it was our fault. It feels sad for me to definitely let go of that part of my life and to recognize that I have done so.

Another pernicious aspect of IDPOL is the now-popular practice of stating one's identity (in terms of the key bases of race, ethnicity, sexual orientation, and class, at the very least) whenever one speaks or writes.[10] For more than a decade it has been customary—sometimes even obligatory—for feminist authors to publicly "situate" themselves in their books and papers, especially if their identities are multifaceted. Thus, a volume of feminist essays on mothering carries a blurb on contributors that begins: "I am a lesbian socialist-feminist mother of a twelve-year-old interracial daughter. . . . "[11] However, the author of this blurb, who is white, played IDPOL imperfectly, since she apparently took for granted, and therefore did not specify, her race. (One may wonder whether, had she not been white, this woman would so readily have announced her daughter's interracial heritage.) And as we have noted, it is customary for feminist reviewers to comment (generally unfavorably) on the identity distribution of the subjects and authors of articles that appear in journals and collections of essays.

Furthermore, group identity is assumed to determine all arguments a person makes or any actions she takes. When practical questions arise, however, identity politics is apt to break down. Which kind of faculty member is most needed as a role model for students: a Native American, a woman with disabilities, a lesbian, or someone from the "Third World"? Who has a better claim on scholarship funds: older returning students with children or young Chicanas for whom English is a second language?

Feminists regularly get themselves tied in knots dealing with such questions. In order to resolve them, it seems that one should have a clear hierarchy of oppressions so that the most oppressed always gets the nod. But no one can agree on how to rank competing oppressions. Black women are widely viewed as the most oppressed, but Hispanics and Native Americans are now putting forward their claims. People are starting to ask: "Is it really true these days that black women professors have a harder time than whites getting tenure, and that they draw lower salaries?"

Meanwhile, some white women with limited financial resources are getting tired of being portrayed as paragons of privilege. A white woman who has worked for years as an activist and lobbyist for Indian causes in South Dakota told us of how "a craze for labels" had disrupted collective efforts. The Native American women in her group began to refer to the white women members as "women of privilege." "For God's sake," the activist exclaimed, in recounting this development to us, "I've been a welfare mother most of my life!" She was also dismayed when a Native American employee of the organization began to reply to every criticism of her work with a shrug and, "You just don't understand how we Indians do things."

Despite their awareness of these difficulties, the primary response of feminists to this—as to any other problem—is to blame patriarchy. As one woman said, referring to the need of different programs at many universities to compete aggressively for special faculty lines for "minority" members: "If there were no patriarchy, there would be no oppression. If there were no oppression, there would be no need for affirmative action. If there were no affirmative action, we wouldn't be here acting like pigs trying to shoulder each other away from the trough!"

Opponents of feminism will indeed be happy to watch the various factions exhaust each other in the fight for scraps. But friends of feminism must begin to ask whether this kind of self-defeating behavior cannot be brought to an end.

THE PRICE OF OPPRESSIVE PRIVILEGE

As we have seen, the strategy of IDPOL is to demand that special consideration be given to the interests and opinions of members of an oppressed group. In addition, such people must be presumed to be especially knowing and virtuous, at least with respect to situations related to their oppressed condition. This strategy of demanding special privileges inevitably leads to hostilities among oppressed groups and to lessened sympathy among those identified as being outside these groups. But IDPOL is destructive in more ways than these. It does harm to the very individuals who identify as members of victimized groups. The price of playing identity politics is the cognitive and moral debilitation of the oppressed.

Why does such harm occur? First, the characteristics forming the basis of membership in oppressed identity groups are, by and large, immutable. One might seek transsexual surgery, dye or straighten one's hair, or lose one's accent and assimilate; but, as a rule, one cannot change membership in the groups under discussion. Class, by contrast—especially in America, where one's social position depends more on income and education than on birth and cultural heritage—is much more labile.

On the other hand, individuals do have a choice in the extent to which they actively identify with the group to which society assigns them. Thus, Gore Vidal, to take an example, has always refused to identify himself as a homosexual. The IDPOL strategy, however, requires that group affiliation become a salient part of an individual's personal identity. We are reminded here of the opening rituals of

Alcoholics Anonymous, where participants introduce themselves as alcoholics; in this context, being an alcoholic is clearly the most important aspect of the person and is the basis for the bonding that such rituals encourage.

IDPOL, moreover, demands that one actively identify with the worst damage that has been inflicted on one's group. As a woman, therefore, I must feel solidarity with females in other cultures—as when the feminist philosopher Mary Daly routinely proclaims in her public appearances that she feels the pain of her African sisters who are undergoing clitoridectomies.[12] But, not surprisingly, Daly's expressions of solidarity sound hollow to many people, and they are particularly objectionable to black women, who see her as "appropriating" oppression that "belongs" to them.

Within Women's Studies, women are pressured not to say things like, "I know many women are discouraged from going on to graduate school, but I always got a lot of encouragement from my male professors." As a result, women learn either to deny, or to feel guilty about, experiences that do not conform to the approved model of oppression. It is assumed that an inability to testify to personal experiences of gender oppression casts doubt on the authenticity of one's commitment to feminism.

Individuals must not only identify with a particular oppressed group but also, as far as possible, existentially participate in the sufferings and injustices of that group. The result of this pressure is that group members are constantly exposed to vivid accounts of incidents of extreme sexism. Women who have been brutalized undoubtedly find it gratifying to learn that others, too, have suffered—this is the consolation of the postsurgical ward. But women who do not feel crippled by sexism must "learn" that in fact they were—and are—victims of this cultural offense. Those whose experiences have been less negative are expected to search their memories for suppressed traumas. If they cannot locate these, they should, at the very least, maintain a sympathetic silence. And until they can come up with the requisite sufferings, they had better mute their claim to status in the identity group.

One effect of these practices is to stretch the meaning of words such as *harassment* and *racism*, so that everyone in the group is able to qualify as a victim. Another is that it hypersensitizes all those who identify with the oppressed group. IDPOL team players learn to be on the lookout for instances of injustice—especially those directed at them personally—so they will have a show-and-tell for the next sharing session.

Any undertaking involving the wholesale substitution of group norms for individual experiences, feelings, and ideas ought to be suspect. But doctrinaire feminism is particularly worrisome because it blocks the individual's ability to evaluate fairly and reasonably the causes of and remedies for her own personal unhappiness or lack of fulfillment. There are many barriers to a satisfactory life—some surmountable, others not. But the one thing all of us can aspire to is self-knowledge, along with some understanding of the constraints placed on us by our situation and of reasonable prospects for overcoming them. Feminist indoctrination inhibits women's ability to reach for this objective.

Feminism begins with the promise of liberating women from the distortions of gender under patriarchy. Unfortunately, however, contemporary feminism also fits women with blinders that keep them from seeing the varied possibilities present in their individual lives. At times this leads to paradoxical situations, as in the incantation that women are silenced and powerless, often voiced and written by highly articulate women in positions of considerable authority.

Silvia, a research biologist and lesbian activist, wrote to us:

> There is no doubt in my mind that women are oppressed. However, one would think, with all of the work in Women's Studies and feminist/postmodernist theory, someone would have made the giant leap in logic that though we may not have much control or choice over the fact that we are oppressed, we do have autonomy and choice with respect to how we will respond to our oppression. *We do not have to act like oppressed people.* I learned this very important lesson from an elderly

black man when I was in my early twenties. I grew up in an urban ghetto. I graduated from high school functionally illiterate. I was filled with anger and hostility, was an alcoholic, and, like most of my peers, could be constantly heard complaining about "the man." But that piece of advice from a man I held in high respect literally changed the course of my life.

When I was focused on my oppression exclusively, my creativity was stifled, I lacked vision for myself, and I lacked empathy for others. I, along with my peers, was constantly policing others for the proper attitude and behavior. Contrary to what most people on the outside believe, the ghetto isn't a place of chaos. It is a place of order. The rules and the manner in which order is maintained may be different than on the outside, but that doesn't mean that order doesn't exist. We all had a desire deep down to get out, but very few ever did, mainly because of the incessant policing of attitude and behavior. The moment that someone shows signs of making something of their life, rather than gaining the support of their peers, they are ostracized and torn down by them. It's a vicious cycle. This, in my opinion, is largely what goes on in feminist and lesbian circles as well. There is a right way to "be" and a wrong way to "be."

A rare attempt to challenge IDPOL's orthodoxy occurred on the Women's Studies E-mail list when, in 1993, the nomination of Lani Guinier as the assistant attorney general for civil rights fell through. Guinier received so much uncritical support on the list that one social scientist was moved to comment: "What troubles me is that the assumption is made by people who have *not* read [Guinier's works] that she is right and the attackers are wrong simply because she is a black woman. This is identity politics at its worst. We need to be discussing ideas, not the identity of individuals." The fact that few people in Women's Studies circles are willing even to entertain such a position, for fear of appearing "racist," merely demonstrates the hold of IDPOL on their minds.

It is indeed much simpler to flaunt an identity than to formulate a winning argument. Long before IDPOL had a name, the writer James Baldwin exposed the game when he said: "Every time I attend a conference of white writers, I have a method for finding out if my colleagues are racist. It consists of uttering stupidities and maintaining absurd theses. If they listen respectfully and, at the end, overwhelm me with applause, there isn't the slightest doubt: they are filthy racists."[13]

Given the crudeness of its categories and the problems it creates, why is IDPOL being played? The answer is that it works in the short term, at least within the progressive and sympathetic setting of the academy. Most of our colleagues—to their credit, it could be argued—*do* feel some responsibility for the past and are highly susceptible to imputations of collective guilt. But IDPOL, which is inherently unstable and promotes internal conflicts, cannot sustain a coherent political movement. Furthermore, by always giving greater weight to the testimony of members of oppressed groups, it tempts the participants to invent grievances. The greater feminism's success in raising our feelings of moral outrage at sexual harassment, date rape, or insensitive remarks in the workplace or classroom, the more likely it is that members of a protected group will find it in their interest to make a false or frivolous accusation. In a rape trial, for example, it is now ironic that, as we—properly—destigmatize the woman accuser, we simultaneously undermine the old feminist argument that the process of accusing someone of rape is so self-vilifying that no woman would ever intentionally make a false accusation.

Similar conundrums can occur with allegations of racism. In very hostile environments a victim of racism must have great courage to speak up. But in a climate in which it is assumed that every white person is a racist, it would be surprising if individuals did not sometimes allege racism when it is to their advantage to do so.

The only remedy for such abuses is to stop using identity as a passkey to all questions of truth or responsibility. Oppression will not cease because special political, epistemic, or moral privileges are awarded to the oppressed. Its elimination must be sought elsewhere.

4

Proselytizing and Policing in the Feminist Classroom

FOR MANY Women's Studies faculty, teaching is a more important, and probably more gratifying, activity than research. Indeed, feminists have been in the forefront of the current movement to give teaching and service greater recognition in the university. It seems likely, therefore, that most Women's Studies teachers start out sincerely intending to act in the best interests of their students. Given the ideology of academic feminism, however, their best instructional efforts have too often succeeded only in subverting both the values of the academy and the goal of improving women's condition.

On the one hand, Women's Studies teachers are deliberately using their classrooms as sites for the recruiting and training of students to be feminist activists. This aim tends to produce standard proselytizing tactics such as providing comfort and support for neophytes, denouncing the enemy, rejecting opinions that contradict or complicate the party line, and engaging in rituals of confession and celebration to keep the faithful pure and committed. These are all procedures that tend to constrict, rather than open, mental horizons, and straiten, rather than enlarge, argument.

On the other hand, since Women's Studies programs function as parts of colleges and universities, they are expected to offer their students at least the semblance of a liberal education; they could not otherwise justify their status within academic institutions. Despite widespread complaints about the erosion of that ideal, college students still expect the classroom to be a place for debate and the free expression and exchange of varied ideas and opinions, especially when the topics under discussion are open-ended and controversial. This opposition between politicized academic instruction and the values of liberal education explains most of the problems that erupt in Women's Studies classrooms.

Many feminists, however, resolutely refuse to face up to these difficulties. Instead, they write theoretical treatises about the virtues of feminist pedagogy and recommend that these methods be exported to the rest of the educational system. Some of the theory behind feminist pedagogy is discussed in chapter 7. What we want to explore now are the games that actually go on in Women's Studies classes, under the guise of pedagogy. Like IDPOL, what might be called FEMPED is a bewildering but destructive array of maneuvers. Who better to provide an initial description of these games than students?

SURVIVING WOMEN'S STUDIES: STUDENTS' PERSPECTIVES

The students we talked to had strong reactions—some positive, some negative—to their experiences in feminist classrooms. Caroline, a social worker in her mid-twenties, says that the one Women's Studies course she took at a private women's college was more than enough. Laura, on the other hand, who recently graduated from a state university with a minor in Women's Studies, "honestly believe[s] that everyone should be required to take a Women's Studies class." Despite this divergence of opinion, their descriptions of what went on in their respective classes are surprisingly similar. It is primarily in their evaluations of these experiences that they differ. Laura describes feminist education as "reverse indoctrination," but she thinks such training is necessary in order to counteract all that "you grow up indoctrinated with." Caroline, for her part, deplores "this ongoing knee-jerk reverse sexism which everyone tolerated and encouraged."

It did not take Caroline long to form a bad impression of Women's Studies:

The course was Introduction to Women's Studies. I was a senior, and I was, I think, pretty confident by that time, and I remember clashing with the professor very quickly. The class made me think of a skit on *Monty Python* which involves a quiz show, except the answer to every question is "pork." And whatever the quiz show host asks—for example, "What's the capital of Pennsylvania?"—the answer is "pork." In the class I took, the answer was always "men." Whatever the question was, the answer was "men." It could be, "What style of architecture is that?" And the answer is, "Men's architecture." Or, "Who contributes to all the violence in the world?" "Men." "Who's responsible for everything that we endure?" "Men" [laughing].

I was involved with a man at the time, and I thought that he didn't fit their categories of what men were like. And I also saw him as having been pressed into stereotypes of his own. When he'd been in high school, he took up computers. He'd been very nonathletic, hated team sports, wanted to read, wanted to fuss with his computers. And he was called a nerd and hassled constantly over this and abused in various ways. And I felt like I really identified with that—I hadn't been all that feminine in high school. I wore a black leather jacket, hung out with the guys, and people had made fun of me. I hadn't been desirable as a woman; he hadn't been desirable as a man. No girls wanted to date him, no guys wanted to date me. So I guess I was interested in a more global analysis, like: What is it in our society that creates some of these tensions? What is it that we're doing to ourselves here? I'm not saying I wanted the whole course to be about this, but these questions weren't acceptable at all, and I felt that the professor responded really aggressively to me.

The time that it really sort of came to a head was when we were talking about rape: "Rape—the act of violence that men do to women, that men do to women because they want to keep them down." And we got all these reasons why men rape women. And I thought, Well, there's this act of violence of men against women, and why don't we explore a little bit why people are so frustrated and so violent and so angry that they do these things? And why don't we take into consideration that men get raped too? I had a friend in high school, a man, who was raped by a bunch of other men of his age, and when I tried to enter this information, it was met with a stone wall: "Those statistics are insignificant compared with how many women are raped." And I thought, Well, how many men are reporting it? And why are you discounting what I'm trying to share here, which would be adding to the picture? And I don't remember the comment that the professor made, but it was very condescending, to the effect: "Are you saying that rapists are just poor misunderstood people who should be patted on the back and sent out?" And I'm thinking: You miserable bitch! You know, she was really like "Let me humiliate you in front of everyone," because, of course, that was not what I was saying!

I have friends who've been raped; it's not like some far-away thing to me. It's something to get really angry about and be upset about, but something to search for a better solution to than castration! But the only solution that the professor was getting at was that men are the problem and without men there'd be a solution. There was no talk of *real* solutions.

Caroline also objected to the constant representation of women as victims:

I didn't feel like a victim. I felt more responsible for the ways in which I messed up my life and the things I'd done wrong than I thought the professor was willing to allow. I find it more empowering to take responsibility for my problems and for the things I do wrong than to say that someone else has done it, because if I've done it, then I have some sort of control over my life. For example, I feel I have to take responsibility for the fact that I read *Cosmopolitan* and I look at the ads and then feel miserable. And that's got to be at least some part of me, and I can't just say, "Well, it's men." There are women in advertising, lots of women.

In her other courses at the "Seven Sisters" college she attended, Caroline had been used to studying with professors who encouraged discussions and arguments in class. But in her Women's Studies class she found a very different atmosphere:

I felt that the professor really controlled the discussion—that there were some things that she thought were appropriate to be discussed, and then there were the wrong answers and she didn't want to hear those and they couldn't be discussed. It didn't really feel like discussion. It felt like a fill-in-the-blank-type lecture, where the teacher kind of tells you what to say and you say it, and then she goes on.

I don't remember ever having the politically correct thing come up in any other class the way it did in that class. The Women's Studies class is the one which sticks out in my head— I felt really attacked as a person in a way I hadn't been in any other classes.

I just didn't feel that these Women's Studies classes had anything to offer. It seemed to me like they were stuck twenty years ago and that I could find out the information I was curious about through history classes, philosophy classes, but not through Women's Studies. There wasn't anything that a

Women's Studies class could offer me that I couldn't get somewhere else better, with less rigidity.

Laura, too, recalls such tensions in the Women's Studies courses she
attended, but she draws quite a different conclusion. She describes the
purpose of Women's Studies programs this way:

> I think that Women's Studies was created in order to
> strengthen women and to strengthen women's position in the
> world. I think it was created to—ideally?—to educate every-
> one, so that things can change, so that people will be equal.
> Practically? I think it appeals to a small base of people and that
> it is very difficult for it to educate the general population
> because the general population is not open to it. I think it
> could be better used to educate men. I mean, men ignore the
> fact that there's a Women's Studies program on this campus.
> And so women are getting all this great knowledge about
> women in the Women's Studies classes, they're learning all this
> stuff that can empower them and help them change, but it
> stays among the women.

She readily admits that men are not welcome in Women's Studies
courses and are sometimes even discouraged from enrolling:

> In the upper-level courses, if a man who's never taken a Wom-
> en's Studies course wants to get in, he has to be very strong-
> willed and has to be determined to do it, because he is going to
> run into a lot of flak—because in Women's Studies classes,
> women definitely feel like they run the show. I mean, the stu-
> dents run the show; they have a right to speak. And if a man is
> going to speak, he'd better have a *damn* good thing to say, and
> it had better be right!
>   I think it's a poor classroom atmosphere. It works for Wom-
> en's Studies only because it seems to balance out the feeling
> that everybody has from the rest of their classes. But overall, as

an education, it's horrible because people who are going to want to speak, to voice something that might differ but is just as valid, are never going to speak up. I mean, it's got to be a scary thing to sit in a room with thirty irate women.

Not that all the women in her classes formed a unified group:

The classroom gets divided. I mean, it gets divided into many small groups. There's always a small group of women who speak out. They always have something to say, they always have a comment on something, and you pretty much get the general feel of all their politics within the first week. After that, it breaks down into other small groups. There's a group that says very little. It comes down to your sexuality and your political views. It's like, it seems a lot of times if you're heterosexual, strictly heterosexual, or conservative, you don't have the right to say much in Women's Studies. You're classified with men.

Sexuality comes up all the time in Women's Studies classes. It's amazing—it just becomes an issue. People are declaring themselves, what their sexual orientation is, right away. I mean, within a week, you *know* what everybody in your class is. I don't think it should matter. And the professor's sexual orientation—that comes up as well. Why should it come up? I think it's an issue in the real world, and it should come up if people are going to be treated fairly, but in Women's Studies people get treated the reverse of what happens in the real world.

Why, then, did Laura resist the temptation to divulge that she was bisexual and thereby counteract the damaging assumptions that she was straight?

Because it seems like a cheap way to get credit. You're buying credit on sexuality. It doesn't make me a better person; it doesn't make me any different. All right, so they look at me and they go, "Ah, she's heterosexual"—great! And I go, "No, actually I'm not." I've come up three rungs on the ladder. I mean, that's reverse discrimination. Who I sleep with makes me a better person? I really believe people should keep their hands out of whatever happens in the bedroom. I think it's nobody else's business, and I'm not going to buy my credit by who I'm sleeping with.

Discussions about style and appearance were also a constant in her Women's Studies classes:

The issue of personal hygiene and what is correct has come up in *so* many classrooms. Why should anyone care whether you shave your legs or not? I wish it were different. Women's Studies seems to get bogged down in pettiness sometimes. And that's just because it becomes repetitive—makeup, hair, appearance, what brand of tampons you use, if you use tampons, all that.

Laura's general enthusiasm for Women's Studies courses evidently did not blind her to their special problems. She had taken one course (taught by a staff member in the Women's Studies program), on women's career choices, that attracted a broader audience with less uniform viewpoints. One young woman, for example, stated that it was her aim to be married and have children. Had she made this admission in the feminist theory class, Laura says, "she might have been torn apart" by the other students, with little intervention by the professor.

That's because [in the feminist classroom] it's mostly an open discussion. Many professors say, "This is your classroom, this is your discussion, I'm here as another participant, not as a leader," which pretty much waives the right of the professor to intervene. So it's very rare that a professor would step in to stop something like that. I mean, it winds up being this conflict between the students. I guess that's going to happen in the real

world. But I think a classroom *should* be a safe area, and I definitely feel like that girl should have been free to walk into a
feminist theory class and say, "Regardless of what anybody else
believes, I want to be a housewife. That would be the most
rewarding life for me."

I think there should be more of that, but it's hard because
you're dealing with a minority opinion, you're dealing with
women who've been oppressed, and you're dealing with explo-
sive issues to women. So any woman who is going to hold a
view that might, in some minute way, support the other side, is
going to be torn apart. And how do you accept her views without accepting the views and actions that have oppressed you?

All the professors would have to be made aware of this—so
aware that they'd have to start really thinking about the
dynamic that goes on in the classroom. I mean, obviously it's
nice to have a safe haven for people, but how do you differentiate between a safe haven that ostracizes people from the program and a safe haven that also works to incorporate other
people in the program?

Like Caroline, Laura objects to the simpleminded habit of blaming everything on men:

A lot of people got triggered by "men men men men men." I
remember somebody just going off and saying, "Can't you
blame anything else but men?" Yeah, sometimes people got
furious. In one class this girl said, "All you do is blame men. I
happen to like men." And she was completely at a disadvantage, because here she is sitting in full makeup, a skirt, heels,
well-done hair. Guns were drawn. She was attacked. There
were mainly three people who jumped in, and they just completely cut her to pieces.

You know, somebody who even looks like that and who
voices this opinion is immediately going to be accused of being
male-identified, which I think she was, and obviously she does

not see the point in all history that men *are* to blame. I was upset by that too. I think one other person said to the class, "I think you do dwell too much on men." But by this time emotions had picked up, the snowball is barreling towards the bottom of the hill, and people aren't going to jump in the way. One guy did speak up and said, "You know, sometimes I have a really hard time sitting here because I feel like you are blaming men for all the problems in the world and here I am, a man, identifying with you, feeling the exact same way you do about feminism." And this one girl—the same girl who attacked this other girl for saying, "You always blame men"— she said to him, "You obviously have no understanding. You *are* a man. You can only try to empathize."

My brother and I are very close, and I would bring up an experience with my brother in my feminist theory class and it was like, "Ugh! You were hanging out with a man." God forbid I should bring him up! I spoke so rarely, and it was like I had to think through everything I was going to say. It came down to hostility—it was like taking a chance, a different kind of chance, in a Women's Studies class to speak out. If it becomes a personal attack and not a political attack, I think the professor should intervene, like, "You're off the subject. This is no longer political." But they very very rarely intervene.

Despite her many negative comments about the Women's Studies program in which she did her minor, Laura ends on a ringing, if somewhat chilling, endorsement:

You scratch the surface and then you go down deeper, and the more you think about it and the more you can see how it personally affects your life and your friends' lives and your mother's and sister's and everybody else's life, it's like, wow! And the whole thing starts to seem overwhelming after a while. . . . I could go into this class and learn about the persecution [of witches] in European history that I wasn't necessarily getting in my classes outside of Women's Studies, so that I know it's happening all over the place, and these aren't just isolated incidents. So, in that sense I got a firm foundation, a factual foundation, which was good.

I really honestly do believe that everyone should be required to take a Women's Studies class. In fact, I would force my friends to take a Women's Studies class if I could.

TRAINING THE CADRES

There is general agreement that students in Women's Studies classes should not merely absorb information about women's oppression and develop strategies for combating it, but should also, in the process of studying these subjects, undergo an intense feminist experience. The precepts of feminism (whatever these are said to be at a given moment) must guide pedagogical practice. As Nel Noddings puts it in *Caring*, "It is time for the voice of the mother to be heard in education."[1] Rules on exactly how political the content of the course should be, and how "maternal" the teaching, vary from program to program. Predictably, however, the ideologically sanctioned intrusion of politics on instruction is frequently disastrous.

Women's Studies professors readily admit to the political aims of the education they offer. In justification, they advance the rather tired argument that all teaching, on any subject, grinds a political axe of one sort or another. Teaching Shakespeare, unless he is read "against the grain," propounds an "elitist view" of literature and condones a hierarchical order of society. In other words, Shakespeare is unavoidably "political." Teaching chemistry without pointing to the necessity of "a science for the people" abets the "military-industrial complex." Because mathematics is supposedly a difficult hurdle for women and some minority students, it is presumed to be an inherently oppressive subject. And so on. In this essentially trivial sense, everything one talks about is political. When it comes to articulating the political ambitions of Women's Studies, however, many feminists have something much more concrete in mind.

Typically, introductory Women's Studies courses include material on rape, sexual harassment, battered women, child sexual abuse, abortion, and reproductive rights, not to mention lessons on all the current -isms such as racism, classism, ableism, and ageism. Often the faculty members or graduate students who teach such courses are not competent in the full range of subjects they must cover, having had little or no formal training in sociology, social psychology, economics, medicine, or criminology. When teaching, they tend to rely exclusively on feminist writings—particularly of the more popular and, hence, accessible sort—as their resources. As a result, students are likely to learn only what feminists say about these troubling and complex social issues. All other research is regarded as inherently biased. Thus, not only the choice of topics, but also the selection of study materials and the methods of instruction are dictated by the objectives of feminist activists, and the range of knowledge communicated to students is tendentious, narrow, and repetitive. Even committed students sometimes complain about tedious duplication, while not realizing that this problem is rooted in Women's Studies' political agenda.

As noted in chapter 1, students in many programs can receive academic credit for doing "internships" or performing community service in feminist agencies, and then submitting reports on their activities. At the university where one of us teaches, for example, a total of fifteen credit hours out of the thirty-six required for a Women's Studies major can be earned in this way, outside the classroom.

Some schools require a practicum and pair their seniors with mentors who are feminist activists in the community. The principle that Women's Studies should train its students for political action is at times used as a justification for appointing to the faculty women from the feminist community who lack even minimal academic qualifications. In such instances, the political agenda leads directly to a weakening of traditional academic requirements. One graduate student (who appreciated the mentoring practice) wrote to us about a lesbian activist brought into her program to teach a course on feminist theory: "She personally knows a lot of the theorists we read, so hearing anecdotes about them and about the movement in the 1970s added another dimension to the class. But there were drawbacks. She wasn't as comfortable facilitating a classroom as 'regular' professors are and had to get a guest lecturer in for the classes on 'postmodern feminism.'"

The importance attached to feminist credentials among both faculty and students is evident in an anxious query from the director of one Women's Studies program in which a prize was to be given to the best graduating senior. The director's problem was that the most deserving student—one who had a straight-A record, had written substantial research papers, and had contributed a great deal to class discussions—was not a feminist! The director appealed to colleagues for advice on how to handle the matter and proposed that the guidelines be tightened so that this situation would not recur.

Of course, the mere fact that Women's Studies has an explicit political aim does not by itself mean that Women's Studies education need take the form it does. As one of the women we interviewed remarked:

> Even if one were explicitly training political activists, one could do it in the traditional liberal arts mode. One would give them general historical and theoretical courses on conflict resolution, attitude change methodology, not only the tactics of Machiavelli and Mao but also those of Gandhi and Martin Luther King. One would also need general philosophical analyses of the concepts of justice, freedom, et cetera. Background in economics and history of technology would be helpful. But as you can see, this is a far cry from what Women's Studies actually is like.

Fulmination and Ferment

A major reason for the transition of Women's Studies from politically relevant instruction to politically correct indoctrination is found in the opportunities created in the Women's Studies classroom for the manipulation of students' emotions. The popular press—and particularly those elements of it that like to excoriate feminism—often portray the women engaged in feminist practice as mad (in both senses), hysterical, and certainly angry. What may be surprising to many people is that feminists of the second wave have proudly "owned" such epithets and even seem to go out of their way to cultivate anger and rage. Sometimes they make their point in jest. One popular bumpersticker, for example, reads: GOD IS COMING—AND BOY IS SHE PISSED. More generally, feminists view anger as a positive, healthy, and enabling emotion, as in the song called "Anger," by Naomi Littlebear:

> *Who says emotions are insane?*
> *Anger in a woman is the birth of freedom*
> *from the chains of your pain.*
> *Anger! Anger! Anger!*[2]

Other writers speak of nurturing their anger or practicing it like the piano. Margaret, the former program director whose story was recounted in chapter 2, commented on her slow realization that she was spending much of her time acting angry:

I was not a person who invited confrontation or felt comfortable with it. But anger was absolutely a measure of one's feminist commitment. It was taken as a sign of one's authenticity, one's radical credentials. I remember sounding angry a lot, and I remember hearing myself and thinking, This has become sort of a way that I talk. It was very strange.

Some feminist writers even speak of "tending" their anger, of periodically stoking the flames to use it as an energy source for political action.

The closest parallel in Western literature to the feminist attitude toward anger is the Greek concept of *thumos*, variously translated as Anger, Spirit, and Honor.[3] For Plato, Anger/Spirit was one of the three parts of the Soul—along with the rational and the appetitive faculties—and was a valuable source of courage and moral indignation. But when unchecked, *thumos* led to the infantile egotistical rage of Achilles (as portrayed by Homer), a man so narcissistic that he was willing to let the Greeks go to defeat in the war against Troy merely because his honor had been sullied. To warn against such excess, Aristotle called for the proper emotional balance: "The man who feels anger at the right things and against the right people, and also in the right way and at the right moment and for the right length of time is commended."[4]

If feminists could bring themselves to overlook the male referent in this passage, they might find Aristotle's message of value to them today. Women obviously are justifiably angry about many things. But to generate and cultivate anger in a classroom setting strikes us as irresponsible, especially since many of the techniques used to arouse and sustain such an emotion are manipulative, and most professors have no special ability to deal with the ensuing problems. Moreover, in the end, all such strategies are bound to prove counterproductive.

Making a fetish of anger—it might well be called ANGER-CULT—affects the Women's Studies classroom in many ways. First, doing so has a direct impact on subject matter. The topics selected for extended discussion in introductory Women's Studies courses are often lurid and charged with high emotion: rape, wife battering, incest, molestation of children, forced prostitution. One reason for choosing such topics may be practical: it is certainly easier to grip students' attention with talk of sexual slavery and clitoridectomy than with discussion of more mundane issues like the need for comparable-worth legislation or prenatal health care. In addition, feminist fac-

ulty often complain that their noninitiated students are too compla-
cent about past disadvantages and indignities, and are apt to dismiss
them as long since abolished (as many communications on the
Women's Studies E-mail list reveal). These faculty members may feel
that such students will not become activists until their sense of outrage is aroused.

Women's Studies seems to need angry students in order to "keep
the momentum going," as one feminist professor put it. Classroom
exercises can easily be designed to elicit strong emotional responses.
Another faculty member posted this on E-mail: "[After discussing
rape,] I had the women in the class do some simple self-defense rituals such as putting our arms around each other in a circle and yelling
'No!' and front snap kicking against the wall. A sociologist who
teaches at [another university] does the same thing."

The perceived need to stir up feelings of outrage among students
is also connected with the feminist sacralization of what is generally
described as a "click" experience. Participants in consciousness-
raising sessions in the late 1960s and early 1970s reported that, as
they compared notes about their experiences and began to discover
patterns in their complaints and relate them to larger political issues,
moments of epiphany would occur when everything would "click"
into place and they would immediately know that they were feminists. Like Saul after his illumination on the road to Damascus, some
feminists, such as the writers Artemis Oakgrove and Elana Dyke-
woman, even took on new names following their enlightenment.

However, while religious conversion experiences are often followed by surges of euphoria and celebration, feminist epiphanies are
more usually accompanied by strong waves of anger. It was a relief
for the early consciousness-raisers to discover that what they had
previously conceptualized as inadequacies that were either personal
or rooted in their "natures" as women were really the effects of systematic cultural and political oppression. But it was also infuriating
for them to realize that they had been dupes of patriarchy for so
long, and to find out how difficult it was to convince others, especially men, of the validity of their new feminist perspective. Hence,

irascibility and ire have come to be seen as indicators of the depth of one's feminist insight and commitment, "a sign of one's authenticity," as Margaret put it. From a feminist viewpoint, then, cultivating anger not only increases the likelihood that students will turn to activism but also serves as a precondition for equipping them with an authentic feminist conceptual framework. Those who are not full of rage "just don't get it."

Even from a feminist perspective, though, anger-based pedagogy can be a dangerous game. Free-floating anger, like lightning, seeks something to discharge itself on; thus, the oft-voiced feminist worry about "horizontal hostility" or "hazing within the community" is well justified. If, however, the anger nurtured in the program is not released, students are apt to become depressed. At the end of one recent semester, Women's Studies faculty on the Women's Studies E-mail list engaged in a long discussion of what to do about students' sagging morale. Had they overdone their emphasis on the atrocities perpetrated against women? Had students concluded that the situation was hopeless? Had they just given up? Sustaining anger, it turns out, is exhausting.

Propaganda and Resistance

The most important goal of any Women's Studies course, as is widely taken for granted, is to convert students to feminism. Feminists answer the charge that they are indoctrinating students by pointing out that all education attempts to change students; to "educate" means to "lead out" from a less into a more valued form of life. Art teachers try to expand students' aesthetic sensibilities; classics teachers try to convince students that the Great Books contain perennially valid insights. What is wrong, then, with exposing students to the sexism, racism, homophobia, and exploitation that pervade society and also affect their own lives? Why not help them change their attitudes?

Of course, feminists themselves realize that many students do not respond favorably to their pedagogy, and the phenomenon of "student resistance" is now the focus of organized discussions and scholarly papers. On the Women's Studies E-mail list an animated discussion recently took place about how to deal with female students who "just don't get it." The example that triggered the dialogue was the following:

> We were talking [in class] about how women are treated, when one student said, "I may be crazy, but I like having car doors opened for me and being put on a pedestal." Another student said, "Thank God you said that. We've [indicating the person sitting next to her] been talking about the same thing.". . . So [in this class I've] got a bunch of southern, traditional students (for the most part) who want equal rights and want to also be "ladies." [I] would like to enlighten them without alienating them.

The network generated many suggestions, ranging from a bibliographic reference to an essay on rape which argues that chivalry is a male protection racket, to a recommended exercise:

> Whenever my students raise the issue of opening doors, we eventually get to talking about holding hands. Ask your students to observe male-female couples walking hand in hand. Malls are a good place to do this. They will see that almost always the man's hand is in front. Then the students will say things like, "Well, it feels most comfortable that way!" Next ask them to observe adult-child hand holding. Again, the adult's hand is always in front. This can help them to see how this puts them in the same position as a child.

This exercise, it is worth noting, while dramatic, is not entirely honest. It is a simple anthropometric truth that when a taller person reaches down and a shorter person reaches up, the hands mesh more easily with the taller person's hand in front. Hand position may have little to do with dominance. It could be, just as the students say, more comfortable that way. Nonetheless, most of the Women's Studies people who got into the ensuing E-mail discussion felt that such a response showed student "resistance," which constituted a serious problem.

The preceding example of "resistance" is rather benign in that neither the degree of student recalcitrance nor the intensity of reaction to it by Women's Studies teachers or feminist fellow students appears to have been extreme. But at times the censoriousness of "enlightened" students toward their classmates can be much more energetic. One of the authors of this book witnessed an interesting scene that illustrates this point. It took place at a meeting at which a new antiracist curriculum was being presented to the Women's Studies students for their comments and suggestions. A white undergraduate who was very active in the program kept insisting that the Women's Studies faculty must "do something" about the many white students who sat in Women's Studies courses and studied racism but just weren't "getting it." "You can't let them get away with that," she said heatedly. "You must do something! You must do something!" Finally, in one of her better moments, a colleague muttered, sotto voce, "A firing squad, perhaps?"

When the political agenda of the Women's Studies curriculum is coupled with the favored therapeutic/confessional model of teaching, serious problems can result. Some students resent assignments they find intrusive, such as the writing of essays in which the student is expected to analyze her own racism, or the common feminist practice of requiring students to keep journals for recording personal reactions to readings. Objections to such assignments often induce attacks by outspoken feminist students, who become impatient when their peers "have trouble coming to terms with" their status as oppressors or oppressed.

One student we interviewed, who considers herself a feminist, told us of her discomfort with the dynamics she observed in some journalism courses she had taken, in which several Women's Studies students were extremely assertive: "I was surprised that they were not very tolerant—I guess that would be the word. They were very

very self-righteous, and I got the impression that they felt they were there to teach the rest of us rather than to learn what the professor had to teach us." This student is not alone in having difficulty adapting to the brave new feminist classroom in which smashing, or at least rearranging, boundaries is the norm.

Confusion and Condemnation

Although Women's Studies faculty worry about how to handle disbelieving "southern ladies," disruptive males, or unenlightened women students, they never take student resistance as a valid indication that there might indeed be something inappropriate about what they are teaching or how they are teaching it. Instead, they piously claim, as did one professor on the Women's Studies E-Mail list: "It is precisely at the point of resistance, of 'ignorance,' that there is the potential for real learning."

But what drove many of the professors and students we interviewed to despair was the "resistance" of the more-feminist-than-thou students who disrupted classes they judged to be insufficiently political. Even faculty who are still happy with Women's Studies sometimes report experiences similar to that described on the Women's Studies E-Mail list by one professor who said, "The resistance I have become most familiar with is that of female students whose expectations of 'feminist discourse' are not being met."

One reason why the views of all these "resisting" students—be they males, not-yet-feminist females, or true-believing feminists—become so visible, and hence so problematic, is the feminist encouragement of or even insistence on self-disclosure in the classroom. Feminism has borrowed pedagogical techniques from a variety of sources: Paulo Freire's practice in adult literacy classes of giving people a vocabulary to describe their oppression, the potent mixture of denunciation and exultation characteristic of revival meetings, and even the dress and demeanor codes imposed in bootcamps and finishing schools. We also find echoes in feminist classrooms of the obligatory self-incrimination demanded in China during the Cultural Revolution, and, of course, of the interventionist techniques of psychotherapy. Students are encouraged to "get in touch with their anger and pain" in discussions inside and outside the classroom, but especially in the journals they are asked to keep. They may be given assignments that require personal disclosure, such as discussing gender roles acted out within their own families, or (this, for white students) their first encounter with a person of color.

Although these techniques are in part derived from one or another of the varieties of psychotherapy, what takes place in a feminist classroom is very different from the true therapeutic encounter, in which the client can explore in a protected environment any thoughts and feelings, no matter how antisocial or bizarre. In the Women's Studies setting, by contrast, there are very definite expectations about, and limits on, the views that are deemed acceptable.

The teacher may explicitly announce, for example, that hers "is an antiracist class." Or, as indicated on the Women's Studies E-mail list, she may include in her syllabus such specific caveats as the following:

> As a white woman teaching feminist literary theory, African-American women's writing, various "minority" writings, and always affirming lesbian writing/writers, who is trying all this in a mostly white, conservative community . . . I've opened my classes and included on my course outline the following statement: "Any point of view will be welcomed in discussion except those that contend that one race, sex, or sexual orientation is superior to another." The students (particularly the young men) may not like it, but they accept it, or they leave. The ideological principle of "equality". . . works to suppress "discussion," which can be no more than a showcase for bigotry and abuse.

In other instances newly canonized views are clothed in a grudging gesture toward openness, as in the case of one Women's Studies professor who told us she said this to her students: "Personally, I can't imagine why any woman would want to have a relationship with a man, but since some do, we have to try to respect them."

As noted earlier, students are often required to submit journals giving their reactions to assigned readings. When doing so, they soon learn that only certain opinions and phrases are acceptable, as did this male undergraduate whose frank reports on his reading in a weekend "training" workshop on racism (offered for academic credit) elicited sharp replies from the two female graduate students who were teaching the course:

> STUDENT COMMENT #1 ON ASSIGNED READING: I am dominant but I am not racist. This article denies that it is possible for me to overcome the prejudice with which I was programmed. This is why the Left is failing: because it reduces all of its subjects to simpering essentialist categories and fails to acknowledge that anyone—yes, even those nasty Anglos—can rise above their cultural morass and effectively reprogram themselves. I really resented this pandering, whiny article: it's Anglo angst in rare form.

> FIRST INSTRUCTOR: How can you help *but* be—when you benefit and receive privileges from this racism? Your defensiveness has prevented you from understanding this article. One of the first signals to me that I have met a racist is when they insist that they are not.

> STUDENT COMMENT #2: In this article, Bell Hooks once again proves her worth to the Black community and to the women's community.

> FIRST INSTRUCTOR: Ugh! What a limitation on her contributions! Again, she is reduced to her race and gender. What a fine example of racism and sexism.

> STUDENT COMMENT #3: To say that all one needs is to be good intentioned is, I think, ridiculous and harmful. Everyone needs to have some sort of theoretical basis from which their action springs, not just a visceral one.

> FIRST INSTRUCTOR: Is this not reductionism at its finest and most limiting? Over time we have found that social change has

occurred as a result of direct action resulting from emotional strength and courage. Often the *theory* comes afterward or gets in the way.

SECOND INSTRUCTOR: "*Yes*—A very European-male opinion."

FIRST INSTRUCTOR'S GENERAL REMARKS ON THE STUDENT'S COMMENTS: Again you have effectively avoided demonstrating *any* personal awareness or at least strategies for personal action. I can acknowledge your need to make sense of such a complex "paradigm"—but I have yet to see that you actually can make sense of it at a personal level. I'm sadly disappointed by your self-protected intellectualizations. I've met far too many white men who bend over backwards to protect their own racism and white supremacy and frankly I'm utterly bored. [emphasis in original]

Students who decline to express personal views may be graded down in such courses or publicly humiliated. Those who express opinions unacceptable to feminist teachers and students are, as we have already noted, either charged with "resistance" or encouraged to drop the course. A male student, a Women's Studies major, told us that in his feminist theory class the professor did not allow discussion of divergent viewpoints and always shut him up when he made criticisms. "What about when women make the same criticisms?" we asked. "They never do," he replied. "I don't know if it's kissing ass or what, but they all seem to be in agreement with her." He was aware that he was not really welcome in the class, he said, but he had decided to stay in it nonetheless; besides, it was a requirement for all majors.

When students reveal, in class, personal traumas exemplifying the sort of damage from sexism that feminists can relate to, they may be hurt in different ways. Nonfeminist students may laugh at them or dismiss them as whiners; but ultrafeminists may also put them down if their anecdotes indicate that they are either too dependent on the opinions of men ("Sounds like you should have ditched that jerk ages ago!") or that their attitude smacks of racist, ableist, or other unacceptable sentiments ("I think we should explore the fact that you described the person stalking you as a 'big black guy'"). Even when no overt hostility or dismissive responses ensue, the student, having made her revelation, may feel vulnerable or exposed. A recent article in the *Chronicle of Higher Education* calls attention to the possible harm done to students who feel coerced to reveal painful personal material to professors, and then are embarrassed or hurt by the professor's attempts to be helpful.[5]

Equally pernicious is the opposite mode, in which it is the professor who "discloses" her personal problems to the class. Here is an example, given in a recent contribution to the Women's Studies E-mail list, by someone who teaches Women's Studies and communications:

> This semester is going wonderfully well, though mostly the reason for that . . . is related to my renewed mental and emotional health, having come to terms with what had been repressed memories of childhood sexual abuse. A good deal of what is different is that I am approaching all my classes from a position of sensuous joy and love. . . .
>
> Tuesday night I had a discussion/activity planned around dealing with a recurring question/complaint from male students (past and present): we shouldn't spend so much time looking at the terrible things men had done to women in the past but instead should focus on changing things in the present. I had the students break down into groups to discuss why it is important for us to examine our past, no matter how painful it may be, and to consider why someone might resist doing so (the "answer," of course, being that our personal identities are tied up in our conceptions of our social and cultural history, so that looking at "the terrible things men have done to women" threatens the positive identity that has been built around history as it has been taught).
>
> I also tried to get them to think about how examining a painful personal history might be helpful for them. Many stu-

dents responded in a very general way. I managed to get a few older students to give some personal examples. I ended with telling them about how I had had to come to terms with an excruciatingly painful past (explicitly identifying the problem as incest), and how until I could do that I had no future, only an endless repetition of old patterns. And now there is joy and hope and boundless energy.

This was the third class meeting (one night a week). They all sat so still, with amazement and wonder on their faces. Afterward an older student thanked me for making myself so vulnerable. I told her I didn't feel vulnerable as I spoke. I felt loved.

We merely note that, in contrast to this instructor's obviously fragile psychological condition, which she considers appropriate to "share" with her class, she holds a tough and dogmatic opinion about "the answer" to male students' legitimate questions.

Feeling Good versus Becoming Competent

Classical psychotherapy (like traditional mothering) is a very demanding endeavor. But a sort of "I'm OK—you're OK, but men are horrible" latter-day variant of it is—as we have seen—very popular in the pedagogy of Women's Studies. On this model, women "empower" themselves primarily by realizing that all their troubles result from patriarchy, and that the key to greater self-esteem is held by feminist political analysis. This can only be developed in association with other women, for many feminists—as we discuss in greater detail in later chapters—claim that traditional schooling emphasizes such "masculine" cognitive virtues as rationality and objectivity, to the detriment of women's own "feminine" cognitive faculties such as empathy and subjectivity. Students are also told that their lives provide valuable data, and they are encouraged to "own," and take responsibility for, their personal opinions.

Taken in conjunction, these propositions result in a serious cur-

tailment of the possibilities for critical debate. The standard procedure of at least trying to separate intellectual positions and arguments from the individuals who propose them, so that the former
may be examined dispassionately, is explicitly blocked. No claim is
evaluated without identifying the person who originated it, and any
judgments about the merits of the claim automatically reflect on the
person making it. According to this way of looking at things, people
and their feelings can never be divorced from their ideas. To argue
otherwise is to run the risk of being dismissed as "male-identified"
and, hence, subject to "compartmentalized thinking."

From a feminist pedagogical perspective, there are two ways to
resolve the conflict that occurs when people make opposing claims.
One can say that each person has her own perspective and all opinions are equally valid (a standard move in family therapy), or one
can give preference to the opinion of the person who is most
oppressed. Critical discussion becomes difficult, if not impossible, in
either circumstance. When feminist classrooms manage to avoid
breaking down into personal hostilities and censoriousness, they
often do so only by sacrificing free and frank intellectual discussion
at the altar of an appropriate feminist ambience. Even those who are
generally enthusiastic about the feminist approach note the absence
of critical discussion, as one student wrote to us:

> I feel Women's Studies classrooms offer a nurturing environ-
> ment in which to learn. I learned a lot more in that class than I
> did in any undergraduate class. On the downside, sometimes
> people are afraid to even disagree with each other, although
> constructive criticism and respectful debates are very useful, I
> find. (Another technique we used was to always own our own
> opinions.) Because of this fear, the discussion sometimes
> lacked the intellectual rigor I craved as a grad student. People
> spend so much time worrying about offending others that they
> often don't disagree at all, and, as a result, the conversation
> does not move to a very deep level theoretically.

One might argue that the feminist approach, whatever its intellectual cost, is not only a more humane form of inquiry but also the one many women feel most comfortable with. For example, the authors of the much-cited book *Women's Ways of Knowing*, which we discuss more fully in chapter 7, note that, when given a choice of classroom assignments, women students rarely opt for projects involving debate. They are uncomfortable with conflict and especially dislike the idea of having to defend a position with which they personally disagree.

It is certainly true that in the domestic sphere, the milieu for which women were traditionally held to be best suited, paying attention to feelings is very important. And it may well be that many women are ill at ease with contentious modes of resolving contradictory claims. But the whole point of education is to introduce students to new ideas and methods, to expand their horizons, to move beyond what they already know and believe. Just because a student "feels uncomfortable" debating, evaluating arguments on impersonal grounds, learning statistics, or honing her skills in disputation by defending a disagreeable proposition, doesn't mean that she would not gain immensely from becoming competent in these ways of operating intellectually.

Moreover, in the name of being "supportive" to women, the therapeutic aims of feminist pedagogy too often collude in inculcating the attitude of "learned helplessness" so deplored by our earlier, tougher, feminist foremothers. Consider, for example, the following policy announced by one Women's Studies teacher, as described on the Women's Studies E-mail list:

> A few years ago I started making it a requirement—a condition of my agreeing to be students' senior thesis advisor—that they had to join, form, create, find—in other words, somehow participate in, a peer support group by, for, and of others who were writing senior theses at the same time. If they ask for my advice on what to do or how they should go about it, I tell

them, as a model, about a group I participated in while in graduate school. The goal of this group was to provide an intellectual community committed to doing whatever was necessary to help one another achieve the conditions necessary for work (whatever those turned out to be). . . . Among other things, one of the explicit (or implicit) goals of such a structure can be to explore feminist conceptions of colleagueship, collaboration, and cooperation in intellectual endeavors.

Is this professor merely helping her students learn how to network? Or is she telling them that it is not possible to work alone, and that one can do nothing without supportive friends? The latter claim is patently untrue (just ask Barbara McClintock!). But beyond the truth or falsehood of such advice, one should consider whether it is empowering for students to believe that they can learn and work only in a cozy Women's Studies environment. When does a support group become a crutch? When do networking and forging consensus stifle innovation and creativity? These are hard questions, but feminist pedagogues have not even asked them.

FEMINIST PEDAGOGY: A MIDTERM REPORT

The most characteristic aspect of feminist pedagogy is the value it places on getting students to "give voice" to their raw, unanalyzed feelings on any topic being discussed. But for those who believe in liberal education, the feminist mode of dealing with these personal reactions has many pitfalls. Any teacher who has ever dealt, in a classroom, with emotionally charged readings or issues knows how difficult it is to balance the students' needs to ventilate their feelings with the academic objectives of analyzing assumptions and evaluating arguments.

When, in 1969, the Ontario Institute for Studies in Education initiated a Canadian Public Issues Project, which developed curricular materials on controversial topics such as abortion, euthanasia, law enforcement methods, cultural diversity, and sex education,[6] those who designed these materials encountered a major problem in getting students to move from a mere blurting out of their subjective reactions to a reasoned analysis of the issues. Their recommendation was that teachers begin the study of each topic with one or two periods explicitly designated for "sounding off," and then—very deliberately—change the classroom atmosphere to one of a calm and careful weighing of pros and cons. The goal was to have students realize the complexity of issues and grasp the strengths and weaknesses of whatever conclusions they, individually, might draw.

Contrast this with the situation in Women's Studies. Consider, for example, a recent communication on the Women's Studies E-mail list, in which a philosophy professor described what she tells her students about the value of small-group discussions:

I always spend time *in class* talking about the reasons why I use that classroom technique (small group discussions), and the reasons that I think it produces a superior learning experience to the one(s) that I'm electing not to use (traditional lecture, etc.). I also talk about what "counts" as "active participation"—and I make it clear that talking, per se, is *not* what is valued, but that "being engaged, both with the course materials and with the learning processes of themselves and others in the classroom" is what matters. I point out that this can include "actively listening" and "giving attentive consideration to questions produced by others" whether or not one chooses to speak up, oneself. But I also point out that this includes "bringing one's own questions, confusions, concerns and insights into the discussion" with the caveat that leaving *oneself* out is not really a way of being well engaged. [emphasis in original]

Another professor complained that feminist pedagogy's stress on personal involvement had led the students in her feminist theory class to a different kind of resistance—namely, an unwillingness to undertake serious intellectual work:

> My Women's Studies students are generally far more interested in discussing "issues" such as pornography, abortion, advertising, rape, personal appearance, and hygiene than in learning about less immediately "relevant" matters. After the first couple of times I taught the course, I realized that the students were, typically, good at articulating their feelings, but far less able to engage in analysis. This meant that assignments to examine the theoretical assumptions of a particular text often resulted in papers revealing "what X [the text] means to me." The discourse of feminism they were picking up elsewhere reinforced their own inclination to concentrate on the confession of personal feelings and to disdain the hard work of intellectual and scholarly critique. Every semester I have had to spend considerable time attempting to undo this tendency, struggling to move students beyond what came naturally to them—voicing opinions on any and every subject, expressing feelings—to what they conspicuously evaded: thoughtful analysis.

Activists will argue that what many women need most is not practice in the subtleties of scholarly analysis, but a nurturing atmosphere capable of leading them to empowerment. But this is a hollow claim. The most distressing aspect of feminist pedagogy may be its tendency to undermine women students' ability to achieve.

If "criticism" is alive and well in Women's Studies in the form of personal assessments by students of one another's degree of feminist enlightenment, it is notably absent as part of a thoughtful intellectual practice. Just as the discourse of feminism today excuses a great many ills, so has it served as an instrument by which students can indulge their own disinclination for hard work. One professor we interviewed—herself a staunch advocate of and participant in the

Women's Studies program at the private "Seven Sisters" college at which she has taught for many years—mentioned her impatience with those students who object to having their writing or other work subjected to criticism because, so they contend, such feedback indicates adherence to the male standards they reject:

> I think it's because we make the students feel safe in doing it. And the other manifestation that I know irritates a lot of my colleagues is that many students assume that feminist teachers don't really mean the rules that they make—"the paper doesn't really have to be in on time," "I don't really have to do all the work," and "oh, but she's a feminist and so her politics will be that she has to be nurturing." That drives us nuts!

A particularly egregious example that this is not merely a "misunderstanding" on the part of students recently appeared on the Women's Studies E-mail list. In a discussion of the "patriarchal assumptions of academia," one contributor offered her own list of just what these assumptions are, and explained the "patriarchal" thinking that lay behind them:

Grading? (hierarchic sorting of students' "worth" on performance measures)

Deadlines? (violence and confrontation implicit in the word)

Focus on performance as opposed to learning? (need for evidence of learning)

Terms? (time chopped up into blocks of arbitrary length)

Specialization vs. generalization? (the very idea of disciplines)

Seeming arbitrary rules of majors and/or graduation?

Focus on preparation for jobs vs. life?

Enculturation to values of rigor, rationality, objectivity, Aristotelian logic?

Enforcement of rules of language and grammar?

Enculturation of rules of citation and promoting "future research"?

The correspondent ended with the question: "Which if any of these are patriarchal in nature, and does it matter?" The fact that it is impossible to tell whether this list is intended as parody or as genuine feminist insight is itself an indication of something deeply amiss within feminism.

The breakdown of a working consensus about the importance of academic achievement is most notable, as we have seen, in the classroom, where those professing feminism act out commitments to constantly challenge "rules and regulations." Not surprisingly, feminist pedagogy encourages faculty to abdicate a "superior" role. Some let undirected classroom discussion go on for an entire semester (which certainly saves the professor much preparation time!). A few take an even more extreme view and do not prepare a syllabus. Encountering such a lack of structure, many of those who enroll in a class, expecting to learn from the professor, may simply decide to drop the course, as one teacher told us happened in her feminist theory class when she informed the students that it was up to them to devise a syllabus for the semester.

Even when professors do not go to such extremes, many seem embarrassed at the thought that they have more knowledge than their students. They work hard to disguise this fact, one technique for doing so being the affirmation that their students' "experience" is as valuable a form of "knowledge" as the intellectual training and specialized learning the professor has (one would hope) painstakingly acquired. Such abdication of expertise, with its concomitant dissolution of identities and roles is, of course, connected to feminism's explicit assault not only on hierarchies generally but also on the boundaries between the public and private, the emotional and the intellectual.

In a 1975 essay, Jo Freeman provides a telling example of a different intellectual climate as she describes a survey conducted at the University of Chicago in 1970 to determine whether women graduate students suffered discrimination or discouragement in pursuing their degrees. The researchers had concluded that, though faculty had offered neither men nor women significant encouragement, such "equality" in fact had a different impact on women than on men because of the "differentiating external environments from which women and men students come." Thus, professors "discriminate against women without really trying" whenever they fail to act positively to help women students overcome this "handicap."

So far, this might sound familiar to today's feminist teachers. But Freeman then moves in quite another direction. In marked contrast to the feminist pedagogical imperatives that developed in the 1980s, she asserts that women, as a group, are "deprived of the rich external environment of high expectations and high encouragement that research indicates is best for personal growth and creative production." "Overt opposition," she continues, "is preferable to motivational malnutrition."[7]

In her particular intellectual setting in the 1970s, Freeman took it for granted that the encouragement women need is provided by the challenge to excel and that teachers' expectations play a prominent role in determining student performance. This is a far cry from today's popular feminist pedagogy, which rejects these "high expectations" or urges women not even to attempt to excel, as such an effort could itself be defined as masculinist or patriarchal.

In Women's Studies' extreme concern for providing students with a sustaining, nonjudgmental, reassuring atmosphere—which can include the tendency to explain away any lack of success as not their own fault—there lurks a highly problematic view of young women. Such educational tactics may seem appropriate for children, who indeed are often short of confidence and need regular and massive doses of encouragement. But to treat university students in this way is to infantilize them, perhaps to drain away their burgeoning confidence by providing too much reassurance, too many acknowledgments that they are not responsible for this or that failure, that someone or something else is to be blamed, and that the academic criteria they are struggling to meet are really obstacles raised against them by an unfeeling patriarchy.

Girls, as they grow up, need to overcome the well-meaning but often ill-advised overprotectiveness of their parents, which sends them the message that they are not quite competent. Do they go to university only to have this message repeated to them in Women's Studies programs?

5

Semantic Sorcery:

Rhetoric Overtakes Reality

WOMEN'S STUDIES originally had two legitimate academic objectives: to find and publicize information about the lives and works of women who had been forgotten or overlooked, and to make women's lives a primary focus of inquiry. But soon the "add women and stir" recipe for doing Women's Studies was rejected as inadequate. As an oft-repeated line in the early 1980s had it, you can't merely *add* the idea that the world is round to the notion that the world is flat. More drastic measures were indicated: the old flat-earthers had to be routed.

Far more important than the recovery of women's lives and past contributions ("excavation work") was the need for a radical reappraisal of all the assumptions and values found in traditional scholarship. As a consequence of this turn in the direction of Women's Studies, what came to be transmitted to students as feminist scholarship was every bit as problematic as the tense and volatile atmosphere of feminist classrooms.

THROWING AWAY THE MASTER'S TOOLS: PLAYING *TOTAL REJ*

TOTAL REJ is our name for the game that results from the feminist move of totally rejecting the masculinist, patriarchal, Eurocentric, capitalistic cultural heritage and trying to invent *de novo* feminist replacements for all that has been discarded.

Earlier generations of feminists believed that if principles of basic decency, justice, and fairness were applied to women, most of women's grievances would be resolved. There was nothing wrong with the principles themselves, according to the older view—it was simply a matter of extending them fairly to women, children, and the disadvantaged.

TOTAL REJ feminists, by contrast, argue that two hundred years of American "enlightenment" have failed to deliver the goods to women—we cannot even pass the Equal Rights Amendment. There are deep reasons, then, why women are justified in doubting that piecemeal modifications of the present society will ever liberate them. Our culture, including all that we are taught in schools and universities, is so infused with patriarchal thinking that it must be torn up root and branch if genuine change is to occur. Everything must go—even the allegedly universal disciplines of logic, mathematics, and science, and the intellectual values of objectivity, clarity, and precision on which the former depend.

A much-beloved aphorism taken from an essay by Audre Lorde is often quoted on this point: "the Master's tools will never dismantle the Master's house."[1] When read in context, it is not at all clear what tools Lorde had in mind. Although her phrase seems to allude to a passage in Frederick Douglass's autobiography, Lorde's intended message is quite different. Douglass fervently believed that the master's tools for enforcing bondage could also become the slave's tools for liberation. He movingly describes overhearing one of his masters explain why slaves should not be allowed to become literate, and then goes on to testify how important it had been to him to learn to read. Lorde proposes a quite different route to liberation. Her remarks appear intended as a call for women not to count on men's help, but to rely on each other for support.

Whatever Lorde's original intention may have been, her words have now been taken up as a slogan by those who find little worth saving in the traditional academic corpus. One contributor to the Women's Studies E-mail list took the suggestion to its drastic conclusion: "I think you could burn the house down. Why would one want to use the master's tools?"

We wish to make it clear that what we are objecting to is the rash nihilism of this game. We have no quarrel with serious debates about feminist challenges to and interventions in traditional disciplines. But in many Women's Studies settings, arguments about traditional knowledge tend to be reduced to avowals of a kind of feminist knownothingness. This is the posture we characterize as TOTAL REJ.

Students sometimes act as if the invitation to engage in a wholesale condemnation of nonfeminist writings and ideas were to be taken literally. Why should they have to read Darwin, Marx, or Freud when those authors wrote only sexist nonsense? A historical shift has clearly taken place when a Women's Studies student feels justified in submitting a paper (as reported by a political science professor we interviewed) consisting of the single line: "Freud was a cancer-ridden, cigar-smoking misogynist." And how reassuring the thought that one can ignore all science, all economic theory, and all technology because, after all, these brainchildren of "malefactors" just oppress women, as some Women's Studies students now write on their affordable, efficient word processors while listening to a CD as their wrinkle-free jeans are being washed in the laundromat and their Stouffer's spinach soufflé is heating up in the microwave.

What young female students in search of meaningful education most need is broad exposure to countervailing ideas. In a normal program of studies they would indeed receive such exposure, at the very least through distribution requirements in a comprehensive arts and sciences curriculum. But TOTAL REJ encourages them to discredit everything that is not feminist, and the highly charged moralistic atmosphere cultivated by Women's Studies throws up hard-to-surmount barriers around the student who might wish to explore other points of view. One pernicious result of this game is the absence from many Women's Studies programs of anything like encouragement of a love of learning. It is very difficult, after all, to invite students to develop curiosity and the desire to learn while hurling anathemas against the academy.

Not surprisingly, Women's Studies students are often criticized by faculty in other departments (and sometimes, as we have seen, by Women's Studies professors themselves) for their disinclination to think hard and work diligently. A knowing and dismissive sneer is obviously far more economical. An even more predictable effect of TOTAL REJ is the absence of critical thinking about Women's Studies' own pet ideas, claims, and arguments, which must rush in to fill the newly created intellectual void. Nor is this tendency to be found only among students.

Older feminist faculty, the pioneers who started Women's Studies programs, had the benefits of a traditional education. With all its shortcomings, such an education seems to have given them the intellectual tools they needed to make good on their challenges to that very education. These women were not as inclined as younger students or activist staff members to reject "malestream" academic disciplines. It is in large part due to the authority of these older scholars that Women's Studies has come into existence. But, more recently, feminist faculty have not followed their example. One Women's Studies professor we know of—with a doctorate in education, no less—proudly proclaims that all the "old knowledge" must be tossed out. Everyone, she says, is now on an equal intellectual footing, all starting from scratch.

It is, of course, impossible to totally reject one's cultural heritage. Therefore, feminist faculty sometimes simply borrow old ideas from the books of the "fathers," repackage them in feminist jargon, and present them to unwary students and colleagues as the original products of sisterly collaboration. This pretense of intellectual parthenogenesis—a direct outgrowth of TOTAL REJ—has a variety of bad consequences. By spuriously presenting concepts as the offspring of a virgin birth, one cuts off the reader (and the student) from the wealth of prior critical discussions of core ideas. The practice also perpetuates the myth that feminism cannot profit from external input. Not surprisingly, it breeds contempt among academic colleagues in other departments, who may conclude that whatever is worth taking seriously in feminist scholarship is only a cross-dressed version of something created much earlier.

By arguing that feminists have not succeeded in starting *de novo* and have instead drawn selectively on the Western intellectual heritage, we certainly do not mean to suggest that there is nothing new under the feminist sun. Feminist scholars have put forth many original proposals—some of lasting value—and these are readily acknowledged even by feminists who walked away from Women's Studies programs, as we saw earlier. But what is too often missing wherever TOTAL REJ prevails is the appropriate acknowledgment of male precursors, which would help students make connections between Women's Studies and what they learn elsewhere in the university. This omission makes TOTAL REJ a game that subverts, in the name of revolutionary political goals, one of the standard obligations of scholarly integrity: acknowledge your sources.

By claiming that the master's intellectual house must be torn down and that we must start over on a new foundation, feminism has attracted, and has for the most part been receptive to, any number of approaches to knowledge that are alleged to be politically liberating. The popularity of Marxism and of French versions of psychoanalysis seems to be waning now, but cultural relativism, standpoint epistemology, social constructionism, theories of linguistic and cultural hegemony, and other progeny of postmodernism are alive and well in feminist classrooms, and are often uncritically embraced there. Flirtations with exotic intellectual approaches are, of course, endemic in the academy, especially in largely interpretative fields such as literary criticism and film studies. Though these approaches may sometimes irritate nonparticipants (perhaps because they require a lengthy initiation process into their special discourses), they generally do little harm and may even yield genuine insights. In feminist settings, however, they are apt to become more than mischievous. In brief, here's why.

Interpretative frameworks work best when they are used like

proverbs. "Look before you leap" is good advice to contemplate when one is feeling impatient, but on other occasions it is well to remember that "she who hesitates is lost." Likewise, aggressive types who believe that only sticks and stones break bones need to be reminded of the power of language, while folks who think words are more important than deeds should be urged to kick a few stones (as in Samuel Johnson's famous refutation of Bishop Berkeley). Radical approaches to knowledge are most effective when they challenge received orthodoxy. Too much feminist theory, by contrast, employs exotic epistemologies that reinforce, rather than challenge, feminine stereotypes and the gender socialization to which many young female students have been exposed. This is most evident in feminism's uncritical embrace of some peculiar ideas about language.

From at least Victorian days it has been the job of bourgeois women to monitor language and enforce norms of what is socially acceptable. The important things these women needed to know about their world—how to raise children, manage the household, and keep their husbands happy—were learned primarily from small, informal community networks or personal experience, not from books. Deprived of political rights, their most effective means of influencing their environment was through rhetorical manipulation. There is a nice irony in the fact that, like their Victorian foresisters, many feminist academics today are intrigued by approaches that focus entirely on the power of language to shape culture. Just what kinds of games are feminists playing with words?

WORDMAGIC AND OTHER LANGUAGE GAMES

Feminism, like many other political movements today, is in thrall to the notion that linguistic reform will not merely reflect social transformation but will actually bring it about. Feminist activists have used language innovation both to promote new feminist ideas and to shame those who resist their agenda. As a political stratagem, this preoccupation with language has had some success, despite the ridicule now being heaped on politically correct terminology. However, attempts to manipulate language have had a counterproductive impact on feminist research and teaching. WORDMAGIC, our general rubric for the games feminists play with words, hurts women in the long run.

Phony Philology

The study of word origins and the evolution of their meanings is indispensable for the historian of ideas. Philology also offers insights into the cultural significance of contemporary usage. Explaining that *philosophy* comes from *philos*, meaning "fond of," and *sophia*, "wisdom," or that the *nomos* in *astronomy* means "law" is a nice way to start a semester. And it is certainly legitimate and relevant to point out that woman (from *wifmon*) is the qualified or marked form of *man*.

But feminists have turned philology from a scholarly tool into a propaganda weapon by creating a game we call Phony Philology. At first it may be amusing to note that *seminar* is etymologically related to *semen*, and to use this observation to talk about the exclusion of women from higher education. But when feminist editors circle the phrase "X's seminal paper," even when X is a woman, and ask for nonsexist rewording, and when feminist students seriously demand that their seminars be called "ovulars," the emphasis on etymology seems just plain silly.

Words may be clues to attitudes, but the correspondence is not so simple. We speak of *seminal* works, but we also say that a phrase is *pregnant* with implications. One does not get very far arguing that it is the male roots or connotations of academic speech that are responsible for the exclusion of females. For every time someone refers to the *thrust* of an argument, someone else will speak of the *fruitfulness* of a discussion or the importance of being *receptive* to new ideas. Feminine metaphors abound as we thread our way through a difficult passage and peel off layers of meaning.

Once one develops a fixation on male imagery, genuine etymology becomes irrelevant, as in the feminist attempt to call feminist historical research "herstory," an action that is intended to radically modify what is presented in departments where "his-story" has traditionally been taught. Does this also mean that "hermeneutics" is characteristically female? Or could it be that the "her" and the "men" in the word imply a transcendent state of androgyny?

Mary Daly's *Wickedary*, which promises to take the "dick" out of *dictionary*, is a confusing mixture of bad puns and provocative but genuine philology, the latter paradoxically showing traces of Daly's impressive Catholic theological training.[2] But in a day when few students have even a smattering of Greek or Latin, and when most are depressingly unsophisticated speakers of their own language, they cannot easily distinguish tongue-in-cheek etymology from the genuine article. By manipulating philology to fit and advance a political agenda, feminist wordmagicians help cultivate in their students an attitude, at best, of indifference and, at worst, of contempt for intellectual traditions.

Metaphor Madness

Closely related to the game of Phony Philology is Metaphor Madness, which privileges metaphors over precise meanings. Teachers love to share examples of misread metaphors culled from student papers. But sometimes mistakes in the figurative use of language become entrenched. Albert Einstein came to regret having attached the name *Relativity Theory* to his equations, which actually describe certain invariant properties of mechanical systems, because poets and homespun philosophers immediately began to say that Einstein had demonstrated that everything is relative.

As for feminists, they have made the magnification of metaphors into a cottage industry. Looking for hidden positive messages, such as the search for clitoral imagery in Emily Dickinson's poetry (the subject of a paper recently delivered at the Modern Language Association's annual meeting), may lead to a rather skewed view of her verses, but it could also be illuminating. More harm is done when feminists search a text for signs of negative masculinist imagery and then use them to discredit the entire work in which they appear.

This is a favorite device of feminist critics of science. An extended example—given here because it is such a notorious one—will show how this game works. Bacon's *New Organon*, a book on scientific method favorably cited by the founders of England's Royal Society, contains some famous passages in which Bacon speaks of putting Nature on the rack in order to extort her secrets, and of prying into her innermost nooks and crannies. Feminists such as Carolyn Merchant, in her book *The Death of Nature*, claim that this and similar passages in the writings of early scientists strongly suggest that modern science has always treated the natural world contemptuously and has viewed nature as a woman who exists only to be raped.[3] And if it is true that the scientific method was originally conceptualized as a form of rape, is it any wonder that women even today often feel uncomfortable in science classes and believe that science is responsible for our present ecological crises—the rape of Mother Earth?

However, the argument from Bacon's metaphors is very weak. In his day, natural philosophy, science, the nation, justice, and the church were also spoken of as though they were female. Does this mean that a reference to the penetration of Nature by Science alludes to a lesbian affair? Moreover, there are other passages in which Bacon speaks very tenderly of Nature: To be understood, Nature must be obeyed. Feminists might argue that this merely means that Bacon is talking about something more like a date rape; let scientists first try seduction, but if teasing out Nature's secrets doesn't work, put her on the rack! What Bacon really meant to convey by these locutions, however, becomes clear if one actually reads his book and does not merely scan for incriminating metaphors.

The *New Organon* is, first, a sustained attack on the Aristotelian account of knowledge as it had been developed and institutionalized in the Middle Ages, and, second, an attempt to formulate a radically new approach. Aristotle's theory of knowledge was a naturalistic one: only sense organs in their natural state could be trusted. Someone who is drunk or dizzy from spinning around is not a reliable observer. In Bacon's time this sensible-sounding precept was used to discredit Galileo's telescopic observations. And the Aristotelian corollary—that only observations made of systems in their natural state could give knowledge of their normal workings—was used to discourage "artificial" arrangements such as William Harvey's experiments showing that valves in the veins allowed blood to flow in only one direction.

Bacon is saying that we must put Nature on the rack of experimentation and use scientific instruments to penetrate her innermost secrets. The violence of his images is directed at Aristotelians, not women. Since Bacon was also a prominent jurist, his metaphors were undoubtedly rooted in then-current legal debates in England concerning permissible methods of gathering evidence for trials; this is how Bacon's contemporaries probably interpreted his metaphors. If feminists were seriously trying to understand Bacon's writings about science, they would have to read him in this light.

When, however, one's main purpose is political, not scholarly, it is easy enough to construct a "metaphorical case" against almost anyone. And, indeed, feminists have turned metaphor against themselves as they have scrutinized one another's writings for lapses into any of the dreaded -isms.

Linguistic Litmus Tests

Closely related to the game of Metaphor Madness is the feminist habit of applying Linguistic Litmus Tests. Ignoring the proverbial reminder that actions speak louder than words, feminists have transformed the sensible biblical counsel "By their fruits you shall know them" into the more dubious "By their nouns and pronouns you will judge them." Thus, a feminist facilitator at a diversity training workshop attended by one of us told students that any (male) instructor who called women "girls" was not only using "unacceptable" language in the classroom, but was likely to be sexist in other ways as well. Someone asked her, "But what if it were simply a case of a kindly older professor calling his eighteen-year-old students 'girls and guys'?" The reply was firm: there is no excuse for ever referring to women students as "girls." And on the Women's Studies E-mail list, a professor "shared" with everyone her clever solution to a male student's insistence on using the generic *he*: she told him she would not grade his paper until he rewrote it without the offending pronoun.

Many publishing houses now insist on "nonsexist" language in the list of books they publish. We know editors who pride themselves on their rigorous application of this policy. Yet it strikes us as a bizarre laundering of texts whose ideological origins ought to remain open to readers' scrutiny. If a writer genuinely conceives of his [*sic*] argument as applying only to men, or has not extended his research to include women, or otherwise has no interest in women's contributions, would we not want to know it, instead of having the evidence for it excised by diligent editors?

Undoubtedly, lexical choices often suggest a great deal about an individual. And in such cases it is a disservice to readers and listeners if revealing language has been "corrected." On the other hand, while lexical preferences are often very telling, the inferences we draw from them are fallible and, as speakers of so-called Black English will testify, can all too easily be used prejudicially. Moreover, there is an important asymmetry at work here: use of a progressive neologism, one that deviates significantly from the accustomed terms or expressions, is a good indication that the speaker has some knowledge of, and is in sympathy with, the innovative trend. Talk of "womanist" theory, for example, tells us that the speaker is at least vaguely attuned to black feminist perspectives. Negative implications, on the other hand, are more hazardous to draw. Saying "feminist" instead of "womanist" hardly signals racism.

Many of the feminist proposals for altering the English language are good ones and are rapidly catching on. Even the *New York Times* some years ago added the useful honorific *Ms.* to its style sheet. Any individual or group can propose and argue for linguistic changes. Often these shifts affect the cultural and social climate for the better. But feminists go wrong when they conclude that anyone who fails to adopt their proposals should be assumed to discriminate against the group on whose behalf the proposal is made.

The use of a Linguistic Litmus Test is especially ill-advised when one is reading works from other cultures or historical periods; grave misunderstandings, not just howlers, are bound to result. Training students in such habits of mental inflexibility hardly contributes to their capacity to understand the "diversity" of human groups and of past societies.

Accordion Concepts

Phony Philology, Metaphor Madness, Linguistic Litmus Tests— these games are irritating, and they trivialize academic feminism. But there are more serious methodological errors than these at work today, which, as one woman we interviewed sadly put it, turn feminists into "victims of their own rhetoric."

A particulary pernicious game is one we call Accordion Concepts, a label we have borrowed from an essay by Wilfrid Sellars in which he observes that "the term 'theory' is one of those accordion words which, by their expansion and contraction, generate so much philosophical music."[4] Somewhat more formally, we might refer to this game as "The Failure to Draw Distinctions."

When this game is played, concepts are stretched so widely that crucial distinctions are obliterated. Consider two examples: the feminist catchphrase "any woman can be a lesbian" and the "art project" recently exhibited on the University of Maryland campus that listed as "potential rapists" male names pulled randomly from a student directory. The latter action raises all sorts of problems about the legal and ethical limits of "performance art" and the political effectiveness of guerilla theater, but our focus is on how feminist claims such as "all men are potential rapists" or "every woman can be a lesbian" are intended to be understood.

The slogan declaring every woman to be a potential lesbian is taken from a 1975 record album called "Lavender Jane Loves Women." The lyrics to the song, sung by Alix Dobkin, turn the tables on the once-common belief that lesbians, if only they tried hard enough, wouldn't be that way. The song is smart and funny, and it contains no manipulation of meaning.

The game of Accordion Concepts gets under way when academic feminists "theorize" the slogan. An example is Adrienne Rich's redefinition, noted in an earlier chapter, of *lesbian* to include all women who put energy into, or who identify with, the life projects of other women, regardless of whom they happen to sleep with or be in love with.[5] On this redefinition, Catharine MacKinnon, the radical feminist legal theorist who has appeared in newspaper photos arm in arm with her fiancé, Jeffrey Masson, becomes a prototypical lesbian because of her intense political commitments to the cause of women. To be sure, Rich's essay is more subtle than this, because she at least introduces a continuum, permitting the drawing of some distinctions. If taken literally, however—which it often is in Women's Studies courses—her extension-by-definition of *lesbian* rules out the possibility of conceiving either of a nonfeminist lesbian or of a nonlesbian feminist. Such semantic sorcery benefits neither the lesbian rights movement nor the cause of feminism.

Even more mischief is done by feminist identifications of "potential rapists." Again, one could gloss such verbal excesses as mere activist hyperbole: the Maryland students, when interviewed on National Public Radio,[6] said they were only trying to make everyone realize that rape is caused by men's aggression, not by women's imprudence. They were trying to reverse our mothers' warnings that every woman is a potential rape *victim*, focusing attention instead on the *perpetrators*. One could even agree that a woman whose car breaks down on a lonely road at night may be well advised to act as if (almost) every man were a potential rapist. Such commonsensical interpretations of the slogan branding all men as potential rapists do not violate our conceptual categories, at least in the current political context.

Mystification begins as feminist alchemists go to work on it. Here's the trick. First they capitalize on the ambiguity of *potential rapist*. What might this possibly be construed to mean? On one reasonable interpretation, *potential rapist* could be used to describe a man who says he would enjoy forced penetration if he thought he could get away with it, and there is indeed a substantial minority of male undergraduates who have checked this response on surveys of campus attitudes. But most men, contrary to the apparent meaning of the claim that they are all potential rapists, do not in fact express a desire to rape. When confronted with this objection, feminist theorists quickly deny that they think all men have such a yearning. Instead, they say, they are thinking of the masculinist *zeitgeist*, which supposedly determines our cultural milieu so extensively that it makes every man a prospective rapist.

One of the correspondents on the Women's Studies E-mail list, where this subject was discussed at length, offered the following explanation to a feminist man who protested that he did not like being called a potential rapist:

> [Men] are potential rapists because our culture defines traditional male sexuality in such a manner as to glorify violence and the oppression of women. The knowledge that you have overcome this conditioning is very heartening. I know a few other men who have also overcome their conditioning, and are kind and gentle people who would not rape. But they are still potential rapists simply because they are men raised in a patriarchal culture that glorifies violence and conditions both men and women to accept a rape model of sexuality as normal. I agree with you that it does not feel good. It shouldn't feel good. Given your level of sensitivity and knowledge about violence against women, though, I hope you will begin to feel less defensive. It SHOULD make you feel more responsible.

Using this analysis, to say that "X is a *potential* rapist" is to say nothing at all specific about X's individual potentialities. The statement simply conveys the fact that he grew up in a patriarchal society in which, supposedly, rape is normal.

But the "theorizing" of the concept of rape does not stop there. In a radio interview, Robin Morgan proposed that the legal definition of rape be extended to cases where women, though not subjected to forced sex, are cajoled into unwanted sexual activities—cases where, as she put it (alluding to Margaret Atwood's dystopian novel *The Handmaid's Tale*), the woman would rather be playing Scrabble.[7] And Andrea Dworkin and Catharine MacKinnon have long argued that in a patriarchal society all heterosexual intercourse is rape because women, as a group, are not in a strong enough social position to give meaningful consent—an assault on individual female autonomy uncannily reminiscent of old arguments for why women should not have political rights.[8] Obviously, rape is an extremely grave crime, and its definition deserves careful analysis and debate. But serious discussion is not advanced by redefining terms in such a way that every time a feminist woman marries a man she is, strictly speaking, a person on the lesbian continuum marrying a potential rapist. By such definitions we would have to say that every offspring of such a union was conceived in an act of rape. Perhaps some radical feminists do hold such a belief, which may explain their hostility to childbearing.

Most feminists would, of course, neither draw such implications nor endorse them. They want to have it both ways. They would like to retain the charge that rape is a terrible violation of human rights and, at the same time, stretch the legal definition of the crime beyond all reason. But even the rhetorical gains won by this sort of concept stretching can backfire. When birth-control campaigns among disadvantaged groups are labeled "genocide," does this extreme accusation heighten concerns about birth control? Or does it merely diminish the horror of the Holocaust and the slaughter of Armenians? How will victims of a brutal rape feel when they are lumped together with people who suddenly discover that some embarrassing episode on a long-ago date should now be reclassified as "rape"? Whose experience is being trivialized in such careless inflation of language? Will social disapproval of sexual harassment not be lowered when the concept is stretched to include even casual unwanted glances or an unsolicited friendly touch?

One certain result of these exaggerations is the kind of cognitive confusion that inevitably will adversely affect the design of research projects. Imagine trying to discover what it is that makes some men commit rape, in the conventional sense of the term, if *rape* is defined according to Dworkin and MacKinnon. Until the relevant concepts are defined more specifically, skepticism about feminist statistics concerning injustices perpetrated against women is warranted. No matter how firmly people are committed to the improvement of women's condition, they are bound to raise their eyebrows when they discover that in a supposedly scientific study of rape, the act was defined so broadly that nearly half of the victims in the sample were able to say that they continued to date their rapists.[9] The recent adoption of the dramatic term *survivor* for those who have experienced even mild sexual harassment is merely another instance of irresponsible concept stretching.

Because *rapist* and *lesbian* are such highly charged words today, people do notice when they are used indiscriminately. But other instances of concept stretching are less likely to be detected and are, therefore, more difficult to counteract. Consider the compromise position arrived at by contributors to the Women's Studies E-mail list in their vigorous discussions of *potential rapists*:

> I have a comment about how I teach the issue of potential rapist and potential rape victims which might be useful. I do not think all men are potential rapists, but I do tend to believe all people are racists and sexists. To be sexist is not the same as to say a person could or would rape under any circumstances. To be a racist is not to say a person could or would participate in lynching or raping people of races other than one's own. What it means is that all people tend (and I stress that word, "tend") to prefer their own groups (those they are taught to identify with from birth). . . . So . . . I teach my students to be aware of their unavoidable racism, classism, sexism (both women and men) because it is ignorance of those preferences that leads people to participate in racist and sexist and classist activities from a belief that what their group wants, knows, believes, or whatever is a generally acceptable action. We all need to be

> aware of our group preferences. . . . If I insist that I am not
> sexist or racist, that is when I find myself most dangerous.

This correspondent correctly diagnosed the absurdities that result when every male is called a "potential rapist." But she assumes that *sexist* and *racist* can be defined so that they apply to everyone. The justification offered for this assumption is simply that our culture, including our language, is permeated with sexism, racism, and other such attitudes. We grow up in this culture; therefore, all of us are unavoidably sexist, racist, and so on.

In this simplistic feminist worldview, conditions such as racism and sexism are original sins of the soul that all individuals must constantly and publicly confess to in themselves and confront in others. This theological postulate is then invoked to prove that every charge of racism or sexism must be true. One may try to dispute details of who did what to whom, but the answer to the question is always given in the premise that underlies it. Such a move, of course, trivializes the very evils feminism claims to oppose. Whatever is meant by calling Women's Studies programs "racist" (which is a currently fashionable charge), it is surely something other than what a reference to the Ku Klux Klan as a racist organization would signify. Furthermore, so many important differences exist between, say, the men who formed the Tailhook gauntlet and the gay men who provide child care at the Middleway House, a battered women's shelter in Bloomington, Indiana, that one wonders what gain can possibly come from calling both "sexist."

Feminists should ponder this question. Once so vehemently critical of the attempts of anthropologists and philosophers to generalize about the human condition, they are now themselves engaged in a most dubious form of universalizing.

The Power of Naming

According to Genesis 2:19: "[God] brought them unto Adam to see what he would call them: and whatsoever Adam called every living creature, that *was* the name thereof." People of most, perhaps all, cultures believe that having the authority to name something, or even knowing the name of something, gives one power over it. In a recent controversial legal case, when the custody of an adopted baby called "Jessica" was transferred to her biological parents, one of the first steps the latter wanted to take was to rename her. Nor is it a mere accident of history that married women in our culture have traditionally taken on their husband's name, and rarely vice versa.

Feminists, however, carry this faith in the sheer power of names to extreme lengths. Ever since Adam, they argue, it is men who have had the authority to define the world by bestowing names. They go on to claim that liberation will never come until we begin anew and let Eve rename every living creature. This idea is a popular theme in feminist literature. One thinks immediately of Adrienne Rich's *The Dream of a Common Language* and Judy Grahn's *Another Mother Tongue*. Suzette Haden Elgin, the author of novels about a society in which women create their own language, has even written a grammar book for Láadan, a language she invented, one especially well suited, she claims, for expressing the thoughts of feminist women.[10]

So far, so good. A feminist Esperanto (non-Eurocentric, of course) might prove a very interesting experiment, but these imaginative musings are transformed into some very strange political practices. It almost seems as if feminists, at least those within the academy, believe that renaming things *is* liberation. Thus, feminists at one university produced a handbook of "preferred" usage that enjoined professors and students from using *rich* as an honorific— as in "the rich tones of the baritone sax"—and *poor* to denote something undesirable, as in "a poor performance of *Tosca*." To use these words is to be "classist." The example would be merely silly but for the strong suspicion that the language patrols actually believe that the avoidance of such terms will improve the lot of the impoverished.

Critics of the politically correct lexicon have mocked feminist-flavored neologisms such as "differently abled," "physically challenged," and "handicapable," and have deplored heavy-handed attempts to enforce their use. But our objection to the practice is more fundamental: By putting so much energy into the efforts to change languages, feminists are diverting attention from real issues.

Administrators find it much easier and cheaper to rename the office that serves students with special needs (for example, substituting *disabled* for *handicapped* in the title) than to ensure wheelchair accessibility or provide telecommunications devices for the deaf on campus. They find it expedient to require faculty, graduate teaching assistants, and students to attend "sensitivity training" sessions, in which people debate the propriety of hyphenating *African American* (as actually happened at one university). But to imagine that a hyphen will alter anything in the world of social and economic relations is scholasticism masquerading as serious politics.

Early in this century intellectuals were captivated by the so-called Sapir-Whorf hypothesis, according to which the structure and lexicon of a language both molds and reveals a culture's basic categories of thought and perception.[11] People quickly realized that the connection was not perfect: German has no single word for what we call "efficiency," but one can hardly claim that Germans have no such concept. The Hungarian language has no gender, yet patriarchy exists in Hungary nonetheless.

Still, there has always been some plausibility to the view that attitudes and ideas are in some ways influenced by language, and no one could dispute the observation that if a new idea emerges or a new artifact is invented, most likely a new word or phrase will be added to the lexicon. The Sapir-Whorf hypothesis was never intended to suggest a simplistic and unilateral link between language and the world, yet this is how some feminists have been using it. They imagine that if they create new terms and make everyone else use them, social change must follow. In real life, things do not happen in such a predictable way. The result likely to be achieved by the language police is either resentment among those whose language is being regimented or—at best—hypocritical acquiescence by those who can be shamed into compliance. Corporation executives are old hands at awarding employees a fancier title instead of giving them greater responsibility or a raise. Feminists need to recover their senses and *smell* the roses, rather than worry so much about what to call them.

6

BIODENIAL and Other Subversive Stratagems

TOTAL REJ AND WORDMAGIC are favorites of feminist players, but by no means are they the only games in town. Other, equally obnoxious, games have won fans and participants from among feminist teachers and scholars. In this chapter our primary focus is on feminists' repudiation of the sciences, especially their refusal to grant any explanatory power to biology. This is a posture we call BIODENIAL. Its obverse, social constructionism, is currently the leading contender in the search for an all-encompassing concept capable of sustaining the feminist worldview.

SOCIALLY CONSTRUCTING THE BIRDS AND THE BEES

It is a basic precept of contemporary feminist thought that both the world and our knowledge of it are socially constructed. But what exactly does this mean? Attempts to answer the question quickly run aground on loose terminology and semantic shifts. *Social construction* is one of those trendy terms in academia today that, while they signal a certain sympathy toward nouveau ideas, have no fixed referent. The core impulse behind its frequent use, however, is easy to detect, and the principle from which it proceeds seems plausible enough. *Social construction* directs attention to those properties of a phenomenon that depend on culture, and are therefore, presumably, amenable to change. Some approaches describing themselves as "social constructionist" are sensible and productive; others lead to extreme or silly conclusions. All too many feminists gravitate to the murky end of this spectrum.

A wide variety of positions fall under the label of "social constructionism," and we begin our discussion with some plausible ones. In his book *Threatened Children*, the sociologist Joel Best argues that what is taken to be a serious social problem at a given period is socially constructed.[1] In other words, the priority ascribed to a problem—for example, the kidnapping of children by strangers—is influenced more by media attention and the rhetorical strategies of activists than by empirical data demonstrating the actual dimensions of the phenomenon. What is being socially constructed is our society's perception of the seriousness of a problem—a problem that is assumed to exist independently of media hype or the preoccupations of our culture. Best's argument is clear and persuasive.

A contrasting, but equally unobjectionable, example of social constructionism is found in a recent newsletter from Iowa featuring a long article on dairy cows. Certain bovine breeds, it appears, have undergone such an intense process of artificial selection, guided by the financial interests of dairy farmers, that they can now hardly survive without being hooked up to milking machines. The cows, in other words, have been genetically constructed to serve a precisely defined social purpose, a process that raises various ethical issues.

In both instances, use of the term *social construction* is uncontroversial. Doubts arise, however, as we move along the spectrum. Michel Foucault's *History of Sexuality* contains the oft-cited claim that no homosexuals existed before the late nineteenth century because "homosexuality" is a social construction contrived by the medical-psychoanalytic disciplines.[2] Much ink has been spilled trying to discover exactly what Foucault meant. Even more puzzling is the question why gay activists should have taken up this claim as a slogan (thereby destroying the continuity between Sappho and Gertrude

Stein or Edward II and Oscar Wilde), but one could supply the following charitable interpretation: Sexual identity, like personal identity in general, is structured by the concepts and beliefs current in the ambient society. The new medical category of "homosexuality as sickness" (as opposed to "homosexuality as sin" or "indulgence" or "sport of nature") was so salient a force that it was incorporated into the very personalities of all people, both homosexuals (who felt afflicted) and heterosexuals (who felt superior by contrast). Foucault might not endorse such a tepid exegesis of his views, and many will find even this modest interpretation historically inaccurate. But at least it puts forward a view worth debating. If a condition is constituted in large part by the beliefs and postulations of the culture within which it exists, then a change in the culture could lead to a reconstruction of the condition, perhaps along more desirable lines.

What are we to make, though, of the claims put forth by certain followers of Foucault? Bruno Latour, for example, contends that no anthrax existed before Pasteur, and Ian Hacking says there were no battered babies before 1962.[3] It is, of course, possible that Latour only wanted to point out that Pasteur's achievement—isolating the anthrax bacillus, growing it in a petri dish, and sharing the specimen with co-workers—was an important contribution to the material culture of science. And perhaps Hacking merely intended to make an assertion similar to Joel Best's, namely, that the battering of babies was not regarded as a serious social problem until physicians defined it as a syndrome in 1962. But each author, in the argument he makes, seems to do his best to block such a charitable interpretation of his work.

If, then, one reads Hacking as making a stronger claim, similar to Foucault's, that the battered-baby problem is constituted in large part by physicians' categorization, does it follow that children would be better off if we changed our conceptual system and ceased speaking of a "syndrome"? In this case it seems that an activist would want to argue that what is at stake here are bruises and broken bones, which exist independently of conceptual schemes, and that willfully causing such injuries is or should be universally condemned. Of course, the die-hard social constructionist could reply that the activist's argument is not meant as a description of reality, but merely as a proposal to the society of readers about an alternative way of constructing the phenomena. We cannot block this rejoinder, but at this point the social constructionist's thesis becomes an idle disclaimer to be appended to every essay.

No other academic program seems to have leaned so heavily and inventively on social constructionism as has Women's Studies. The theoretical bedrock of the current wave of feminism is the claim that gender itself is socially constructed, and that the different roles played by men and women in society, and the personality characteristics, attitudes, and behaviors ascribed to them, derive largely from conventional social arrangements, which vary dramatically from culture to culture. Such differences can be neither explained nor justified by making reference to innate biological sex differences. This is as nontendentious a statement of the social constructionist interpretation of gender as one can make, and we ourselves have used the phrase "social construction of gender" in precisely this sense.

As in the old nature-versus-nurture debates, however, controversies arise about how far the social constructionist approach may be pushed. No one denies, for example, that the division of labor between women and men varies from society to society, and so is, at least in part, socially constructed. But is it legitimate to relate all aspects and expressions of gender to social forces? Does biology have *anything* to do with gender? And if so, what?

Women's Studies is very strongly committed to taking an extreme social constructionist line. Here is a docudrama specimen of the kind of discussion this commitment provokes in introductory classes:

Q: Isn't it a fact that men are stronger and run faster than women, and might not this fact have something to do with traditional work assignments, at least in preindustrial societies?

A: No one knows how strong and fast girls would become if they were encouraged as much as boys are. Besides, women have more endurance and a better ability to survive cold and famine. It is merely a social convention to place such a high value on speed and strength.

Q: But only women get pregnant, and, until recently in human history, infants had to be nursed or they would die. Surely these biological facts explain *some* of the differentiation in gender roles.

A: The effects of pregnancy are certainly socially constructed. Until recently, middle-class women in this country had to quit their jobs as soon as they began to "show." Working-class women or, at earlier times, slaves, by contrast, did heavy work up until it was interrupted by the "labor" of childbirth. It all depends on what society thinks pregnancy consists of.

Q: But even so, those women had to either stay close to home to nurse the baby or else carry the infant with them. Surely it was only rational to take that physical fact into account when setting up a society!

A: You're taking an essentialist, biological determinist line, and we've already seen how this leads to sexism, racism, and homophobia. Besides, what makes you think men can't lactate? Some can, you know. Even scientists admit that. And, anyway, none of this is relevant to the construction of women's roles today in our society.

This exchange represents a relatively moderate defense of claims for the social construction of gender. But Women's Studies abounds with much more startling assertions, such as the insistence of Women's Studies students in a class taught by one of us that the pain of childbirth is socially constructed by patriarchy and would not happen in a feminist society. These same students also argued that there was little infant mortality in the past until childbirth was "medicalized" by men—another notion the students had picked up in an earlier Women's Studies course.

One way feminists have tried to break any possible connection between gender and biological sex is to point to the existence of societies with three or more genders, such as the *berdache* in some Native American cultures (on which there is by now a significant literature) or the *Hijras* in India.[4] Another way is to deny the legitimacy of the dichotomous categories of "male" and "female," as done by Anne Fausto-Sterling. In a recent *New York Times* article, she noted that as many as 4 percent of neonates are born as hermaphrodites but are surgically altered to force them to conform physically to male/female body stereotypes. She goes on to argue for the social acceptance of biologically intermediate sexes.[5]

Bold and speculative claims that challenge current scientific views are or should be welcome in the academy; they often provide an impetus for investigations that advance knowledge. Valuable insights may be gained when feminists point out the conventionality of sexual dimorphism, or propound adventurous theories about the possibility of parthenogenesis and male lactation, as long as this is done in a forum where ideas can be critically scrutinized and debated. As the nineteenth-century philosopher of science William Whewell observed, truth can survive the struggle, while error will fall apart in confusion. What we object to is the pedagogical practice of presenting unsubstantiated ideas to students ill-prepared to examine them, and dressing these notions up as well-founded and properly documented feminist correctives to "malestream" prejudice. Equally deplorable is the habit of branding any disagreements with these ideas as demonstrations of a lack of genuine commitment to feminist aims.

Again, there is nothing wrong with pursuing even crazy-sounding, half-baked ideas. They *may* turn out to be fruitful in some way. The eccentric German archeologist Heinrich Schliemann believed the Greek myths and ended up discovering Troy. Perhaps feminist archeologists will eventually unearth compelling evidence of lost matriarchies, and feminist biologists will overthrow our current theories of human sexual reproduction. However, it is dishonest not only to pretend to students that speculative fancies are well established in scientific or scholarly consensus, but also to dismiss criticism of them as inspired by sexism or "backlash," and hence unworthy of reply. In maintaining this pretense, feminist intellectual separatists are reinforced by a second tenet of constructionism, which is that not only social categories but knowledge itself is socially constructed. If this were taken to be axiomatically true, there would be no reason for attempting to reconcile male-constructed knowledge claims with those put forward by feminists. By embracing such a position, the social constructionist can argue that, in addition to gender itself, our best scientific theories of gender or sex chromosomes or infinite sets are the products of specific cultural beliefs and interests.

As with all the other articles of social constructionism, this claim comes in mild and wild variants. Again we start with the tame versions. We recognize that scientific knowledge or other expert opinion always depends in part on what problems particular patrons of research regard as important at a particular time. The problems favored for investigation may well reflect the patrons' own economic and political interests. Moreover, scientific output is influenced by the technology available to experimenters. In more subtle ways, too, the social context influences how knowledge is constructed. A tradition of open critical debate, and of institutions in which such debates flourish, will lead to a kind of research very different from what can be done in a stifling, suppressive setting where researchers must fear punishment for producing unpopular results. This rather commonsensical view of how knowledge is produced we might call the mild or moderate form of the theory affirming the social construction of knowledge.

But a stronger, more radical social constructionist position holds that all knowledge is so deeply imbued with the cultural norms and personal identities of its producers that it can never be true or—without far-reaching modification—even useful for individuals not belonging to the producers' own group. This more extreme position is invoked in some feminists' wholesale dismissal of science, which would have it that it is neither necessary nor productive to attempt detailed and precise critiques of specific scientific doctrines because all of them are equally tainted by their patriarchal origins. Taking this view, one can reject science and all other forms of specialized knowledge simply by pointing out that they have been constructed by males (and a few women who made their accommodation to the patriarchy) and therefore are *a priori* of dubious worth to feminists. Students who are invited to accept this radical version of social constructionism, and who act on the invitation, are thereby excused from learning anything beyond that which is offered to them in the setting of Women's Studies. Moreover, they are likely, when emerging from such an education, to distrust and reject whatever deviates from the party line they absorbed in Women's Studies. And there *is* a party line. As will be noted in chapter 7, feminists have, through an NWSA report, made both epistemological relativism and the denial of biology integral parts of the official corpus of feminist theory. Any challenge to these strong forms of social constructionism is taken as a sign of backsliding from feminist commitment.

IS THE MIND THE ONLY SEX ORGAN?

Arguments for the social construction of reality are very old, but it is only since Marx that they have gained the kind of intellectual substance to win them broad support. To a socially conscious and responsible person, it is certainly appealing to be able to demonstrate that a human problem is amenable to remedial action because it has its roots in the conventions of society and culture, and not in some immutable biological order. For progressives, in particular, the promising outlook opened by this demonstration creates the temptation to look for cultural explanations of phenomena and to be intensely suspicious of invocations of biology or other sciences.

As a general argument, however, the case against biology fails. Near-sightedness, for example, leads to all sorts of undesirable social consequences, such as being unable to read or to remove splinters from babies' toes. Near-sightedness is biologically determined, and that very fact helps make it correctable. Xenophobia, on the other hand, is certainly in large measure a social construction, yet we seem to be very slow in correcting this condition.

Feminists would reply that in the case of social differences between men and women, any assignment of these to biology has always oppressed women. Examples of this abound, from the time of Aristotle to the present. But, again, as a generalization, this argument fails. The phenomenon of morning sickness in early pregnancy was for years given a social constructionist interpretation. It was sometimes taken to be a sign of women's innate fragility, an indication of how reproduction put such a strain on women (of a certain class) that they could not possibly bear children and hold down a job at the same time. It has also been construed as a sign of psychological weakness, an indication of women's tendency toward hypochondria and mental instability. But all such constructions can now be relegated to the dustbin, in the light of recent biological research showing how nausea in early pregnancy is triggered by certain substances that are dangerous to the developing fetus. Morning sickness is a natural response that has survival value for the species as a whole, and women can avoid it by following a carefully controlled diet.

In fact, if we want to understand a phenomenon fully, perhaps in order to change it, political touchstones will not lead us to a solution. To reject a promising avenue of research because it smacks of the bugaboo of biological determinism is to privilege dogma over the welfare of the very people one is trying to help.

Feminists who are seriously into BIODENIAL will, of course, look for the ulterior patriarchal motives behind the research on morning sickness just mentioned. They would see this as one more attempt to blame women who bear an unhealthy fetus. This was the knee-jerk response to the research on fetal alcohol syndrome and the adverse effects of nicotine and other drugs. Luckily, the extremists who criticized this research did not draw the most drastic conclusions from their distaste for science; they opted for the slightly more plausible and less harmful argument that patriarchy should be blamed, instead, for driving women to substance abuse in the first place.

BIODENIAL may be part of the reason why feminists have yet to produce a positive model for heterosexual sexuality. If heterosexual intercourse, under patriarchy, is a form of rape, what should it be like in a society based on feminist values? Feminist literary utopias usually simply reverse the present hierarchy, making men into gentle sources of semen, or they dispense with men entirely in favor of parthenogenesis, the merging of ova, or some similar mechanism. Where are the novels or theoretical models that describe healthy relationships between people who are political equals but biologically dimorphous?

Feminists sometimes seem to interpret the sexologists' slogan "The most important sex organ is between the ears" as implying that the mind is the only sex organ. But their position on nature versus nurture is shifty. When it suits them, many feminists—though ostensibly committed to strong social constructionism—surreptitiously slip back into biological essentialism, as, for example, when they totally deny that male-to-female transsexuals, no matter how thouroughly socialized, could ever be "real women."

In a similar vein, one Women's Studies professor reports:

It constantly happens in class that students argue for social constructionism on the one hand but revert to essentialist ideas quite opportunistically. It's as if everything they dislike about "women" gets dismissed as social construction, while all the rest is the Real Thing. As for men, most everything about them is not socially constructed, since that would, in some sense, let them off the hook, so men get heavy doses of essentialist attributions while the students imagine they're espousing a straight constructionist line of analysis.

What amazes me is that these students would rather believe men are evil than that they can change. The intellectual opportunism, as well as the illogicality, of these proceedings are stunning, but any effort to discuss these contradictions in class is, in my experience, futile. People already resistant to unilateral explanations hear the contradictions. The hard-line feminists, on the other hand, simply dismiss the teacher as not feminist enough or not the right kind of feminist for them. Their unwillingness to examine their own ideas is one of the things that clearly sets the Women's Studies students apart from the others.

As an illustration of this tendency, the professor recounted this episode:

In one recent class on women's fiction, I was discussing a British feminist writer's description of women's complicity in men's wars. From the back of the room, one of the few Women's Studies majors shouted: "That's bull!" When I invited her to elaborate her criticism, she explained that women only supported men's wars as a result of coercion, propaganda, social pressure, and economic insecurity. I agreed that these were real factors, but added that young men might be exposed to comparable pressures—as well as additional ones. This she hotly denied, asserting, in that tone of utter certitude which had by then become familiar to me, that men simply *were* to blame and women simply *were* the victims of patriarchy.

This is not just a matter of impressionable and literal-minded undergraduates speaking from ignorance. Important women scholars who have actively supported feminism have found themselves unwelcome in Women's Studies programs because they did not adhere to social constructionist dogma.

For an extended example of this academic form of shunning, consider the case of the sociologist Alice Rossi, the president (1983–84) of the American Sociological Association (ASA), a pioneer of second-wave feminism, and a founding member, in the mid-1960s, of the National Organization for Women. Professor Rossi explained to us the trajectory that led her away from both

Women's Studies and the usual sociology meetings (she is involved, instead, in international multidisciplinary projects that promote a biopsychosocial approach to human behavior):

> My interests have shifted very much in the direction of trying to build bridges between the biological sciences and the social and behavioral sciences. In fact, my presidential address at ASA was on a biosocial perspective on parenting, which is extremely controversial. And yet the impulse for that really came out of the more radical wing of the feminist movement.
>
> I could not accept the idea that gender differences reflected merely the ghettoization and low status of women huddling together as a discriminated-against group, because I believe that some of the things I admired most in myself and in other women were rooted in more fundamental aspects of gender differences. Once I began thinking seriously about that, I had to inform myself in the areas of neuroendocrinology, reproductive biology, evolutionary theory, and that just led to a different direction of interest, a direction so controversial at that time that I would get notes from former feminist colleagues in the profession and outside it, saying that I had turned conservative and had given up on the "good politics."

Debate became impossible as the pressure increased to deny any biological role in social and individual phenomena. Students who had taken several Women's Studies courses would sometimes come to Professor Rossi's classes with the fixed sense that they had "discussed all that already":

> It was all settled in their minds. You didn't have to know any biology, you didn't have to know anything about genes, you didn't have to know anything about how your hormones worked, what the influence on behavior is, or the lack of influence. I've had endless discussions, not with faculty in Women's Studies but

with students who were in the program, [and when pressed,] they just came back at me all the time with the same argument— "Well, there's no reason to deal with anything biological because that only takes away from the *real* factors. The real things that determine things are social and political." I said, "Look, that's based on an erroneous conception of the relationship between the body and the mind and the spirit. It's a two-way street."

As Professor Rossi sees it, the critique of a strict social constructionist view has significant political (and policy) consequences:

In terms of being interested in activism, if you believe there are some innate tendencies that come out of a very long evolutionary process, then things like unisex education just are not the solution. You need *compensatory education*. I believe that very strongly and deeply. And it isn't just a matter of giving girls a doctor's kit and boys a nurse's role. It's more important than that.

A careful evaluation of Professor Rossi's position can only come in the course of a debate in an appropriate scholarly forum. But we do not for a moment doubt that her views, backed as they are by her substantial research and that of others, deserve to be considered seriously. Once again we observe that feminism, which began its career as an enormous opening out into the world, an expansion— and in many cases, a correction—of existing knowledge and perspectives, has ended up leading to a narrow, blinkered approach. Much of the original feminist work on gender was excellent, but when social constructionism turns doctrinaire, it ceases to be a useful thinking tool and becomes one more intellectual straitjacket to be cast off.

As the flip side of social constructionism, BIODENIAL has done its share to bring on the stultification so pervasive in Women's Studies today. BIODENIAL, however, is not the only self-defeating game feminists play with the vexing problem of gender.

GENDERAGENDA: CLEANSING THE CURRICULUM OF PHALLIC PHANTASMS

All revolutionaries, political or intellectual, would like to raze the existing system and then build afresh, doing things over according to the revolutionary blueprint. Feminism is no exception, which was our point in describing the game of TOTAL REJ. But it is one thing to call for a brave new feminist world and quite another to actually construct one.

In the heady early days of Women's Studies, gender analysis seemed to cast a totally new light on every subject, and some enthusiasts even talked about establishing feminist universities in which every discipline would be newly founded, using gender as the fundamental and overarching concept. But certain subjects remained more or less impervious to change by either the search-for-missing-women or gender analyses. Because few forgotten women could be reclaimed in the natural sciences and mathematics, some feminists argued that the traditional definition of the scientist was too narrow, and they urged the admission of midwives, lab technicians, and home economists into the pantheon of science. Gender historians uncovered some sexist howlers, such as Aristotle's theory of reproduction, in which a passive, nutritive role was assigned to the female—she was the fertile soil quickened and formed by the male seed. But once one moved from biology to chemistry or physics, what possible relevance could gender have? Goethe may have compared double decomposition reactions to the switching of marital partners, and electricians refer to male and female circuit connectors, but there seemed to be very little gender imagery within the actual *content* of science, except when one was studying sex differences and reproduction. Metaphors were a different matter, of course, and, as we saw in WORDMAGIC, feminists made much of these.

The gender analysts then made a crucial move. Perhaps the place to look for gender in disciplines such as physics and mathematics was not in the subject matter itself, but in the very methods used by scientists and mathematicians as they posed their questions and sought answers. If it could be shown that the entire enterprise of science and mathematics, as well as the traditional canons of rationality embodied in logic and statistics, incorporated patriarchal assumptions, the gender agenda would be vastly expanded. Far from being gender neutral as compared to the humanities, the sciences would at one fell swoop be revealed to be the most sexist disciplines of all. Then it would be obvious why women had traditionally avoided the physical sciences in favor of the liberal arts and "soft" sciences.

There were problems, however. Is there a real difference between the claim that syllogistic reasoning or the methods of controlled experiments are inherently sexist and the arguments of nineteenth-century chauvinists who were sure that the diversion of blood to the womb made women ill-suited for abstract reasoning? Contemporary feminists have never managed to escape from this dilemma, but they have raised enough smoke and mirrors to hide the cracks in their position. It is with such evasive and equivocating moves that the game of GENDERAGENDA is played.

How "Feminine" Tunes Are "Brutally Quashed"

For a relatively simple example of how GENDERAGENDA works, and—presumably—how it is enjoyed, let us examine a recent book on classical music called *Feminine Endings: Music, Gender, and Sexuality*, by Susan McClary.[6] Musicology and music theory are as exacting in their methods as the hard sciences and, one would suppose, just as resistant to the GENDERAGENDA. But such an assumption underestimates the ingenuity of feminist critics, as McClary's book demonstrates.

McClary begins by admitting that she felt envious of friends in literary studies and art history for their ability to use the new tools of feminist criticism in their work. It was difficult for her, at first, to imagine how classical music, with its vaunted attributes of objectivity, universality, and transcendence, could be susceptible to a feminist critique. But once she had pried open the forbidden door, she began to realize that the "structures graphed by theorists . . . are often stained with such things as violence, misogyny, and racism."[7] In the first part of her book, McClary briskly catalogues a number of straightforward complaints: Women musicians have been systematically discouraged from entering the profession or developing their talents, on the sexist grounds that they could not be truly creative. The works of female composers have not received just recognition. The librettos of many operas are egregiously misogynist (Bartók's *Bluebeard's Castle* is described in grisly detail). Furthermore, the technical terminology is sexist: opening themes and strong endings are "masculine," "feminine" endings finish on a weak beat, "feminine" themes are subsidiary, and so on.

So far so good. But not content merely to show (as others have done) that women have not always been made to feel welcome in the classical music scene, McClary goes on to make a move characteristic of GENDERAGENDA. She grants that males prefer the so-called masculine endings, but insists—without offering evidence—that females are in fact more receptive to endings that finish on a weak beat. Therefore, she concludes, the formal structure of classical music is intrinsically gendered and cannot, for this reason, have any universal, objective, transcendental merit rooted in its aesthetic worth. Whatever appeal music has depends on the match between the gender of the composer and that of the listener.

Some extravagant gender interpretations follow. McClary says that "many of Beethoven's symphonies exhibit considerable anxiety with respect to feminine moments and respond to them with extraordinary violence."[8] Furthermore, "Beethoven's Ninth Symphony unleashes one of the most horrifyingly violent episodes in the history of music. . . . The Ninth Symphony is probably our most compelling articulation in music of the contradictory impulses that have organized patriarchal culture since the Enlightenment."[9] In the Unfinished Symphony of the sexually ambiguous Schubert, on the other hand, "it is the lovely, 'feminine' tune which we are encouraged to identify with and which is brutally, tragically quashed."[10] In addition to such observations, McClary describes the radically different formal devices used by contemporary women composers such as Janika Vanderwelde and Laurie Anderson.

It is important that we be very clear as to what makes a book like *Feminine Endings* troubling within the context of Women's Studies. Taken as a speculative musicological exercise, McClary's book might provoke some interesting discussions among experts. Music students familiar with Beethoven and Schubert, and with analyses of their music other than McClary's, will be able to refer to the scores to test her notions of the phallic significance of climaxes in romantic music. They may also ask why Bach and Haydn could express their masculinity in a very different musical idiom. In such a knowledgeable setting, there is no chance that the book will be taken as the new orthodoxy.

But in the happy-go-lucky world of Women's Studies, where interdisciplinarity reigns and no professional caution keeps anyone from using material from fields in which they have little or no learning, the book is likely to be read quite differently. There, it will be taken as showing not only that women have often been excluded from the profession of music, but that the best of classical music contains in its very essence, and expresses in its musical aesthetic, the violence of patriarchal misogyny. Since McClary is obviously inspired by feminist ideas and clearly intends her analysis as a weapon in the liberation of women, her book will be assumed to be useful reading for the aspiring female musician. It may cause some harm there. But its worst injuries will be done to the nonmusicians among Women's Studies students, who will simply add classical music to their already long list of areas with which they need not bother. GENDERAGENDA dictates that no contrary interpretation need be offered, and once again young women will have learned that unless the thing is of woman born, it is worthy only of their contempt.

McClary's book is probably the first comprehensive attempt to apply a gender analysis to music. It is, therefore, not surprising to find that, in its organization and thematic arrangement, it recapitulates the whole history of Women's Studies. It begins with the search for forgotten foremothers, describes how women have been excluded, then looks for and, of course, finds ugly male attributes at the very heart of the activity, and finally declares that women cannot participate successfully without making great compromises (thereby— rather problematically—implying that the forgotten foremothers were dupes, not heroines). The conclusion reached is that if women are to be an authentic part of the music scene, the profession will have to change drastically. Until that happens, women with feminist sensitivities will take up music at their peril.

"Logic . . . Is Insane"

The pattern just described is also present in recent feminist critiques of logic. The old gender stereotype employed to discourage or excuse women from studying logic is a familiar one: women are not adept at abstract thought or formal analysis. Earlier feminists would have bristled at these assumptions. They would have pointed at the sexist content of the homework exercises that, until very recently, were standard fare in logic books. Quite understandably, female students might resent having to analyze the structure of sentences like the following: "If any husband is unsuccessful, then if some wives are ambitious he will be unhappy." "Women without husbands are unhappy unless they have paramours." "If either red-heads are lovely or blondes do not have freckles, then logic is confusing."[11]

However, in a recent book by Andrea Nye, *Words of Power: A Feminist Reading of the History of Logic*,[12] we are given a feminist critique, not of the exclusion of women from logic, but of logic itself. In her first chapter, Nye tells the story of her experiences as a student in her logic class: Only one other woman was in this class. Nye was too unsure of herself to raise her hand. She found it immensely difficult to think in the way required. When confronted with the example "Jones ate fish with ice cream and died," Nye, who had come to philosophy from literature, found her mind wandering off to speculations about why Jones should eat such a bizarre dish and why death was the consequence. The difficulty she experienced in representing the structure of the sentence with p's and q's raised a troubling question in her mind: "Is it because I, as a woman, had a different kind of mind, incapable of abstraction and therefore of theorizing; is it because I was too 'emotional'?"[13]

Many women have had such doubts. The liberal feminist reply to them is to analyze how pedagogical styles in logic classes, as well as societal gender stereotypes, make women feel alienated from logic. Nye's response, however, is to put the shoe of blame on the other foot. She argues that, given its historical development from ancient Greek times, logic, as we know it today, is not only alien to women but also has been, and continues to be, a weapon of oppression used against them.

Nye begins her interpretation of the history of logic with an attack on Aristotle's Law of the Excluded Middle, and concludes by suggesting a link between Frege, a giant of twentieth-century logic, and Hitler:

> Hitler, . . . guided by sentiments not unlike the ones expressed in Frege's diary, worked out the master-logic of National Socialism. . . . National Socialist thought, like Frege's, did not concern itself with empirical content. . . . No personal experience could negate [its] body of truth. The applications of logic to action that Frege had promised came readily to hand. If Jews are a mongrel race, they must be exterminated. "A thought like a hammer" [Frege's phrase] demanded instant obedience to the dictates of logic.[14]

Following this extraordinary association, Nye concludes that "logic in its final perfection is insane."[15]

Nye's unusual reading of the history of logic will be submitted to the normal tribunal of her peers, and the process of critical evaluation has already begun. At the 1992 Pacific regional meeting of the American Philosophical Association, for example, the philosophers Don Levi and Daniel Merrill commented on the book at an Author Meets Critics Symposium. Pointing out that Nye is shifty in her use of the term *logic*—it is absurd to pretend that *Principia Mathematica* and *Mein Kampf* are both logic books in the same sense of the term—they proposed that logic as taught in critical-thinking courses can be a tool of liberation. But, again, it is one thing to submit Nye's book to a panel of philosophers, and another to present it to untrained and suggestible students. We can easily imagine how such a book will be taught in Women's Studies classes. Nonspecialist teachers will mine it for ammunition to use against their usual target. Is it likely that logic will survive such treatment as a subject worth studying, or will it be discarded by the GENDERAGENDA as yet another example of patriarchal thinking?

Opposition to Exact Science

It is interesting to note that in their assault on science, feminists have managed to hold on to many of the stereotypical notions concerning cognitive skills that used to disfigure masculinist thinking on this subject. Take the dichotomies devised long ago to help demonstrate the superiority of the male mind: abstract versus concrete, logical versus intuitive, objective versus subjective, analytical versus synthetic, quantitative versus qualitative. Once these pairs are set up as opposites, ancient gender stereotypes allow the labeling of one pole as "masculine" and the other as "feminine." Not surprisingly, the attributes designated "masculine" are the ones thought of as more characteristic of, and desirable in, science. Females, according to this view of the world, are uncomfortable with quantities (they prefer "so hot I can barely handle it" to "T = 66° C"). They respond naturally to anecdotal evidence but are unmoved by statistical data. And so on.

One would think that those who remain unconvinced by this argument for women's defective reasoning ability would respond by offering counterexamples, such as the market women in Tangiers who compute prices in several currencies without the aid of a calculator, or Katharine Bement Davis's 1926 study of the sex lives of 2,200 women—a survey that predated the Kinsey reports by more than two decades.[16] But the GENDERAGENDA promotes a different strategy: Gladly granting that there is indeed a link between gender and reasoning style, this game preserves the old dualistic categories but reverses the value signs associated with each of them. All the "male" attributes now bear a minus sign, while the "female" attributes are given a plus sign. Thus, intuitive impressions come closer to the truth than logically constructed arguments, and qualitative and anecdotal studies are more humane than—and therefore superior to—statistically rigorous quantitative ones, because the latter ignore the rich peculiarities of individual cases. So the argument rushes to its inevitable conclusion: the very tools of male science are in this way proved deficient and must be replaced by female instruments.

Now, interesting things are to be said about the comparative value of contrasting cognitive styles, and philosophers and scientists have long debated the proper roles they should play. Early in this century the British philosopher of science Norman Campbell argued with Pierre Duhem about the relative merits of physics represented as abstract formulae (the French style) as opposed to physics instantiated in mechanical models (the English style). Long before Barbara McClintock and her "feeling for the organism," scientists spoke eloquently about the need for *Fingerspitzengefühl* and *Empfindung*. Einstein remarked on the importance of having a "nose" for good problems. And biologists have long debated the respective advantages of experimentation and naturalistic inquiry.

Feminists are welcome to enter these discussions, and they may wish to press the argument that the prevailing methodological orthodoxy has sometimes adversely affected women. But nothing is gained by insisting that methodologies are intrinsically gendered and that their value can be determined by their place on the scale of gender stereotypes.

Feminist academics were understandably excited about the significance of gender as a lens through which to view important segments of traditional scholarship. But somewhere along the line they fell victim to a sort of "gendelirium," no longer fueled by solid scholarly achievements but fed by anger and the wish to repudiate wholesale the entire academic tradition. The results have been a few spectacular polemics and some livening up of scholarly journals, but for the Women's Studies student, the outcome has been less fortunate. She learns that traditional disciplines, by the very methodologies they employ, oppress women and that, if she studies them at all, she may lose her feminist soul unless she does so as a subversive agent, a mole burrowing from within to destroy the patriarchal paradigms.

Nor is this burden lifted as the student leaves the university gates. Silvia, the research biologist quoted in chapter 3, spoke to us of the attitudes displayed toward her profession by feminists whom she meets socially:

> There's an antagonism toward people who do science. If I were a sociologist or labeled myself a psychologist—which I sometimes do these days, by the way—or an anthropologist or some of the other disciplines traditionally considered to be more feminine or feminist-oriented, I'd be accepted right away. The problem is that I do biology. Basically, people don't talk to me. There's a general mistrust of anything I do or say. I'm perceived as being poisoned by the patriarchy, because biologists and hard-core scientists are trained in such a way that we're absolutely poisoned, and so we have little or nothing to offer. I find it interesting that women who are medical doctors aren't viewed the same way. I don't know why. Or they may get a similar treatment, but for a different reason—because they are perceived as making a lot of money, and we feminists have the downwardly mobile aspect, too—but not because they've been necessarily poisoned in the way that they think in general. It's almost as if hard-core science and feminism are like oil and water—they simply can't mix, and if you're one, you can't be the other.

In today's professional and graduate schools, logic and science are prerequisites for many fulfilling and important pursuits such as medicine, economics, biochemistry, engineering, law, and computer science. Logic and mathematics often serve as gatekeepers because many students, not only women, find them difficult to master. To tell a young woman to resist logic because it is a tool of domination that will poison her mind is to put yet another barrier in her path. Although the Hippocratic physicians did not always live up to their oath, their injunction to "At least do no harm" has much to commend it. Feminist teachers might think about adopting as their motto "At least do no harm to women," for it is young women who will most suffer from the feminist repudiation of science and critical thinking. In this respect, the presence of feminism in the academy emphatically does not liberate it from past narrowness. Quite the contrary, it introduces a new constriction.

Despite the feminist rhetoric about encouraging a less doctrinaire, more dialogic approach to education, we find, instead, a contemptuous dismissal of great chunks of invaluable knowledge. This affects not only attitudes toward science but, much more generally, the ability to select appropriate research methodologies in all disciplines. Again we cite the words of Professor Rossi:

> I've no argument with good qualitative ethnographic in-depth study—absolutely none. But it's not the be-all and end-all, and what was developing, at least in terms of feminist sociology, was a belief that quantitative work is sexist. I think I'm a good feminist and I am also a good survey designer and a good data analyst and I see things because I *do* have female eyes and a feminist lens, and it has nothing to do with the method. But dismissal of a method just is anathema to me. And that's what I was encountering—*ideological* opposition to quantitative analysis. And the graduate students reflect it. My God, if anything, that's the domain within sociology that women should be encouraged to master. They need to know the possibilities well enough so that they can make a decision—"the problem I'm interested in requires only a personal in-depth approach," fine. But to never learn this method over here, and then not only go your own way but condemn people who made another option—that's intellectual Stalinism to me.

7

"Mirror, Mirror on the Wall": Feminist Self-Scrutiny

IN THE PRECEDING CHAPTERS we portrayed feminist ideology and its academic pitfalls through a description of games popular in Women's Studies programs. These games are waged more single-mindedly and with greater ferocity in the more self-consciously "political" programs. But they are played, with varying degrees of aggressiveness, everywhere.

At this point in our argument, the sincere feminist reader, one sympathetic to both the legitimate achievements of feminist scholarship and the urgency of the real political and economic obstacles still faced by women, might well be thinking: Yes, you've captured the ethos of all too many Women's Studies programs. But isn't the public perception of an enterprise usually set by the distortions of extremists in its ranks? (This is always an issue in gay-pride marches, for example: How do you keep the media from reporting only on rowdy drag queens, dykes on bikes, and S-M aficionado/as, while overlooking the rank and file?) Surely, such a reader might object, most Women's Studies faculty deplore the games you have described. And now that these idiocies and abuses are being brought to light, will they not move quickly to root them out or at least curtail them?

We sincerely hope our friendly feminist reader is correct in her assumptions. But unfortunately, the actual situation appears to be otherwise. If there is opposition to the processes we have described, it has not been evident in the pronouncements coming out of Women's Studies programs.

To indicate the extent to which the official line is still unreconstructed, let us consider now a report on recent policy trends in Women's Studies programs. This report, along with other internal documents representing attempts by programs to evaluate and improve themselves, suggests that the games feminists play are indeed the current sport of choice in Women's Studies.

ASSESSING WOMEN'S STUDIES

In 1992, the National Women's Studies Association (NWSA), in collaboration with the Association of American Colleges, published the results of a three-year evaluation project financed by the Fund for the Improvement of Postsecondary Education of the U.S. Department of Education. The report was promisingly titled *The Courage to Question* and was issued with a companion volume, *Students at the Center.*[1] The project's goal was to determine how Women's Studies programs across the country were doing, primarily with an eye to improving them. The publication was designed to provide a model for programs seeking to do a self-evaluation. Participating schools included small liberal arts colleges, land-grant universities in the prairies, and inner-city branch campuses.

The Courage to Question and *Students at the Center,* written in an informal and personal style that makes for pleasant reading, are cast as sincere attempts at self-scrutiny on the part of Women's Studies programs. We therefore approached them hoping to find some signs of feminists' attempts to remedy or address some of the difficulties we have been documenting in this book. However, as we read the books it became increasingly clear that the real goal of the self-evaluation was to provide ammunition with which to answer outside critics. Close inspection revealed that the model program goals proposed in these volumes not only fail to alleviate the ideological excesses we have described, but in fact reinforce them.

The authors of the study were evidently pleased with the results they had obtained. The students they polled were, by and large, very positive about their experiences in Women's Studies; some were even ecstatic. They praised the Women's Studies classroom as a place of affirmation and validation where they could find their personal voices and strengthen their identities. They gave high marks to the analyses they were taught to make of sexism, racism, ableism, ageism, classism, and heterosexism. These, they said, revolutionized their views of the world.

All assessments begin by referring to the question of method: How can one best ensure that the data collected and the conclusions drawn are accurate? In *Students at the Center*, Caryn Musil, who edited the two volumes, and the other project directors described their decision to use *feminist* assessment methods: "Feminist assessment begins with and enacts values. It does not presume to be objective in the narrow sense of the word, nor does feminist theory believe there is any such thing as a value-free 'scientific' investigation."[2]

In feminist assessment, narratives count more heavily than statistics, a point the authors drive home with the obligatory reference to the impossibility of dismantling the master's house by using the master's tools.[3] They indicate that evaluation methods "*should be compatible with feminist activist beliefs*" and with the aims of "emancipatory pedagogy."[4] In addition, the assessment should also be based on research that is "central to this interdisciplinary area":

> To be successful, feminist assessment must be compatible with feminist scholarship. It should take into consideration such concepts as maternal thinking, caring, concern and relatedness, and women's ways of knowing or connected learning. These concepts can serve as the theoretical framework for feminist evaluation, a process more concerned with improvement than testing, with nurtured progression than with final judgments.[5]

Since the idea of *connected learning* referred to in this passage plays a central role in *The Courage to Question* and in feminist pedagogy generally, we need to analyze it in some detail. The foundational document on this concept is *Women's Ways of Knowing*, by Mary Field Belenky, Blythe McVicker Clinchy, Nancy Rule Goldberger, and Jill Mattuck Tarule.[6] We argue that the *connected learning* model promoted in *The Courage to Question* is an unfortunate oversimplification of *Women's Ways of Knowing*, but that the latter readily lends itself to such a distortion. It must also be said that *Women's Ways of Knowing* itself is based on inconclusive research and draws too uncritically on the work of Nel Noddings (*Caring*), Sara Ruddick (*Maternal Thinking*), and Carol Gilligan (*In a Different Voice*).[7] Serious flaws in these books, especially Gilligan's, have been repeatedly pointed out in mainstream psychology journals, and even in *Signs*, the premier feminist periodical. But because of the opportunistic eclecticism of Women's Studies (which somehow manages to coexist with academic feminism's doctrinaire assumptions and assertions), these writers' claims are rarely qualified or bracketed. As long as they have intuitive appeal and serve an apparently useful and immediate political purpose, they find wide and uncritical acceptance.

What follows, then, is a case study of how an ideologically inspired conjecture, having evaded the usual mechanisms of scholarly appraisal—largely because Women's Studies rejects these mechanisms—emerged, nearly a decade after its first appearance, as an allegedly well-confirmed discovery, one sound enough to serve as the foundation of far-reaching academic policy.

"WOMEN'S WAYS OF KNOWING"

Women's Ways of Knowing is considered an exemplar of feminist scholarship. Composed collaboratively and dedicated to the four authors' mothers and daughters, it is written in an engaging style without the use of statistics (not even in an appendix), and with surprisingly few qualitative comparisons. The book is based on open-ended interviews with 135 women of diverse ages, classes, ethnic backgrounds, and social circumstances. It offers a blend of quotations from the women themselves with the authors' interpretive comments. These, in turn, are followed by policy recommendations.

The book has been very successful. It received the 1987 Distinguished Publications Award from the Association of Women in Psychology and has become a popular text. For example, in 1993 the biology department at Indiana University used it in a course for prospective teachers, as did the School of Education. The book's authors propound two major theses. One is the descriptive claim that women "have cultivated and learned to value ways [of knowing] which are powerful but have been neglected and denigrated by the dominant intellectual ethos of our time."[8] The second is the pedagogic contention "that educators can help women develop their own authentic voices if they emphasize connection over separation, understanding and acceptance over assessment, and collaboration over debate."[9]

The first mode of knowing described in *Women's Ways of Knowing* is simply called *silence*, which applies to women who think of themselves as "deaf and dumb." They can neither learn by listening to words ("Someone has to show me—not tell me—or I can't get it") nor use language to accomplish their goals. The second mode, called *received knowledge*, grows out of women's passivity: "Hav[ing] no opinions and no voice of their own to guide them, women in this position listen to others for directions as well as for information." Women who take this approach to knowledge are easily confused when experts disagree. When asked what she would do if advisors from a children's center gave conflicting advice, one woman exclaimed, "'Oh, that's never happened! I don't know what I would do. . . . Maybe I'd go eeny, meeny, miny, mo. I don't know really.'"[10]

The most prevalent mode delineated in *Women's Ways of Knowing* is labeled *subjective knowledge*. One of the few semiquantitative assertions in the book tells us that "of the 135 women . . . inter-

viewed, almost half were predominantly subjectivist in their thinking." In this mode, the absolute authority of the expert has been
replaced by an inner voice, variously described by the interviewees
as instinct, intuition, or "know[ing] with my gut": "It's like a certain
feeling that you have inside you." Some of the women classified as
subjective knowers had gained confidence in their "inner voices"
through the process of escaping from physically and sexually abusive
situations. Others had struggled with their fear of being wrong or of
being laughed at. All the women reported a great feeling of elation
and empowerment as they discovered their inner voices and no
longer felt trapped in silence or enthralled by outside authority. But
the authors stress that, at least in our society, these subjectivists are
at a serious disadvantage: "[I]n a world that emphasizes rationalism
and scientific thought, there are bound to be personal and social
costs of a subjectivist epistemology."[11]

A more complex kind of knowing is the mode the authors called
procedural knowing. Women in their survey whose mental habits
exemplified this way of knowing were primarily college students
who were "privileged, bright, white, and young." Often, as a result
of encountering the divergent procedures and methods for investigating the world employed by academic disciplines, such women
have come to realize that neither external authorities nor inner
voices are infallible. They "engage in conscious, deliberate, systematic analysis. They have learned that truth is not immediately accessible, that you cannot 'just know.' Things are not always what they
seem to be. Truth lies hidden beneath the surface, and you must fer-
ret it out."[12]

What makes *procedural knowing* distinctively female? The answer
is that most of the procedural knowers in the sample felt uncomfortable with the methods and approaches they had had to acquire to
succeed in the traditional classroom, and it is assumed that these are
somehow masculine modes. The authors explain:

> In general, few of the women we interviewed . . . found argu-
> ment—reasoned critical discourse—a congenial form of conversa-

tion among friends. The classic dormitory bull session, with students assailing their opponents' logic and attacking their evidence, seems to occur rarely among women, and teachers complain that women students are reluctant to engage in critical debate with peers in class, even when explicitly encouraged to do so.[13]

These students realized that there were often conflicting points of view, and that not all of these could be equally valid. They also thought it worthwhile to try to sort through the positions in hopes of bettering their understanding. But what they were reluctant or unable to do was to separate the ideas from the individuals who held them. "Teachers and fathers and boyfriends assure them that arguments are not between *persons* but between *positions*, but the women continue to fear that someone may get hurt."[14]

Because not all women resist distinguishing thought from thinker, word from speaker, the authors posit two subcategories of *procedural knowing*, as indicated in the following table (based on stages described in *Women's Ways of Knowing*):

MODES OF KNOWING

1. Silence
2. Passive Reception
3. Subjective Knowing
4. Procedural Knowing
   a. Separate
   b. Connected
5. Constructed Knowing

One of these subcategories, which involves separating a critique of ideas from a personal attack on the people who propose them, is called *separate knowing* (4a). This is the traditional approach, but it was not the one that most women in the sample preferred. Instead, they opted for the other subcategory, called *connected knowing* (4b), characterized by the qualities of empathy, trust, and forbearance. Criticism is possible, but only in a supportive setting created once the members of the group have come to know each other well. An art student said, "'[I]f you've gone along since the beginning with the same people it never comes across as this awful criticism.'" And the authors comment: "People could criticize each other's work in this class and accept each other's criticisms because members of the group shared a similar experience. *This is the only sort of expertise connected knowers recognize, the only sort of criticism they easily accept.*" The authors point out that *connected knowing* works well only in small groups whose members are familiar with one another. One student described her seminar in this way: "'It was like a family group trying to work out a family problem, except it was an idea.'" The authors note, however, that "in most educational institutions there is no chance to form such family groups."[15]

Several intellectual and practical factors would seem to limit the applicability of the *connected knowing* model, perhaps even placing those who subscribe to it at a serious disadvantage. By cutting herself off from data gathered by people she does not know personally, or from the ideas of people with whom she cannot empathize, the *connected knower* is severely limiting her sources of information. In other words, she, too, is separating herself! And if women hope to participate in knowledge networks that extend beyond their families or immediate circles—that is, if women want to function effectively in law or politics or in a business larger than a mom-and-pop store— they will have to learn to operate in a broader and more complex arena of information and ideas.

But even in a family situation (as anyone who has lived with an alcoholic relative knows), it is not wise to rely uncritically on empathy, trust, and forbearance. It is somewhat surprising, therefore, to see the authors of *Women's Ways of Knowing* treating *connected knowing* as on a par with, and perhaps even superior to, the *separate knowing* mode. At the very least, it seems to us, they should have urged women (and men, too) to learn to be comfortable with both approaches, and to use each model, as appropriate.

However, the authors stop short of doing this, perhaps because they believe women are extremely comfortable with *connected knowing.* "Women have been practicing this kind of conversation since childhood," they say, and "women seem to take naturally to a nonjudgmental stance."[16] The authors may also prefer the connected mode because of the neat parallels that can be drawn between it and the propositions of Gilligan, Noddings, Ruddick, and others concerning the moral reasoning of women. Gilligan's research, for example, portrays women as so preoccupied with the intricate web of personal relationships that they are unwilling or unable to invoke abstract norms of justice and fairness when reasoning about a moral dilemma such as abortion.

When we return to *The Courage to Question* later in this chapter, we will see that it is *connected knowing* that is taken to be the epistemological goal of Women's Studies. But *Women's Ways of Knowing* still has one more mode to describe: *constructed knowing.* According to the few women who achieve this modality, the transition to it is spurred on by their perception of the inadequacies in *connected knowing. Constructed knowing* seeks—and when it is accomplished, achieves—an accommodation of *all* the components that were selectively invoked in the other modalities. It is a "voice of integration" that "find[s] a place for reason *and* intuition *and* the expertise of others." In addition, "there is ... an emphasis on a never-ending search for truth, which is coordinate with a never-ending quest for learning. . . . When truth is seen as a process of construction in which the knower participates, a passion for learning is unleashed."[17]

With *constructed knowing* (not to be confused with the social construction of knowledge discussed in chapter 6), we seem to have returned to a conception of knowledge that fits in well with the academic tradition. However, the authors emphasize the differences. "Among women thinking as constructivists . . . knowing is not simply an 'objective' procedure but a way of weaving their passions and intellectual life into some recognizable whole." The "empathic potential—the capacity for ... what Ruddick identifies with 'maternal thinking'. . . —is particularly characteristic of constructivist women," and these women "usually resent the implicit pressure in male-dominated circles to toughen up and fight to get their ideas across." "Constructivist women aspire to work that contributes to the empowerment and improvement in the quality of life of others." These sentences alert us to the realization that this final modality is still tinged with stereotypical feminine virtues—and vices. The authors of *Women's Ways of Knowing* make no attempt to explore exactly how the discordant voices of reason, feeling, authority, and experience are to be brought into harmony; they all must be listened to. We are given a list of ingredients, but the rest of the recipe is missing.[18]

Women's Ways of Knowing effectively documents the severe learning disabilities some women bring with them to Women's Studies classrooms: Such students may be silent; they may only speak by parroting authorities; some may lapse into a solipsistic state of subjectivity; others may be so fragile that they cannot learn without receiving constant support and approbation. The authors make a strong case for the contention that some women have been epistemologically crippled, but they offer no foundation for any claim that the previously ignored "ways of knowing" bestow power on women. Nor do they explore the best techniques for helping learners progress from less to more adequate ways of knowing. And like nearly all feminist research in this area, the authors fail to undertake comparative studies to see whether male students fall into similar patterns.

Women's Ways of Knowing invites the conclusion that some women are attracted to Women's Studies because of a history of personal trauma, and that these students may well have some learning disabilities that will need to be corrected before they can cope with the atmosphere of vigorous debates and critical discourse characteristic of the best university education. In short, the book should be read as a warning that some women need compensatory education, though the authors fail to say which women, how many, or exactly how they can be helped. But, as we will see by returning to *The Courage to Question*, these are not the lessons that Women's Studies faculty have drawn from their reading of *Women's Ways of Knowing*. Instead, they offer it as proof of the superiority of women's wonderfully different and rewarding ways of knowing, and as a celebration of this difference.

THE MISSION OF WOMEN'S STUDIES

As noted earlier, the team that produced *The Courage to Question* followed evaluation procedures growing out of feminist theory and compatible with feminist activism. According to the companion volume, *Students at the Center*, the team decided "not to create a unified, standardized assessment plan."[19] Instead, each participating campus was encouraged to design its own instruments for judging its performance. The consultants, for their part, writing in a chapter titled "Seasoning Your Own Spaghetti Sauce," provide some spices to flavor the various projects, recommending techniques such as open-ended oral interviews and portfolios of student work, as well as the usual questionnaires.

At each of the participating schools, however, the project directors met together on a number of occasions and, after consulting with their local constituencies, drew up a list of key questions intended to guide all seven programs that eventually participated in the assessment project. These questions, indicated in the following list from *The Courage to Question*, provide a summary of the aims and objectives considered essential by this sample of Women's Studies programs. (Numbers have been added for convenience.)

1. Does women's studies cultivate personal empowerment and social responsibility?
2. How successfully does women's studies support students as they express their feminism on campus?
3. Is the authority of experience legitimized and are students urged to comprehend the experience of others?
4. Does women's studies foster connected learning?
5. Are students introduced to the constructed and situated character of disciplinary knowledge?
6. Are students encouraged to reconstruct knowledge from multidisciplinary and cross-cultural perspectives?
7. How do programs navigate tensions between creating safe but challenging classroom space?

8. Finally, how do we shift and make explicit the power relations both in the classroom and the institution?

9. All of these questions [are] understood to be posed within the larger framework in which gender, race, class, sexuality, and other categories of analytic differences intersect.[20]

Nothing in these programmatic questions suggests that it might be the business of Women's Studies to foster research in, or at least make students aware of, women's history, women's literature, or recent social science work on women and gender. Instead, all stated goals seek to promote processes and attitudes, and to stake out psychological and pedagogical "space." Strikingly, these questions assume that an academic department should, as a key part of its mission, support student activism and the shifting of power relations within the institution. Sometimes such efforts take a very concrete form. Hunter College, for example, reported on the establishment of a mentoring program for its students, drawing on "alumnae who are doing feminist advocacy in New York City." The program at the University of Missouri–Columbia listed as its first two goals to "support our students as ambassadors of feminism [and to] continue to address the campus-wide problems of sexism, racism, and other injustices."[21]

The assessors' questions to students were designed to determine how effectively this political agenda was being implemented at the respective institutions. One sample instrument asked: "Can you identify one or two significant experiences at Oberlin (a course, an event, a professor, friendship, membership in political organizations, etc.) that most influenced your feminist consciousness?"[22] The authors of *The Courage to Question* shrug off the concern expressed by a mathematics professor at Oberlin who thought it inappropriate for academic programs to function as political parties.[23] Clearly, political commitment is considered a valuable and central part of the public mission of many Women's Studies programs.

A second major theme of *Students at the Center* is the special quality of feminist pedagogy. Oberlin asked flatly: "Do you believe that women's studies courses differ in pedagogy—in how students learn—from non-women's studies courses? If yes, how?" Old Dominion wanted to know whether "the learning environments were different," and Wellesley asked how the Women's Studies courses had affected the students' personal lives and changed their political beliefs.[24] One of Oberlin's questions encapsulated the central aims of feminist pedagogy, and then asked the student directly how successful she herself thought she had been in achieving them:

> Goals of the Oberlin Women's Studies Program include self empowerment; recognition of differences; collaborative learning; understanding interdisciplinary connections in the analysis of gender, race, class, sexuality; and linking personal with social responsibility. Which of these goals are most important to *you* and which do you feel you have accomplished as a student in Women's Studies?[25]

Many of the buzz words of feminist pedagogy—*empowerment, collaborative learning, personalized learning, connected learning, coming to voice, personal transformation*—evoke memories of progressive education movements dating back at least to John Dewey. When we look carefully at their use in this document, however, we find that the recommended feminist practices are quite different from the rather permissive, individualized, student-centered teaching methods associated with "progressive" education.

First, in feminist pedagogy, students are expected to structure any and all inquiry in terms of overarching concepts such as gender, race, and class (as stated in item 9 of the preceding list). Second, and more important, students are encouraged not only to begin their investigations with personal reflections, but also to continue throughout the stages of their education to make tight connections between what they hear or read and their own day-to-day lives. Third, they are expected, and sometimes required, to voice their personal reactions to their classmates, as well as to listen receptively to the personal comments of others (as in item 3).

Most of the students cited in these assessments were Women's

Studies majors or minors; hence, it is not surprising to learn that they liked this intimate touch. As shown in *The Courage to Question*, they criticized classes that merely talked *about* racism and classism, instead of "really dealing with an issue." What they clearly meant by this expression was "connecting it to one's own experience as oppressed and oppressor." In principle, this sharing of personal viewpoints is intended to lead to "mutual discovery," in the course of which the group generates knowledge about racism, classism, or whatever other -ism is under discussion, by piecing together the testimonials of people in the class who occupy different sites on the web of oppression.[26]

Naturally, when students are actively encouraged by the instructor to relate course materials to their personal lives and speak out about the connection, the classroom atmosphere can get rather intense. All of the participants in the assessment project commented on this (in response to item 7). At Oberlin the atmosphere was described as "searing." Intriguingly, when asked if they felt "pressure to give 'politically correct' answers" in class, 30 percent of the Women's Studies students who participated in the Wellesley study said they "felt silenced or at risk expressing unpopular opinions." An indication of how tense the classroom atmosphere can become appeared in a footnote reporting that, in one Wellesley class, nineteen out of twenty-five students replied yes to a question about pressure to be "politically correct." There is no reason to think that the atmosphere at Wellesley was unusually fervent, but one cannot say for certain, since none of the other assessment teams raised such questions.[27]

Given the intensely experiential character of Women's Studies classes and the pressure faculty exert on students to face up to their status as oppressor or oppressed, it is understandable that, as reported in the study, one of the most satisfying rewards of empowerment that students noted was their increased ability to confront people who told racist or sexist jokes. This response confirms the claim upheld by feminist pedagogues that their classroom techniques are directly conducive to successful activism.

CONNECTED KNOWING AND THE
"BELIEVING GAME"

Connected learning, even if seriously oversimplified as a concept by the assessment project, is considered so important by the authors that they include a complete tabular version of it in each volume.[28] Lewis and Clark College used this model explicitly in evaluating student portfolios to determine whether students exhibited signs of *connected knowing*, as was expected of them. In addition, assessment teams were urged to engage themselves in *connected learning* in the process of finding out about their own programs.

The model that forms the basis for the study posits two epistemological styles: *Connected knowers* are said to play a "Believing Game" in which they engage in collaborative inquiry in order to "construct meaning—to understand and to be understood." *Separate knowers*, on the other hand, are playing a "Doubting Game." They are trying to construct truth, rather than meanings, and so they adopt a critical stance as they attempt to prove or disprove claims and refute or convince their adversaries.[29]

Connected knowers are further characterized by a dozen additional oppositions. "Believers" are said to prefer "narrative and contextual" discourse about material to which they feel close attachments. "Doubters" prefer "logical and abstract" reasoning and try to distance themselves from the subject in order to bring "impersonal and universal standards" to bear.[30]

There have been many previous attempts to characterize diverse thinking styles—mathematicians contrast algebraic and geometric approaches, biologists talk about "lumpers" versus "splitters," and there is the old tradition, dating back at least to the Greek mathematician Pappus, of drawing a distinction between analysis and synthesis (or resolution and composition, to use Peripatetic terminology).[31]

But what is unique about the model presented in this two-volume assessment study is the complete repudiation of the path of *separate knowing* that takes as the basis of its authority "mastery of relevant knowledge and methodology." The authors opt instead for basing one's beliefs on "commonality of experience," which may sound innocent enough until one realizes that these shared experiences are to be elicited in an accepting, noncritical atmosphere, in which emotions and feelings are assumed always to "illuminate thought," not cloud it.[32]

Throughout the discussion the goal is to privilege *connected knowing* and to make it the predominant learning mode, not merely give it equal time or due recognition among the variety of epistemologies.

Nowhere in *The Courage to Question* or *Students at the Center* is any recognition given to the most mature model of knowing presented in *Women's Ways of Knowing*—that of *constructed knowing*, the one that attempts to integrate the best features of *connected* and *separate knowing*. As we pointed out, this modality may not match our highest philosophical and scientific norms, but it is certainly much more adequate to them than the *connected knowing* model fostered by the NWSA assessors. The fact that it is not mentioned by the authors tells us much about their assumptions concerning women's mental processes.

If Women's Studies is indeed successful in transforming its students into *connected knowers*, then feminism becomes a Believing Game, one that disdains proof, disproof, and criticism. It incites students to become personally and emotionally invested in the intellectual positions they explore, and it discourages them from trying to detach or distance themselves from the issues under discussion. At most it urges them to modify their own subjective opinions by expanding them so as to include other women's viewpoints, but never are they encouraged to appeal to, or even to recognize, expert learning or to practice methodological rigor. Discourse must never be logical or abstract. It must always be narrative and contextual.

Such a form of inquiry might possibly be useful for a team of feminist evaluators sitting around the kitchen table, or for a family trying to decide where to go on vacation—although even here a bit of detachment and logic often comes in handy. In a situation where the only issue is the reconciliation of preferences, it is perfectly reasonable to try to come up with a solution that includes everybody. But when the conflict is over rival empirical claims or the constitutionality of a proposed ordinance, expert knowledge *is* relevant, and one party's deeply held subjective opinion on the question may simply turn out to be objectively wrong. It is not a crime to have false beliefs—we all have them. Students need to learn to be gracious when refuting other people's pet convictions as well as modest in defending their own. They need to realize that no proofs or disproofs are infallible. But the *last* thing they should be taught is the dangerous proposition that all subjective opinions are equal.

The *connected learning* model goes a long way toward explaining the unstable atmosphere that pervades many Women's Studies classrooms and faculty meetings. As long as positions are not too far apart, the model of sympathetic inclusion works well, and everybody feels validated and cozy. But as soon as sharp conflicts arise, absent the normal modes of conflict resolution—striving for personal detachment, trying to look at the evidence objectively, calling for further study, attempting to be as methodical and logical as possible—the result is likely to be not just a breakdown in sisterly connectedness, but outbursts of extreme rudeness and insoluble conflict.

Defenders of the *connected learning* model might object that recourse to empirical investigations or expertise is never really helpful because, as pointed out in item 5 in the list of key questions ("Are students introduced to the constructed and situated character of disciplinary knowledge?"), all disciplinary knowledge is socially constructed. This elastic notion is repeatedly pressed into service. As reported in *The Courage to Question*, the Lewis and Clark faculty, for example, in describing how student essays were scored, merely said that by the time students were seniors they should have "move[d] . . . to a meta-analysis of how knowledge is socially constructed and not simply 'there' to be discovered." Old Dominion was pleased to find that many Women's Studies students had learned that gender is constructed (women do not mother because of maternal instinct), had "realize[d] that sexuality too, is socially constructed," and had in general "switched to socio-cultural as opposed to biological explanations. The troubling exception to this was students' persistence in the belief that violence against women is best explained by the pathological impulsivity and aggressiveness of some males."[33]

We are glad that this team picked up on this common contradiction, but our main worry is that an exaggerated emphasis on social constructionism has contributed significantly to the alienation of Women's Studies students from traditional disciplines. Such an emphasis suggests a rather simple and tempting syllogistic argument:

If all knowledge is socially constructed, and women and blacks were excluded from participation in the construction of the disciplines, then, since any enterprise that excludes women and blacks is sexist and racist, it follows that the knowledge in all books except feminist ones is sexist and racist. Therefore, to use sexist or racist textbooks (except to critique them) is to expose oneself to immoral and misleading tracts. In light of such an argument, is it any surprise that many Women's Studies students consider the only legitimate stance toward most of the courses at the university to be an oppositional one?

CRITICAL THINKING, FEMINIST STYLE

The Courage to Question begins with the acknowledgment that critics accuse Women's Studies of being "a grievance industry" specializing in "oppression studies."[34] A female humanities professor who responded to the survey at Oberlin said: "[It has had a] terrible impact—the program has politicized and ideologized students instead of promoting objectivity in education. . . . I must withdraw my support for this program until it becomes less ideological and more in line with the spirit of true academic excellence at Oberlin."[35]

The advocates' major defense against the charge that they were giving their students "propaganda" and "unintellectual, touchy-freely stuff" and were "silenc[ing] everyone who disagrees" was to claim that Women's Studies teaches its students *critical thinking*.[36]

This phrase appears repeatedly both in students' responses and in the comments of the faculty assessors. Since critical thinking is specifically ruled out by the model of *connected knowing*, one might well wonder exactly what the Women's Studies advocates have in mind when they use this phrase. Perhaps they think that Women's Studies students learn not merely the courage to question, but also the audacity to question everything—because patriarchy is everywhere.

We believe the advocates are right when they contend that this is by and large what their students learn. But we also think that the critics are correct when they object that Women's Studies turns many of the same students into uncritical ideologues. Religious fanatics are adept at thinking and speaking critically about secular society. They are not so inclined to turn their scrutiny on themselves. The skill of Women's Studies students at repudiating all traditional knowledge as socially constructed and their ingenuity in ferreting out the hand of the devil patriarchy in every sin and crime of society are not an exhibition of critical thinking at a very significant level. The fact that students have abandoned received views (and have some good reasons for doing so) is no indication that they have not, at the same time, uncritically locked themselves into another framework, which is at least as deeply flawed. What needs to be investigated is whether students are at all receptive to reasoned arguments against the basic tenets of their own framework or, to the contrary, have learned to deploy various criticism-deflecting strategies in an effort to keep their acquired ideas inviolate. Such an investigation, unfortunately, is nowhere to be found in *The Courage to Question* or *Students at the Center*.

The NWSA report is probably accurate in stating that students who major in Women's Studies are largely getting what they want and what the faculty think is important for them. As long as this is the case, reforms are not likely to come from within. Quite the contrary, one can expect the dominant internal ethos to be further solidified and institutionalized. This is exactly what we find as we turn to the issue of how Women's Studies goes about deciding who and what is to be included in its programs.

"QUALITY CONTROL": BIG SISTER IS WATCHING YOU

Since most courses offered in Women's Studies programs originate in other departments and are only cross-listed with Women's Studies, questions often arise as to which classes should, and which should not, be admitted. In a recent comprehensive essay titled "When Is a Women's Studies Course a 'Women's Studies' Course?: Issues of 'Quality Control' of Cross-listed Courses," Lynne Goodstein of Pennsylvania State University tries to come to grips with the problem of "controlling" the Women's Studies curriculum.[37] Her essay, laudable for its clear and forthright presentation of the issues, warrants close attention here.

Goodstein gives three examples of courses that do *not* count at her university. A course on the biology of sex that devoted equal time to males and females was "declassified" on the grounds that "the bulk of course content" did not focus on women. Her Women's Studies program also rejected a proposed course on the sociology of the family, which, though concentrating on women's experiences, merely gave sociological analyses of women's traditional roles and was not "informed by feminist critiques." Goodstein notes, in this connection, that, to be approved in her program, courses should not merely increase information students possess about women, but should also aim to change students' views of themselves. Merely adding women writers to a literature course is not "feminist," she says. A course must show how gender, race, and class, and not any imputed inferior writing ability, have constrained women's literary production in the past.[38]

In each of these examples one wonders whether the "quality control," for which so much concern is expressed, is not really a euphemism for ideological policing. In fact, the shakiness of the entire effort at quality control is indicated by the shifting vocabulary Goodstein employs to make her argument. Her terms range from "curricular integrity" through "exacting criteria" and "integrity of courses" to a "commitment to feminist theory and pedagogy." The

first three of these terms are never defined, merely declared, while
the last appears to serve, as Goodstein's careful research has
revealed, as the chief touchstone of the effort to set the proper goals
for a Women's Studies program. But is there, in reality, general
agreement on what these "commitments" are?

The most intriguing part of Goodstein's essay is a description of
the seven key points that her program at Penn State designated as
essential to Women's Studies courses. A duly appointed Curricular
Affairs Committee conducted a survey of all faculty in the program,
evaluated the nineteen responses it received, and came up with the
following seven themes or goals, which range from the innocuous
and tautological to the tenditious and dogmatic. These goals, with
some comments of our own, are as follows:

1. *Emphasis on women's status,* arising from the "need to recognize the existence of patriarchal structures in defining values
   and social roles. It focuses on gender disparities in social
   power and influence and recognizes that women's status in
   virtually all contemporary cultures is unsatisfactory and in
   need of special attention."

2. *Valuing women's perspectives and experience,* affirming "the
   importance of women's experiences, perspectives, and accom-
   plishments as subjects of study. Emphasis would be placed on
   the historical role of women in the world, the contributions
   made by women intellectually, artistically, and politically. To
   accomplish this goal, the bulk of course content would focus
   on women."

3. *Praxis:* "This theme reflects an attempt to move beyond
   analysis into some form of development or change, either
   personal, social, or political." More than conveying "a passive
   belief in gender equity," a course incorporating this theme
   "assumes that women's studies education would encourage
   students to work toward the realization of these goals." The
   hint, in this passage, of required political good works is soon
   undermined by the qualification that "praxis" (contrary to

what the term means) does not necessarily "require that specific projects geared to social action be included in courses. Rather, praxis implies that course participants will be challenged to consider the implications of the material covered for their lives and the lives of others."

4. *Counteracting male bias in scholarship*; that is, rejecting traditional white male Eurocentric values, assumptions, and perspectives in research. This goal "affirms the importance of incorporating the new scholarship on women and feminist critiques of traditional research concerning women and gender into women's studies courses." Here, as elsewhere in the paper, despite the feminist taboo on "linear" and "dichotomous" thinking, a simple opposition is set up between "traditional" male scholarship and the "new scholarship on women." The former is always and necessarily defective, while no indication is given that the latter should ever itself be the object of critique.

5. *Valuing women's self-determination.* Women's studies courses must "empower women students to seek their own paths and define themselves as entities separate and apart from roles that patriarchal societies dictate. [This goal] reflects the corresponding need for courses to encourage reassessment among men students of their perspectives on entitlement to power and privilege." Here again, a gulf exists between, on the one hand, the freedom supposedly offered to female students to select their own paths and, on the other, the pressure to define themselves according to the current feminist line and in opposition to "patriarchal societies" and their decrees. If, for example, a woman were to decide to become a traditional housewife, has she failed to become "empowered"? Has she ceased to "seek her own path"? Will she need additional "feminist pedagogy" to help her recuperate from this expression of disempowerment?

6. *Inclusion of other "isms"* within the concerns of feminism, stressing "the interconnectedness of the operation of sexism

and other 'isms.' [This goal] recognizes that feminism also functions to critique other forms of oppression, including racism, national chauvinism, class and ethnic bias, ageism, heterosexual bias, and other ideologies/institutions that have consciously or unconsciously oppressed and exploited some for the advantage of others. It recognizes the importance of structuring course material which is inclusive across all lines of 'difference.'" A good illustration of what may be called the "totalizing" impulse in feminism, this description also clearly reveals the intellectual arrogance that sometimes seeps into feminism when it represents itself as self-invented, heir to nothing, and stakes its claims so broadly as to encompass all other social and moral concerns.

7. Finally, *feminist pedagogy* "emphasizes the importance of using techniques which recognize and validate students' life experiences as legitimate data. . . . It underscores the need for classes to operate on principles of mutual respect, equalitarianism, a critique of the traditional teacher/student authority relationship, and student empowerment."[39]

None of these seven themes or goals appears to aim at providing students with the intellectual tools that would allow them to make their own analyses. Rather, they all seem designed and intended to enforce what this decade's feminist orthodoxy considers to be appropriate existential models. Goodstein fails to address the dangerous terrain entered by those who take it upon themselves to dictate approaches and course content according to such manifestly ideological criteria.

More alarming still, Goodstein—apparently without meaning to—divulges the inevitable transition to surveillance that must occur if quality control is to be made effective. In order to obtain information for use in the review process, looking at course proposals and syllabi is insufficient. Instead, "treating the instructor rather than the course as the 'unit of analysis' for evaluation is desirable and increases the potential that cross-listed courses will consistently fulfill Women's Studies program goals." But in the end, even this procedure will not suffice, in her view. "[P]robably the most valid means of determining whether a program's goals are met by cross-listed courses" is obtaining information directly from students, since "even personal interviews with instructors are not always adequate, as they yield information about what the instructor says she or he does, not what the instructor actually does." At Penn State, Goodstein reports, the evaluations in use measure "the extent to which students experience a class as embodying feminist pedagogy as well as other aspects of the seven curricular goals."[40]

We have never encountered, in our readings or in our combined four decades of working in the academy, another document like Goodstein's essay. In it, the drive toward "quality control" seems totally unrelated to legitimate concerns about academic standards. Rather, it represents an attempt to define Women's Studies in ideological terms, which is why doctrinaire criteria are considered indispensable. Instead of delimiting the field of study in terms of subject matter, the emphasis unfailingly falls on a *core cluster of perspectives*, which, in the description of them, often reduce to attitudes. This emphasis cannot be defended as promoting "critical awareness" or "analytical abilities" in students, since that awareness and those abilities are being encouraged in one direction only. Nothing is said about promoting a critical examination of feminist discourse itself. In fact, the preferred methods of feminist pedagogy seem expressly designed to make such a critique impossible.

In her conclusions, Goodstein acknowledges that the "healthy and empowering" process of articulating goals can also be frustrating and possibly demoralizing, as it may "bring to light underlying differences among women's studies faculty and between program faculty and others within academic institutions." This admission seems to presuppose that, ideally, Women's Studies faculty should all hold identical views. Her subsequent remark that "unfortunately, there will be no quick solutions to the problem of 'quality control' of cross-listed courses" reveals the blinders that insulate the entire discussion of control over Women's Studies courses.[41] What other field of study would conceivably create this problem for itself? No doubt many people in Women's Studies see nothing awry in Goodstein's description of "quality control," as is confirmed by extensive communications on the Women's Studies E-mail list expressing the same anxiety about how cross-listed courses can be "controlled." But this general agreement, in our view, is a large part of the problem.

Finally, an important piece is missing from Goodstein's discussion. If surveillance is so indispensable for cross-listed courses, why is it not also necessary for core courses taught by the regular Women's Studies faculty? Surely one cannot assume that all of these individuals, merely because they have appointments or adjunct status in Women's Studies, are in conformity with the feminist perspectives and pedagogical demands set forth in Goodstein's work—unless, of course, such conformity was a condition of employment in Women's Studies in the first place. And what if faculty members in Women's Studies backslide? Shall they, too, then be subject to "quality control"? And shall student spies be commissioned to report back to some central committee on their professors' ideological heresies and pedagogical deviations?

Will Women's Studies, coming full circle, settle comfortably into the practice of bias and ostracism that it originally attacked in androcentric education? If we have moved no farther than "Our picture of the world may be a bit distorted, but it's better than their distortion!" how far have we progressed?

8

Cults, Communes, and Clicks

ACADEMIA, long a sheltered site for radical research and adventurous speculation, has been extremely receptive to the products and producers of feminist theorizing. And this habit of accommodating novelty is appropriate for academics, for it is surely one function of the ivory tower to be an experimental workshop where new ideas are forged, tested, and judged against the old.

There are, however, circumstances in which the spirit of open inquiry essential to the academy is threatened by a worldview. Such a threat materializes when a set of ideas loses its heuristic or experimental character and turns into a dogma that suppresses criticism of itself and blocks alternative paths to discovery. The variants of feminism brought together in Women's Studies programs fit this description of a closed worldview. They are not merely about equal rights for women or the empirical and theoretical study of gender roles and their pervasive effects in society. Feminism aspires to be much more than this. It bids to be a totalizing scheme resting on a grand theory, one that is as all-inclusive as Marxism, as assured of its ability to unmask hidden meanings as Freudian psychology, and as fervent in its condemnation of apostates as evangelical fundamentalism. Feminist theory provides a doctrine of original sin: The world's evils originate in male supremacy. It regards the male's (usually: the white male's) insistence on maintaining his own power as the passkey that unlocks the mysteries of individual actions and institutional behavior. And it offers a prescription for radical change that is as simple as it is drastic: Reject whatever is tainted with patriarchy and replace it with something embodying gynecentric values.

The information we have brought together in this book suggests to us that the feminist persuasions prevailing in U.S. colleges and universities today often lead to consequences deeply subversive of the best academic traditions. Intolerance, anti-intellectualism, and ideological policing produce work that is shaped—we would say, distorted—by an ideological agenda. This may be acceptable in an institution whose denominational affiliations and instructional mission are a matter of record. But it hardly seems appropriate to require teachers in a state university or a private liberal arts college to profess adherence to feminism or to monitor the sex, race, or ethnicity of the authors on their syllabi. Nonetheless, as our investigations have shown, these practices are proudly "owned" by many feminist faculty.

As it pursues such actions, Women's Studies apparently disregards all historical evidence warning of what happens when ideas and those who express them are placed under ideological restrictions. We are concerned that the attempts to set up feminist alternatives to traditional disciplines, each with its own support networks, conferences, and journals, are all too reminiscent of the efforts of "creation scientists" to represent themselves as the intellectual and professional equals of mainstream researchers. In both instances the methods of established science and rigorous intellectual inquiry are dismissed as biased, and radical departures from these methods are proposed to replace them. Creationists say that radioisotope dating must be thrown out because it is sheer atheism to assume that the laws of nature, including those governing radioactive decay, are time invariant. Could God not change the half-life of carbon-14 if he so desired? Many feminists, for their part, find the values of objectivity, parsimony, and consistency shot through with patriarchal bias, and they argue—with breathtaking simplicity of mind—that these intellectual virtues were designed, and are being used, to enforce the entrenched power of the white male European elite.

The harmful pedagogical effects of such positions are obvious. Far too many Women's Studies classes now provide their students with what might be called "negative education." Instead of "learning to learn" (to use a slogan once popular in schools of education), these students are being taught to scorn both the content and methods of the liberal arts and sciences. But the classroom is not the right place for obeisances and anathemas. And it is intolerable that Women's Studies students can come away from their courses with the unshakable conviction that all women are victims, and that victims are, by virtue of their persecuted status, a morally superior breed. It is a fact, however, that Women's Studies classes instruct women in the use of coping strategies to deal with the "oppression" they are being taught to recognize; many feminist teachers pride themselves on this. It should come as no surprise, then, that some students insist on special dispensations to compensate them for past injustices, and claim that if a demand, such as the requirement to become competent in mathematics, is too exacting or a job too taxing, it is because women's different ways of "knowing" and performing are slighted by the entrenched patriarchy (as discussed in chapter 7).

But a feminist education along these lines is sure to impede women's ability to function in the world at large. As a preparation for life, it is counterproductive in the strictest sense of that term. A faculty colleague concerned about the likelihood of this outcome told us about a conversation she had with a graduating senior:

> The student told me she had a good job with a big company in a nearby city—actually it was just what she wanted—better than she had expected. But when I congratulated her, she looked worried.
>
> "Well, there's just one problem," she said. "You know, sexism, job discrimination, all that patriarchal stuff."
>
> I asked her if anything weird had happened at the interview.
>
> She said no, but maybe that was because they saw on her resumé that she had a certificate in Women's Studies and were on good behavior.

I tried to reassure her: "You say they interviewed lots of people for the job? It sounds to me like you were the person they wanted and that they'll make some effort to keep you. I don't think you should expect trouble."

"But it's still a patriarchal world out there," the student said earnestly. "And I'm just afraid that there will be sexist stuff on the job—maybe even stuff that I won't even recognize as being sexist."

I mumbled more words of reassurance, but the image which came to mind was that of certain holy men in India—I think they're called Jains—who walk around with gauze over their mouths to prevent them from accidentally inhaling a gnat and killing it.

We fear that all too often the "empowerment" promised by Women's Studies in fact has undermined students' ability to function effectively and has diminished their life options. Hypersensitizing young women to the obstacles they face may have gained feminism some docile converts, but the initiates have had to pay a steep price.

As a way of trying to map out the main features of the terrain cultivated by Women's Studies, three models seem to us especially useful. One derives from the history of religion; the second, from the experience of communes and utopian social experiments. What these two have in common—with one another and with feminism—can, in turn, be illustrated by a third model, one that has been developed by social psychologists.

TRUE BELIEVERS ALL

Religious movements provide an instructive comparative case to help us make sense of the more disturbing traits of academic feminism. Our frame of reference for drawing analogies and suggesting caveats is the history of Western churches with their tendency to spawn dissenting splinter groups. New movements, whether religious or social, always undergo an initial period of struggle when the intellectual and psychological resources of their members are absorbed by the effort to gain recognition, and when energies are directed mostly against enemies outside the ranks. Ideological positions are kept simple at this stage; there is little discussion of the fine points of belief. Internal cohesion is not difficult to maintain because all who belong accept the movement's survival as a paramount goal. The movement's spokespersons tend to make far-reaching claims for the rights and liberties needed to gain legitimacy, chief among them the freedoms to be self-determining in matters of conscience, to propagate ideas, to voice criticism, and to speak and act on the basis of conviction.

During the period of consolidation that follows, mundane tasks begin to predominate: the need to organize, define the faith, and clarify ambiguities as beliefs are being formalized into a creed. Theological elaboration results from the movement's drive, as it becomes established, to enumerate the articles its followers must accept if they are to remain members in good standing. Hence an orthodoxy arises, as well as a hierarchy of persons entitled to declare and guard it. This development, in turn, leads to attempts to obtain conformity and enforce discipline and—inevitably—to inhibition of deviant beliefs. Tolerance is now seen as worse than weakness; it is a betrayal of the faith. To the true believer, there cannot be more than one valid truth or more than a single way to reach it.

In the later phases of a movement, therefore, declarations of faith tend to be much less inclusive than they had been during the movement's earlier years. Those who cannot agree to them quit, or they are expelled or at least silenced. Means of identifying and separating deviants are implemented so that discipline may be enforced. Deviance itself is demarcated by defining heterodoxy as well as orthodoxy. Proselytizing usually wanes at this stage, as energies are absorbed in the effort to unify and purify the movement internally and as intellectual homogeneity comes to matter more than diversity of ideas and the free discussion of them.

Unless a movement finds some way of accommodating the diversity of views that will always surface in a group not under siege, it survives—if it survives at all—as a sect. A sect sees itself as voluntarily and necessarily separated from the larger society, which it regards as beyond redemption by conversion or other means. Its members are encouraged to view themselves as a righteous remnant. Its saving message, which is utterly exclusive, suppresses debate and criticism. As a result, there is little intellectual development. Ideas tend to atrophy into fundamentalism, showing the mistrust and paranoia that usually accompany a narrow religiosity. Mandated beliefs and coercive institutions are used to erect protective ramparts around the group in order to keep enemies out and followers in. Intolerance is flaunted: one must believe all or one believes nothing. Sects are interesting historical phenomena, and often very moving ones, but because of their intransigence and isolation they have rarely had any major impact on world events.

Such a development is not inevitable. The history of Western religion offers a few notable exceptions to it, such as the Quakers and the Unitarians, whose trajectory from oppositional faction to established denomination evaded the extremes of political orthodoxy and sectarian isolation. But the process described here has been a common one in both the Catholic and Protestant traditions, and its cautionary importance for movements borne by ideological zeal is, we believe, considerable.[1]

It will seem a familiar pattern to many who have been involved with Women's Studies. Similarities are readily apparent. As talk of women's oppression, exclusion, and silencing at the hands of the patriarchy gained prominence in the late 1960s, sufficient cohesion developed for Women's Studies to get under way in the early 1970s—if not yet as a widespread movement, then as a tenacious force and an insistent voice for reform in the academy. Shared beliefs were abundantly supplied by the developing discourse on feminism, in which the imperative to action, when not asserted outright, was always implicit. As the movement gained strength, the emerging agenda, kept simple at first (for example, "integrating women into the curriculum"), expanded in response to the hardening of ideological lines. The sense of mission that legitimized a growing obduracy of thought and speech was noted by most of the women we interviewed, although for some this sense was a nostalgic memory, while for others it acted as an incentive for them to dissent.

Feminism was not slow to develop its corps of theoreticians. But in the accommodating world of Women's Studies, "theory"—recently transmogrified into the more active-sounding "theorizing"—did not always demand a high level of analysis or substantive learning. In many programs, it meant little more than a tethering of precepts to simplistic ideological presuppositions. Instead of expanding intellectual horizons, this, in turn, led to intolerance, the presence and corrosive effect of which were mentioned by nearly everyone we spoke to. Attempts were made to expose and label heterodoxy. Deviant opinion was dismissed as "liberal" or "radical," depending on who was dismissing whom; "false" feminists were distinguished from "true" ones; slanderous comments about one another by faculty members were replicated in students' mean-spirited badmouthing and their censorious behavior in the classroom. One professor described her own growing awareness of this process:

> I don't recall now how long it was before I realized that the intolerance and smugness of many of my students was a mirror image of feelings I had experienced privately and had heard my colleagues express publicly. I recalled the sense of self-satisfaction and complacency I felt when another woman—especially one who described herself as a feminist—revealed, through some word or gesture, the "limits" of her feminist understanding compared to my own. In retrospect, it seemed to me that this smugness had, in fact, been an important component of my own identity as a "feminist."

Thus my students taught me, painfully but unmistakably, about another aspect of feminist identity. The lesson should have been obvious from the beginning, given feminism's often illuminating deconstruction of oppositional terms. What I learned was that our own identities as "feminists," too, depend in a deep sense upon the creation and maintenance of a polarization with something that was not-us. And because so many women (in the university and outside of it) were not feminists, or not the right kind of feminist, the opportunities for indulging this private sense of superiority occurred virtually on a daily basis.

Like religious groups as they splinter, feminism also developed competing creeds, each rigidly embraced by its adherents, each dismissive of the others, each undebatable. Not surprisingly, excommunication, in the form of shunning and scapegoating, became common. The effort to propagate ideas broadly—once a major part of the agenda—tended to contract as the curriculum was pitched more and more narrowly to a self-selected audience of students who seek out the program on their own and form a preidentified group of potential converts.

The insularity of such procedures, along with a certain proclivity in the women's movement to separatism, gives Women's Studies programs a strong resemblance to religious sects. But the historical experience of sectarian groups ought to serve as a warning example, as should their tendency to slip into the kind of intellectual fundamentalism in which a handful of unexamined and unquestioned truths is believed to answer every question, solve every problem, and fend off unwelcome criticism from the malevolent forces outside. This may sound excessively alarmist. Women's Studies programs do not, at the moment, have the means to transform their ideas into forced behavior patterns. But we should not therefore be lulled into complacency about the kind of world that would result if the power to impose and control were ever to be given to them.

PROBLEMS IN THE PROMISED LAND

To supplement the religious analogy, we offer another model, again with strikingly suggestive parallels for feminists. This is the model of communes and intentional communities that seclude themselves from the larger world and attempt in their daily lives to act out alternative values.

Women's Studies has always argued that it has fashioned—or at least embraces—a communal ethos. If we take this claim seriously enough to ask how Women's Studies is actually doing as a community, we notice some interesting similarities between the academic programs we have examined and communal groups as studied by historians and sociologists, or as imagined by writers of utopian or dystopian novels. Like most of the communes examined by Rosabeth Moss Kanter, for example, Women's Studies seems to have purchased what little group harmony it has been able to achieve at the cost of setting limits on personal choice and creative debate.[2]

We have also been struck by the prevailing adoption of negative instruments employed by historical communes in their effort to achieve cohesion, among them renunciation of links to the outside world and to one's former life in it,[3] and "mortification" practices such as mutual criticism, surveillance, denunciation of deviants, confession, and so on. These are practices that serve to strip away much of a person's previous identity. They transmit the message, as Kanter says, "that the self is adequate, whole, and fulfilled only when it lives up to the model offered by the community."[4] Here the communal model and the religious cult model clearly meet.

Women's Studies programs not only show some of the isolationist tendencies of experimental communes; they also too often exhibit an anti-intellectualism and, more specifically, an antiscience animus. This is a theme that can also be traced in the history of communes in America and was already evident to scholars long before the present proliferation of emotionally based self-improvement groups brought it to general attention. Such moves are clear reactions against the world "outside," which is viewed, as in the case of religious sectarianism, as antipodal and inimical.

Communes frequently manifest a preference for an activist over a contemplative, or intellectualizing, ethos. As Kanter writes: "The intellectual who sees several sides to every issue may also be out of place in a utopian community."[5] By contrast, the embrace of labor and an "active" life is a common theme in both real and fictive alternative communities. Knowledge is often represented as dangerous to the life of the experiment, and even of the species, as reflected also in the many imaginative post–nuclear holocaust dystopias in which science has proved itself to be the work of the devil and must therefore be stifled. Such scenarios' dislike of the past leads to a suppression of information about it. In Women's Studies, this has sometimes meant that—as we have seen—both specialized expertise and general knowledge are made suspect and are tagged as the products of men, who are blamed for the corruption or suppression of the female wisdom that would have made the world a better place. Antagonism to theory, unless it can simplistically be reduced to practice in accord with the feminist tenets of the moment, is a further aspect of this tendency.

Along with activism, the communal persuasion also favors a drastic leveling of social and personal distinctions—vigorously promoted in actual communes and utopian novels, and often parodied in antiutopian fiction. What is interesting about this for our purposes is that the concept of leveling exists in incipient form in the rhetoric of feminism, and that this sets Women's Studies constantly at odds with the meritocratic principle inescapable in a university—even in the United States, where (unlike the rest of the world) a very large percentage of high school graduates at least enter college. In the academic setting, therefore, the equalizing impulse is fulfilled more by lip service than by structural alterations. As one woman we interviewed noted, the "teaching collective"—comprising faculty, staff, and undergraduate students—in the Women's Studies program of which she was a staff member could not seriously expect faculty to participate in it if salary sharing were implemented. It hardly needs to be said that material and other inequalities persist; that is the reality. In opposition to it, students within Women's Studies programs, caught up in academic feminism's spurious political rhetoric with its promise of leveling, write papers such as one we have read that takes feminism in the academy to task for failing to repudiate academic emphases on effective writing and reading. Such values, the student argued, not only leave dyslexic and other individuals who have communication difficulties at a distinct disadvantage, but also lower their self-esteem.

ARRESTED DEVELOPMENT

A third model, found in the research of black social psychologists working on social identity theory, seems to be especially useful in drawing the lesson of the two analogies presented so far, because it offers a paradigm that has direct relevance to feminism, and also suggests ways in which feminism needs to grow up.

According to this model, as outlined by Audrey Murrell of the University of Pittsburgh, the move from a negative to a positive group identity involves five distinct stages:[6]

1. *preconsciousness*, characterized by denial and feelings of marginalization and alienation because of the stigmatized identity;
2. *emergence/awakening*, in which a critical consciousness dawns;
3. *confrontation/internalization*, the strident militant stage, belligerent and separatist; and
4. *integration*, in which a more holistic view begins to emerge, leading to:
5. *double consciousness*, with separatism now devalued as dual identities become internalized, finally culminating in an identity of a broader sort.

If feminism is viewed in terms of these stages, it becomes obvious that the familiar "click" phenomenon, in which women, having come out of stage one, find their dawning critical consciousness constantly reaffirmed by the sexist world they see around them, is a characteristic manifestation of stage two. Recurring "clicks," in turn, are preconditions of the belligerent stage-three attitude, where rigid distinctions between "us" and "them"—the characteristic dualism of religious and communal movements—are carefully nurtured.

We believe that Women's Studies programs, if they are not strongly focused on educational goals, transform themselves—and not very subtly—into sites of indoctrination to stage-three attitudes. A recent study of the effectiveness of Women's Studies courses in promoting "feminist identity development," using a similar model of stages of development, confirms that these courses are indeed successful in leading students into—but not beyond—stage three.[7] What is chilling to realize, however, is that the authors of this study never question whether such transformation is an appropriate goal of education, or address how it might be said to differ from other forms of indoctrination aimed not merely at the intellect but at the whole person: the creation of a New Man or New Woman. It simply takes for granted that the development of a "feminist identity" is an unproblematic and desirable objective for an academic program to pursue.

Nothing we have seen in our investigations of Women's Studies suggests that the higher stages of identity development, involving synthesis and integration, are anywhere on the horizon. Perhaps young people will simply have to work out a broader, more integrated identity on their own, once they leave the university. This appears to be the only hope. Meanwhile, their training may well have helped them arrive at stage three—but only to remain stuck there.

Nor is this a mere accident. There seems to be a general awareness in feminist circles of the utility of stage three for Women's Studies classrooms. Moreover, when the stages-of-development model is applied to faculty members themselves, we can see that something else, strongly suggestive of manipulation, is going on as stage-three commitments are pursued. Whether Women's Studies professors are genuinely situated at this stage or simply act as if they were—perhaps more effectively to awaken students to women's oppression, or for the satisfaction of enacting their own *echt* feminist personae—is a question we cannot answer.

But stage-three commitments (among both faculty and students) seem predictably to turn the us-versus-them division inward, as if the "them" at the gates are not enough of a threat (perhaps because they are too remote, or perhaps because they are simply too strong) to promote group loyalty and cohesion at the fever pitch at which the greatest emotional intensity can be sustained. As the us-versus-them opposition is replicated within the original grouping, policing actions get under way. This is a form of behavior that, in addition to allowing some people to be censorious and aggressive toward others, reflects a presumption of rights and wrongs: We are right. You are wrong.

Many feminists have trouble swallowing this. As a political science professor from Texas (who has a bumper sticker on her pickup truck saying FEMINIST REDNECK) wrote to us: "At 50 years of age, I have not thrown off the yoke of one master to have it replaced by another, even if its name is feminism." But in such a judgmental climate, appearances of proper group identity must be maintained, hence the endless discussions and criticisms of how particular women dress, look, and behave. Petty surveillance becomes a mechanism for maintaining group solidarity, because it separates authentic members from questionable ones. But it has a costly consequence: Over time, it drives away those who are negatively categorized, and this reduces the group's numbers and alienates potential supporters.

On a more abstract level, censorious vigilantism forecloses discussion of diverging group goals, leads to ever-greater rigidity and uniformity, and saps the group's vitality—a high price to pay for "harmony." At the same time, an excessive concern with the trappings of group identity prompts members to examine not only others but themselves as well. Here, too, the analogy to religious group behavior holds, for punctilious inspection of every aspect of one's inner and outer life has been an obligation placed by the more rigorous movements on their adherents. Calvinists' self-examination and the Jesuits' insistence on the constant exploration of the state of one's soul come to mind as examples. The aim, in each case, was an attentiveness to the self that allowed not the least detail to escape scrutiny.

One feminist scholar, who is now in a Women's Studies program that she strongly supports, recalled precisely such an atmosphere in her consciousness-raising group in the 1970s, as members acted out their stage-three personalities:

Looking back now, I think, psychologically, the vehemence came out of a sense of fragility—in other words: If we don't all agree on this, then something will crumble and I'll slip back into the alienated person that I just escaped from being. So somehow, unless I get validation from everybody else and a mirroring of my choices, I'm in danger of slipping back into patriarchal violence. I'm just guessing that the anger, that you have to do X, you have to see it this way, comes out of feeling, Well, I've only just gotten here, look at the wicked past I've just escaped from, when I was totally socialized into thinking that makeup was fine.

And I remember the kinds of debates we had in my C-R group. There was one woman who wore makeup, and we were down on her like a ton of bricks! We said it was a betrayal of feminism and so forth. At one point she literally said to us, "If you're going to say that I can't put eye makeup on when I come to this group, you're not going to see me." And in fact shortly thereafter she was gone. We didn't ease up.

I look back at that now and I'm horrified at myself. I always associate that with a form of competitiveness, a kind of pressure to be the most pure and the most ideologically untainted, and, now, I just don't see how you can build a movement like that.

Women's Studies programs, in their bunker mentality and tendency to cut themselves off from the rest of the university in the name of feminist commitment, do function in some respects like cults and communes. In saying this, we are by no means deploring the existence of deeply held shared beliefs, or of groups based on them. Communes, in particular, are fascinating social experiments with considerable relevance to feminism. Our point is simply this: It is not, and it should not be, the mission of a university to lock students into one stage of emotional and intellectual development, or to inculcate attitudes of hostility and condescension to all prefeminist knowledge and nonfeminist individuals. To the extent that Women's Studies programs intentionally cultivate such a mentality (and many certainly do), they have no place in the university. Their ostensible reason for promoting such a posture has everything to do with political aims and with the efforts to indoctrinate in accordance with these aims, and very little to do with the goals of a liberal education.

"FOR FEAR OF FINDING SOMETHING WORSE"

Hillaire Belloc once wrote a cautionary tale about a child who ran away from a strict British nanny, only to be eaten by a lion. The poem ends with these words: "And always keep a-hold of Nurse / For fear of finding something worse." We have not investigated the ethos of other kinds of "oppression studies" or "activist" programs in detail, but there are many indications that these are burdened by problems very similar to those of Women's Studies. Conflating Women's Studies with such programs would, we suspect, only make things worse. Ideals turning into frustration, enthusiasm and dedication lapsing into despair, doctrinaire attitudes driving out the spirit of inquiry—it is, alas, a common story.

We were particularly moved by an interview with a woman who began her career as an enthusiastic supporter of a Marxist approach to education but is now surprised to find herself espousing some traditional liberal values. We offer her story as a kind of parable.

Angela is a literature professor who has for years been involved in the Feminist Studies program of a small, private liberal arts college. She was hired nearly fifteen years ago for a position that specified "a Marxist and a feminist." Because of the college's self-conscious stance as a progressive and experimental school, she has encountered many of the problems that also characterize Women's Studies programs, but in a more complex and supposedly more hospitable institutional framework. Her comments have direct bearing on both the possibilities and limitations of a political model of education.

Angela turned down two other offers at more prestigious universities to accept this position, mainly because she wanted to join an "extremely politicized faculty," and the college seemed to offer the possibility of a fully integrated life: "I took the job to sort of 'be' what I was teaching. But now I very much would challenge the idea that you have to be what you teach, or even that I could really fully understand what that might mean." She also imagined that the college would provide a more relaxed atmosphere than that of a research university. This turned out to be wrong. Her teaching load was very demanding because, in addition to conducting classes, professors were expected to work intensively with individual students. She did not find much support for her interest in scholarship:

> There's a kind of surveillance that women do in relation to each other. When some of my work was published and I began giving papers, I very often wouldn't say anything about it at all. It was a kind of underground activity for me. . . . The challenge was to work as hard as the others did, trying to make myself indispensable in that same way, and then to get something going on the outside too. But I did put the teaching first.

The antischolarly bias of the school took the usual form: suspicions and insinuations of "careerism."

> It would have been extremely hard to have just come in with scholarly concerns, because there was a kind of rhetoric about people who are just looking out for themselves or their careers. There's still a lot of that rhetoric of "using" the school to launch a career. I've heard that expression, not applied to me but applied to others. I hope that's changing.

Her women colleagues, even early in their careers, seemed to compete over who was the most tired and stressed out. Less often did they discuss ideas, and her hopes for a lively intellectual exchange at the school were not fulfilled. As for the Feminist Studies program, it showed the usual conflation of functions:

The program was loosely organized, a few years after I came, to do various things. One thing was to be a kind of caucus and to organize around issues like salaries and working conditions, partly because we thought we all actually knew something about overwork. Then there was a loose curricular component, and we also have a women's center which is run separately by a staff person. Anyway, the program has been in crisis for about five years now. It doesn't function so much as an academic program, any more, but as a kind of gathering place.

The naming of the program was itself a deliberate act of proclaiming its politics:

It was called "Feminist Studies" because we perceived that "Women's Studies" sounded like a kind of content rather than an ideology. In other words, there is such a thing as women, and Women's Studies is the study of that thing. And we wanted to distinguish ourselves as a very politically motivated, ideologically motivated group. Ha! I'm laughing because of all the problems that I, at least, didn't foresee in terms of what a political academic culture would be like or could be like.

She offers the following example of how a thoroughly politicized academic culture operates:

At the point at which I started asking myself questions, the issue was no longer senior male colleagues who were teaching courses on autobiography and not putting a single woman on their reading list. Instead, I was seeing myself as a senior colleague looking at a young man who had put two or three women in his syllabus, and the question was: Should he have put in only white women? Did he have a woman of color in his syllabus? Did he have a this, a that? Were all possible, or many possible, sexualities represented?—and so on.

When I found myself in the position of scrutinizing somebody who, in fact, was not my superior, I felt very, very uneasy.
And then, when it became possible to vote against reappoint-
ing somebody on those grounds, I became very unhappy.

Initially, Angela had been enthusiastic about coming to the college as an "ideologically marked person, whose cards were on the
table politically," and excited "about the possibilities of hiring like-
minded people." Her experiences modified her fervor: "But I now
think there are incredible problems with that, that it's gone crazy,
this hiring of people who are only going to be judged on grounds
that are political, ideological." Some people left the college voluntarily because of the pressure they experienced to "be" a particular
kind of person:

> There was another case, a woman who left. With her, it wasn't
> identity politics in the normal sense, since, as a black woman,
> she was formally the right identity. So it was something else.
> She said there should be no greater pressure on minorities to
> get along with each other than there would be for, say, the
> white faculty, white male faculty, or women, or whatever the
> category would be, to get along with each other. She used to
> wear a T-shirt that said "I am not your Third World expecta-
> tion," so she was not the most popular person in certain circles
> either. There were two negative letters about her in her file. I
> remember one of them said, "I have had no experience with
> this person, which is odd because I'm a whatever [group mem-
> ber]." So this was taken as evidence of her not getting along
> with her "community."
>   Sure, some of this stuff goes on elsewhere, too, and maybe if
> I were in a different sort of institution, I would recover my ear-
> lier fierceness in terms of an ideological push. But I can only
> say now that I've seen something I don't want to be a part of.
> It's very troubling.

Would she still consider identity or political commitments to be appropriate criteria for selecting candidates?

> I am not uncomfortable with affirmative action goals in choosing among candidates, as long as these goals are the ones outlined in the affirmative action guidelines of the institution. But I now think that a person's work has got to be judged on its own merits. If someone is a liberal historian, for example, they should be judged in terms of how well they do that kind of history. If you're hiring somebody to teach the history of the novel and they do that very well, and students are generally satisfied, but maybe it's not the kind of literary history I'd prefer, with social history included, or—say—this person is not interested at all in sociology, just very well trained in a kind of formalism, I think that's fine.

Angela has thought carefully about the troubling ways in which identity politics were being played out at her school: "This 'speaking as a . . . ' routine is very familiar. I certainly see knowledge as belonging in a place and specificity. But I also need to see the difference between that and a kind of central casting notion of what intellectual life is." Far from waning or vanishing, however, the "central casting notion" of intellectual life has spread, though Angela cannot be sure whether faculty or students were its original promoters:

> I teach critical theory, and I think there's an ongoing and sometimes very interesting pedagogical problem of responding to demands for a multicultural, multisexual, multiwhatever classroom. In other words, I think the point is well taken that the inclusion of only white women writers in a course is simply not enough, and I never did think it was enough. I especially think that some of the pressure around race and gender and sexuality has been terrific. It brings a very interesting tension to bear. On the other hand, I think that teaching as I do—I team teach

with the philosophers sometimes, and sometimes I teach alone and I do critical theory texts—there is a real problem now in getting students to read texts for the ideas and not simply for the imaginary identity of the author.

I taught a course on postmodernism, and we read a book that emphasized class, written by an economist. And one of the students, a white woman, said, "Why should we care about some white guy in the Midwest who's out of work?" I always feel somewhat disappointed when there isn't more cross-identification in the classroom. I find I spend quite a bit of time trying to displace notions of identity rather than shore them up.

But this narrow-minded categorizing is also found among the faculty:

Let me give you an example. It was a faculty seminar we had, and we read something by a man who happens to be Indian, and there was a scathing critique of this piece done by a colleague who mistook the name and thought it was written by a white Irish guy! It was ridiculous—the author wasn't Irish. But somebody had imagined that he was Irish and white, and had written an essay on multiculturalism and a critique of pluralism. It was very funny, actually, a nice moment for some of us in the seminar.

Identity politics, in Angela's view, has come to replace critical exploration of ideas:

What I just can't stand is a kind of crude bottom line, when people make peremptory challenges and say, "What about such-and-such a group?" Now I think there is a mimicry between our students who do that and a certain style that has developed in the academy. It's got to do with this kind of peremptory challenge, "Well, what about X?"—as if saying it is enough. It isn't seriously about what could be called dialogue.

I'll give you an example. We were reading a work of fiction, and one of the students—a white woman—said, "Well, look, a white woman and a black woman are never going to be equal." And so my colleague with whom I was teaching the course, who's a philosopher, said, "What white woman, or what black woman?" And the student said, with real anger, "Well, a white woman is privileged in this society." Then she repeated that white women always felt superior to black women. I said, "Are you kidding? You mean you can't imagine being in a room with a black woman who was more talented, more beautiful, more elegant, articulate, and whatever, and would make you feel less that way?" And there was complete silence. Then two Indian students who were there started laughing hysterically, and they said, "Yes, we're just so tired of hearing this in the United States. We feel very superior to all of you."

But I think there was a kind of self-satisfaction in the white student's statement, and I asked myself: What is the satisfaction she is feeling? And I'm not sure, except that it is simple, it gives a kind of righteousness to the person who says it.

However, at the same time that rigid lines were being drawn in relation to identity, other boundaries were erased that Angela believed should have been left intact:

I never thought I would hear myself say these things. One sort of boundary has to do with authority—the authority of the various fields. Women's Studies has been a place where a lot of disciplinary boundaries have broken down, and I think in general that's been to the good because of what's happened to people's work and also in terms of the way that's going to impact throughout all the fields. On the other hand, if there is no—or, as at this school, only very little—possibility of making an argument based on knowing something, on having some authority, or even credentials, in a profession—if in fact all of those kinds of authority are broken down—I think there is a real danger. How can you make a case for a program if you recognize no other value than feeling comfortable around somebody?

I'll give you an example. Two years ago I went to a showing of a video that was made about MTV. It points up the sexism that exists on MTV. And the women's center coordinator was there. To my amazement, she stood up and said, "If any of you would like to see this video just with women, you can go to room 101." I was amazed by that. Then, after the video was shown, she said, "If anyone feels uncomfortable, we have co-counselors standing by." I had thought we were going to have an interesting political discussion of that video. "We have co-counselors waiting!" So the whole thing was treated as personal, the discomfort was seen as symptomatic of maybe an individual problem, abuse perhaps, or something in their past, and not a political and intellectual issue about the politics of representation and the industry of popular music, which is what I thought we were going to be talking about. And in fact, many, many people joined this group of women alone, or went to talk to the counselors. And I thought, If this is feminism, it's not what I'm interested in.

Angela tries to walk a fine line between viewing politics as entirely separate from education and yet wanting to preserve some sort of independent space for intellectual work:

I think that what's happened is that there has been such a proliferation of political criticism, political work, that I sometimes feel there just isn't any space to sit back and really reflect, to just be out of the fray, in the sense of *not* having to think about what this might sound like or who I am if I say this, but just to have a little room, in fact, to make some mistakes, some political gaffes if they are that, or to go in a different direction. I think that intellectual work can seem like so many identified points on the map, so that everything is mapped out too much. There's a kind of surveillance and a kind of mapping that has gone on.

Angela is clear about who is doing the surveillance:

We are, of ourselves. It's a kind of internalization, finally. I'm not sure why this hasn't been widely discussed: What's the difference between lively debate and the kind of devastating character assassination and posturing that I can't stand anymore? I'm so tired of it. It seems so predictable, it's more like a setup than a real debate. This goes on in scholarly cirlces, but also in the classroom, I think. I can imagine if I were teaching a course that had all the women and men who were interested in women's studies or gender studies, it would be really horrible and impossible and difficult, because of the attitude they would bring.

Still, she has hopes that a different climate will develop:

Maybe now there'll be time out or space or something that I think a lot of us yearn for right now. Whether that means an exile or estrangement or whatever, I don't know. But for a lot of us, I think, there's a certain kind of fatigue.

I can't imagine going back in any institutional way to a kind of pre-political state—if that ever existed anyway. I cannot imagine saying, "well, there is some kind of neutral, unpolitical, or apolitical default you can go back to." But I *can* imagine in my classes, and I think I do it more and more, trying to make room for ambiguity, for confusion, for more patient working-out of issues and not jumping to the bottom line. I see that as a part of my work, now, as part of my intellectual work, which I wouldn't have thought of before.

The moral we draw from Angela's story is this: It is not a narrow emphasis on women that bedevils Women's Studies. The problem is the whole tangled web of a politicized academy, paradoxically imbued with solipsistic feel-good practices, which we have tried to unravel in this book. One would find it hard to imagine an environment less likely to lead to an energetic and open-minded pursuit of knowledge.

Conflation of educational and political aims has characterized Women's Studies from the beginning. For many feminists in the academy, this conflation has served as an important source of pride. Rarely has it been identified as a problem—certainly not by feminist scholars. Even responsible feminist writers have felt obliged to celebrate the "specialness" of the close link between "scholarly feminism and the activist movement."[8]

The rhetoric of feminism obviously has worked as intended: It has muddied the waters of already difficult concepts such as "excellence in scholarship." Feminist scholars who do not agree with the antischolarly and generally doctrinaire proclivities of their programs, and who do not wish to be constantly embroiled in internal conflicts, tend to walk away—as painful a step as this often is for them to take. And it *is* painful, since it means abandoning students to more militant colleagues, as well as letting go of much that was formerly believed, hoped, and worked for. This book has given instances of their departures. To the remaining true believers, of course, such departures merely serve to confirm that the exiles had never been "real" feminists in the first place.

9

From Dogma to Dialogue:
The Importance of Liberal Values

THE CENTRAL AIMS of feminism (or the women's liberation movement, as it used to be called) were and are exemplary: to end discrimination against women, to protect women from sexual assault and economic exploitation, to transform traditional attitudes about gender roles, to help women gain the confidence and skills they need to pursue their life projects, to make our society truly one of equal opportunity, and to discover what sort of society men and women, working together as equals, might construct. These are noble and urgent goals.

It was also appropriate for feminists in the academy to explore how they might bring their research and teaching to bear on the pressing issues raised by second-wave feminism. And much of the ensuing research on all aspects of women's lives and the effects of gender has been of major significance. But, as we have described in this book, Women's Studies was, from the outset, drawn into an aggressive stance of professing and proselytizing for the feminist movement. The result, as our cautionary tales vividly reveal, has been not only a subversion of scholarship but also a rancorous classroom environment which, far from preparing women students to lead effective lives, disempowers them by depriving them of a liberal education.

We have argued that these highly problematic developments are not the accidental or unintended result of growing pains likely to be remedied once Women's Studies faculty become aware of them. Quite the contrary. They are the direct consequences of a dogmatically entrenched and ultimately debilitating ideology. Many women and liberal male faculty members know all this. But while dismayed by Women's Studies practices, they are hesitant to speak out for fear of being labeled reactionary or antifeminist. Deans and other college and university officials, who are certainly aware that all is not well, prefer to maintain a position of "plausible deniability" similar to the one they favor with respect to flawed collegiate athletic programs. Administrators are under pressure to meet affirmative action goals, and where better to situate a minority representative or woman than in a marginal, nondisciplinary program where "they" teach students primarily like "them"!

So what is to be done? Ultimately, local conditions must dictate particular tactics. In some Women's Studies programs, in universities that have managed to keep their balance, the adherence to rigorous scholarship and open inquiry may be strong enough to sort through the deluge of propaganda being published and taught under the general rubric of Women's Studies and gender studies. In such situations, feminist faculty who have the stomach will stay and fight the good fight—by opposing ideological policing, by refusing to let classrooms be turned into indoctrination sites or therapy sessions, and by resisting politically based hiring.

In conditions where things are too far gone, feminist faculty who are revolted by what is happening in their programs will probably withdraw their support. We hope they will make it clear why they are doing so.

There are now a few possibilities for those feminists who believe in the values of liberal education to organize nationally. The Feminist Anti-Censorship Taskforce (FACT) has for some years provided a feminist voice in opposition to Catharine MacKinnon's and Andrea Dworkin's more visible and audible views on pornography. Just as this book went to press, we learned of the newly formed Women's

Freedom Network, which espouses a philosophy that defines women and men as individuals rather than in terms of gender and believes that there are no "male" or "female" standards of excellence, morality or justice.[1]

Alternative feminist forums are also available at some professional meetings. For example, as the Society for Women in Philosophy (SWIP) turned its attention more and more exclusively to radical feminist issues and modes of philosophizing, many women (and some men), feeling the need for a new type of venue, started the Society for Analytic Feminism (SAF). At this point, the relations between SWIP and SAF are still cordial (and SAF has even been invited to edit an issue of SWIP's journal, *Hypatia*), but there are dramatic differences in both style and content between the two organizations. SAF, for example, routinely has male speakers on its programs, while SWIP has a caucus called NCLI, for the "Not Currently Lesbian Identified."

But, as sensible feminists have known all along, making a society where women have equal opportunities for life, liberty, and the pursuit of happiness is not a project for women only. Too often second-wave feminists have told men of all political persuasions to butt out. This is unwise. On the other hand, we do not want to reproduce the current generation of "wanna-be-sensitive" university men who uncritically acquiesce in the most ludicrous of feminist demands. It is high time that progressive women and men stopped waxing sentimental about both the plight and the latent virtues of the oppressed and started exercising a little tough-minded common sense in proposing realistic, workable reforms.

Given our bleak analysis, friends have asked us, "Aren't you really saying that Women's Studies programs should be disbanded altogether, and that students should no longer be permitted to pursue a bachelor's or a graduate degree in Women's Studies?" We find this question difficult to answer. We do not entirely agree on this between ourselves, and each of us has repeatedly modified her own position. But we can say the following: In the 1970s there was a vigorous debate within the National Women's Studies Association between those who favored a "mainstreaming" strategy for Women's Studies, with the goal of integrating research on women and gender with the general curriculum, and those who favored "autonomy" for Women's Studies, which would separate it from the mainstream. The "mainstreamers" lost the argument, and perhaps, given the climate of the time, they deserved to lose. But things are different now. Whatever the situation was in the 1970s, in today's tense and constrained academic climate it is difficult to justify setting up new degree-granting programs in Women's Studies with tenured lines and professional staff—even at institutions with a record of animosity toward women, for it is exactly in such "chilly climates" that Women's Studies programs are most likely to act as sites for polarization and nonproductive political agitation. It would be far better to introduce courses on women and gender as part of the regular curriculum, insisting on sound scholarship and high professional standards on the part of those who teach and those who learn. Students and faculty should be encouraged to fight sexism and other injustices on their campuses and beyond, but they should not expect to receive academic credit or tenure for doing so. Life, after all, exists outside the academy too. Advocacy is often appropriate, sometimes necessary, in the street. But in the classroom, the more flexible values of liberal education should prevail.

If there is ever to be an enduring field of scholarly research and teaching called Women's Studies, it must find its way out of the ideological maze thrown up by true believers and self-serving activists. The path it must take has to lead, by way of a reconsideration of fashionable feminist phobias, blind spots, and prejudices, to a new (or old!) kind of feminism—a humanistic feminism that can at least recognize within the complex legacy of "patriarchy" the many liberal principles and enlightened attitudes worth preserving.

It is a fact—though feminist ideologues are reluctant to admit it—that feminists have inescapably drawn on liberal ideas as they have attempted to alter curricula and departments. They have had to argue, even when their practices have fallen far short of the ideal, that the education they were offering would prepare young women for the greatest possible number of experiences and activities, and for exercising independent and critical judgment on them. This is precisely what liberal education is about. Feminists have had to demonstrate that traditional education, with its masculinist bias and misogynist prejudices, failed to live up to this standard—failed to live up to its own standard, one might say.

All arguments that support such a position are rooted in liberal values. That is why these values have been so useful, so strong a tool, for feminists. And even the most radical politicos among feminists, those most likely to sneer at every mention of the L-word, grow outraged when they feel their point of view is not being given a fair hearing. For all these reasons, feminism in the academy should abandon its simplistic and debased notion of the "political," its grandiose claims, its know-it-all strictures, and its radical rhetorical flourishes and return to professional practices consistent with the principles of liberal education.

Women's Studies grew out of a political movement. Without that movement, Women's Studies programs probably would not have come into existence at all. But origins and aims are not the same. We live in a culture that holds intellectual and educational work in low esteem. The rhetoric of Women's Studies—the embarrassment some colleagues seem to feel at *not* being political in the approved way— clearly reveals just how *undifferent*, how reflective of the culture at large Women's Studies is. So does the predilection for therapeutic, rather than intellectual, interventions. In too many Women's Studies programs, one does not find a love of learning or a respect for intellectual achievement. But the costs of this uncritical capitulation to the anti-intellectualism of American culture are high indeed.

When insisting that Women's Studies must serve a political or therapeutic purpose, Women's Studies programs are sadly failing to perform what should be one of their vital functions: to act as independent critics of an important political movement that is going on all around us. From this point of view, the statement that Women's Studies is the academic arm of the women's movement, far from being a cause of celebration, actually undermines the great potential utility of Women's Studies as a forum in which criticism and exploration can take place.

But to say this is to resurrect, as we intentionally do, a number of fundamental liberal ideas: tolerance, the cultivation of a distanced and disengaged analysis, and a degree of skepticism toward one's own positions, and not only those of others—traits, in short, that feminists have too often insisted on repudiating because they judged them to be nothing more than fraudulent fronts for academic masculinism. It is ironic, and tragic as well, that feminism, which originally denounced traditional education for its failures to act in accordance with its self-proclaimed precepts of justice, fairness, equality, and dispassionate evaluation, has so enthusiastically trashed the very principles on which its early (and, on the whole, warranted) denunciations rested. As one of the women we interviewed, Anna, the social science professor introduced in chapter 2, put it:

> Liberal is nearly the worst thing you can be. It may be due for a resurrection, but it will probably be some deformed version of liberalism. Certainly I don't know where else people are going to go with their politics but to liberalism. It's not clear to me what else to do with our views than to say: "Well, this needs to all be out in the open, and we need to convince other people of it." And when you start talking like that, that sounds a lot like liberalism.

It is hypocritical, though not altogether surprising, for feminists (especially those most in favor of a politicized program) to join in the derisive dismissal of liberal education now that its utility to them has been exhausted and they are securely entrenched in Women's Studies programs throughout the country. Where they are not in such positions, it is obvious that they must still plead liberal values to make their case. Given the rhetoric prevalent in Women's Studies, however, what is more predictable than that, a little farther down the road, these same petitioners will brand such values, their former allies, as a cowardly failure to challenge the masculine reality?

But this is a self-defeating strategy. Sooner or later, the antiliberal rhetoric will estrange the audience at which it is aimed. As Jeanne, the historian who left Women's Studies, observed:

> I think the university is, now, perhaps the *only* remaining place in society where people can explore ideas and have differences of opinions without consequences for themselves. That is its strength, exactly. And there are few places in society where that is possible. The fact is that at universities we have unusual freedom to say what we believe and to act on that belief. Even junior faculty! To claim otherwise is just crazy.
>
> There are increasing numbers of people—and I'm hearing them, a lot of them are my friends—who are not only critical of these kinds of dogmatic programs, but who are beginning to speak out against them. Whatever courage they needed, whatever critical mass of people needed to develop, I think increasingly there is going to be a critique. And I hear this criticism all over the place.
>
> What that ultimately means, I don't know. I don't think it will mean a return to some prior state, because we have so many people working on women and gender, people who have been influenced by feminist discourse, however they identify themselves. That will not change. That is now institutionalized. But it may be that there will be a rediscovery of disciplines, a reengagement with departments.
>
> You know, all this has been fundamentally destabilizing to my notion of my own politics. I once was a very strong critic of liberalism. I had certain socialist commitments. But now I am much more willing to embrace the label of "liberal" than I ever was in the past. Those liberal values are, to me, in such need of defense, and that's where I find myself at this moment. And I think a lot of us are engaged in a major political shifting, and something will come out of that. People won't be silenced forever on these issues.

Not only women such as Jeanne, however, now find themselves
ready to defend liberal values. Angela, the Marxist and feminist
humanities professor introduced in chapter 8, slowly discovered the
unavoidable conflicts of her political commitments with other values
that she only then recognized she held:

> Academic freedom, for instance, is a liberal value that, I
> thought, was taken for granted, to be defended by other peo-
> ple. I thought it wasn't for me to do. It didn't seem to be any-
> thing I'd have to worry about. But I now think that actually
> preserving the space for academic culture and academic—
> whatever you want to call it—free speech, is a very important
> issue. It seems so banal, but I never thought that so much of
> my institutional thinking and energy would get down to that—
> that sort of very liberal issue.

Because Women's Studies programs have in so many instances
repudiated liberal values and fallen prey to the dangerous amalga-
mation of political, pop-therapeutic, and educational objectives,
they cannot, at this moment, be considered successful. Too many are
in crisis, and the causes of the crisis, as we have argued, lie within
feminism itself, which should never have been embraced in its ideologically inflamed form by institutions of learning. Those students
who seek the single correct path—true believers already or young
people demanding the security of ultimate enlightenment—will have
to go elsewhere. They can join political groups. Nothing prevents
them from becoming activists, even extremists. If feminist seminar-
ies or cadre training camps are to be set up, however, they should be
clearly identified as such. It is not the function of a university to
sponsor them.

When it becomes impossible to decide whose truth, whose politics, whose identity shall prevail in the academy, what will we then
do? Resort to censorship? To arms? Drive people from their jobs?
What will we then have? Models abound: the Aryan university of
Nazi Germany; Stalinism and Maoism; lily-white institutions in the

pre-1960s U.S. South; the purges provoked by McCarthyism; East German universities whose faculties first had to embody Marxist-Leninist truths and were then removed wholesale when that ideology folded; ethnically pure enclaves in the former Yugoslavia. Think about these, and a chamber of horrors opens. We must back away from particular ideologies to see what they all have in common, and that is the tyranny of politicized education by means of indoctrination, and the even more pernicious faith that someone holds the key, knows the truth, has the answers, and is empowered (whether by our will or against it) to impose them on the rest of us.

How can such an arrogation coexist with a genuine call for multiculturalism and diversity? It cannot. Only that weary adjective *liberal*—much maligned and battered but still bravely insisting on tolerance, mutual respect, and an open mind—can lend to education the power to overcome ignorance, prejudice, and hypocrisy.

As long as Women's Studies offers an academic home to the latter traits while distrusting or openly repudiating the former, it will continue to produce students who, like fundamentalists of every stripe, use their small store of fixed ideas to build walls around their tiny enclaves, not realizing that within these walls they themselves must live as prisoners. Women—and men—deserve better.

POSTSCRIPT

IN WRITING THIS BOOK, we found that a tone of irony was often more conducive to our work than one of dejection. But as we approach the end, we cannot avoid expressing the sadness and dismay with which this task has filled us.

Like the other women who walked away, we once shared the great aspirations and hopes that have inspired and sustained Women's Studies programs for over twenty years. We too believed that the lot of women in our society and around the world could be improved through a new kind of teaching and research. No one likes to see dreams turn sour. It is tempting to pretend that something so simple as a renewed faith in sisterhood or a little more patience with one another would set aright the house that feminism has built within the academy. But we are convinced that the task is not so simple and cannot even be broached until the fundamental errors, double standards, false paths, zero-sum games, and pious dead-ends that we have revealed are acknowledged, understood, and repudiated. Until then, stories of pain and disillusionment will continue to emerge.

Just as we were putting the finishing touches to this manuscript, we met a woman in her seventies who told us how, with much anticipation, she had enrolled in a feminist theory class a few years earlier. Straight out of high school she had gone to work in an office and had become involved with union organizing of white-collar women workers like herself. She had been active in women's causes for decades thereafter. The feminist theory course, she thought, would finally place a lifetime of concerns and commitments in a broader perspective. But, though she liked the readings for the course, she found the atmosphere intolerable. After being reduced to tears in one class, she quit attending. In telling us her story, this woman groped for words: "The atmosphere was so . . . so hostile." She did not, however, place the blame for the class's endless divisiveness entirely on the professor. Rather, she said, the professor herself had seemed intimidated by some disruptive women in the class, and had allowed them to take it over and set both the tone and the terms of discussion. "I'm still a feminist," this woman said—as did every one of the other women we spoke with—"but that class can't be what feminism is all about. I went there looking for some answers, and all I found was the same old struggle for power and dominance."

This woman provided us with one more expression of the deep longing many women have to think of themselves as feminists, dedicated to the dramatic overhaul of so many of our society's retrograde attitudes and routine discriminations toward women. She also reveals how natural it is for such women to think that Women's Studies will help them in understanding what has happened historically to women and in thinking clearly about the issues involved. And, finally, she illustrates how amazement and sorrow can replace hope and anticipation once it becomes apparent to them what is really going on in Women's Studies. Such women wonder: Am I crazy? Old-fashioned? Do I still harbor ancient sexist instincts? Am I alone? It is for these women, too, that we have written our book.

To the enemies of all feminist initiatives, the folks who will say, "See, we knew it all along—feminists are a bunch of wild-eyed weirdos," we have this to say: No. You did not read our book carefully. What we are calling attention to are not the deficiencies of the fundamental feminist goals for political and social reform. Nor are we repudiating the study of women's lives or denying the central role of gender in human societies. What we are decrying is the unfortunate path Women's Studies has taken; the attempt to be revolutionary in all respects all at once; the insistence on mixing politics and scholarship in a manner that is detrimental to each; the sacrifice of intellect to emotion; the tendency to turn the very simple basic moral claims of feminism into an esoteric dogma that can be understood only by the indoctrinated and accepted only by the initiated. This is what we are against.

It's all about ends and means. The foes of feminism do not accept the basic goal of the liberation of women from all that impedes their ability to lead full and productive lives. It is the friends of feminism who are best situated to argue about the means for realizing that goal. We are feminists and we are friends of feminism, but we submit that the methods of teaching and research and of self-governance that have become normative in many Women's Studies programs are ill-advised and destructive to women in the long run. That is why we wrote this book.

NOTES

1. Introduction to the
World of Women's Studies

1. Cited in Adena Bargad and Janet Shibley Hyde, "Women's Studies: A Study of Feminist Identity Development in Women," *Psychology of Women Quarterly* 15 (1991): 181.

3. Ideology and Identity:
Playing the Oppression Sweepstakes

1. Adrienne Rich, *On Lies, Secrets, and Silence: Selected Prose 1966–1978* (New York: Norton, 1979), p. 189.

2. Renée R. Anspach, "From Stigma to Identity Politics: Political Activism among the Physically Disabled and Former Mental Patients," *Social Science and Medicine* 13A (1979): 765.

3. Quoted in Allan Hunter, "Missing in Action: Radical Feminism and/or Poststructuralist Feminism in the Academy," unpublished ms., Department of Sociology, SUNY Stony Brook, Summer 1992, p. 13.

4. Ibid., pp. 1–2.

5. Erving Goffman, *Stigma: Notes on the Management of Spoiled Identity* (Englewood Cliffs, N.J.: Prentice-Hall, 1963).

6. Rich's essay was first published in *Signs: Journal of Women in Culture and Society* 5:4 (1980): 631–60. It is reprinted in *Powers of Desire: The Politics of Sexuality*, ed. Ann Snitow, Christine Stansell, and Sharon Thompson (New York: Monthly Review Press, 1983), pp. 177–205.

7. Lillian Faderman, *Odd Girls and Twilight Lovers: A History of Lesbian Life in Twentieth-Century America* (New York: Columbia University Press, 1991), p. 212.

8. Combahee River Collective, "A Black Feminist Statement," reprinted in *Feminist Frameworks: Alternative Theoretical Accounts of the Relations between Women and Men*, 2d ed., ed. Alison M. Jaggar and Paula S. Rothenberg (New York: McGraw-Hill, 1984), p. 204.

9. Alice Walker, *In Search of Our Mothers' Gardens: Womanist Prose* (New York: Harcourt Brace Jovanovich, 1984).

10. On this subject, see Daphne Patai, "Sick and Tired of Scholars' Nouveau Solipsism," *Chronicle of Higher Education,* February 23, 1994, p. A52.

11. In *Mothering: Essays in Feminist Theory*, ed. Joyce Trebilcot (Totowa, N.J.: Rowman & Allanheld, 1983), p. 332.

12. One of us heard her make this statement in public lectures at Indiana University in 1986 and at the University of Massachusetts in 1993.

13. Mario Vargas Llosa, "El intelectual barato," in *Contra viento y marea*, vol. 2 (Barcelona: Seix Barral, 1986), p. 151 (our translation). In this article, written in May 1979, Vargas Llosa affirms that he heard Baldwin say these words, but does not specify where or when. Our thanks to Will Corral of Stanford University for bringing this passage to our attention.

4. Proselytizing and Policing in the Feminist Classroom

1. Aphorism cited in Mary Field Belenky, Blythe McVicker Clinchy, Nancy Rule Goldberger, and Jill Mattuck Tarule, *Women's Ways of Knowing: The Development of Self, Voice and Mind* (New York: Basic Books, 1986), p. 214. See also Nel Noddings, *Caring: A Feminine Approach to Ethics and Moral Education* (Berkeley: University of California Press, 1984).

2. Naomi Littlebear, *Hermanas: Songs Written by Naomi Martinez Littlebear* (Portland, Oregon: printed by Olive Press, distributed by Riverbear Music, 1979).

3. Plato, *Republic*, IV.439.

4. Aristotle, *Nichomachaean Ethics*, IV.5.3.

5. Susan Swartzlander, Diana Pace, and Virginia Lee Stamler, "The Ethics of Requiring Students to Write about Their Personal Lives,"

Chronicle of Higher Education, February 17, 1993, p. B1.

6. See John Eisenberg and Gailand MacQueen, *Don't Teach That!* (Don Mill, Ontario: General Publishing, 1972).

7. Jo Freeman, "How to Discriminate against Women without Really Trying," in *Women: A Feminist Perspective*, ed. Jo Freeman, 2d ed. (Palo Alto, Calif.: Mayfield, 1979), pp. 217–32.

5. Semantic Sorcery: Rhetoric Overtakes Reality

1. Audre Lorde, "The Master's Tools Will Never Dismantle the Master's House," reprinted in *This Bridge Called My Back: Writings by Radical Women of Color*, ed. Cherríe Moraga and Gloria Anzaldúa (Watertown, Mass.: Persephone Press, 1981), pp. 98–101. We are grateful to the Women's Studies E-mail list for the many interesting comments posted about the essay, and especially for the information concerning Frederick Douglass's quite different view of the "master's tools." We note, however, how quickly the comments appreciative of Lorde's phrase degenerated into a reductio ad absurdum, by which it would be impossible for women to use language at all, let alone typewriters and computers.

2. Mary Daly, *Websters' First New Intergalactic Wickedary of the English Language* (Boston: Beacon Press, 1987).

3. Carolyn Merchant, *The Death of Nature: Women, Ecology and the Scientific Revolution* (San Francisco: Harper & Row, 1980). A further appraisal of this view appears in Noretta Koertge, "Methodology, Ideology and Feminist Critiques of Science," in *PSA 1980: Proceedings of the 1980 Biennial Meeting of the Philosophy of Science Association,* vol. 2, ed. Peter Asquith and Ronald Giere (East Lansing, Mich.: Philosophy of Science Association, 1980), pp. 346–59.

4. Wilfrid Sellars, "Scientific Realism or Irenic Instrumentalism," in *Boston Studies in the Philosophy of Science*, vol. 2: *In Honor of Philipp Frank*, ed. Robert S. Cohen and Marx W. Wartofsky (New York: Humanities Press, 1965), p. 172.

5. Adrienne Rich, "Compulsory Heterosexuality and Lesbian Existence," in *Signs: Journal of Women in Culture and Society* 5:4 (1980): 631–60. It is reprinted in *Powers of Desire: The Politics of Sexuality*, ed. Ann Snitow, Christine Stansell, and Sharon Thompson (New York: Monthly Review Press, 1983), pp. 177–205.

6. National Public Radio, "Morning Edition," September 1, 1993.

7. Ibid.

8. See, for example, Andrea Dworkin, *Intercourse* (New York: Free Press, 1987), and Catharine A. MacKinnon, *Feminism Unmodified: Discourses on Life and Law* (Cambridge: Harvard University Press, 1986).

9. See Mary P. Koss, "Hidden Rape, Sexual Aggression and Victimization in a National Sample of Students in Higher Education," in *Rape and Sexual Assault*, vol. 2, ed. Ann Wolbert Burgess (New York: Garland, 1988), p. 16. For critiques of this and other rape surveys, see Neil Gilbert, "Realities and Mythologies of Rape," *Society* (May/June 1992): 4–10; and Del Thiessen and Robert K. Young, "Investigating Sexual Coercion," *Society* (March/April 1994): 60–64.

10. See Adrienne Rich, *The Dream of a Common Language: Poems, 1974–1977* (New York: Norton, 1978); Judy Grahn, *Another Mother Tongue: Gay Words, Gay Worlds* (Boston: Beacon Press, 1984); and Suzette Haden Elgin, *A First Dictionary and Grammar of Láadan* (Madison, Wis.: Society for Furtherance and Study of Fantasy and Science Fiction, 1985).

11. See *Selected Writings of Edward Sapir in Language, Culture and Personality,* ed. David G. Mandelbaum (Berkeley: University of California Press, 1949); Benjamin Lee Whorf, *Language, Thought and Reality,* ed. John B. Carroll (Cambridge: MIT Press, 1956). For a summary of recent assessments of the hypothesis, see Jean Aitchison, "Sapir-Worf Hypothesis," in *The Oxford Companion to the English Language,* ed. Tom McArthur (New York: Oxford University Press, 1992), p. 886.

6. BIODENIAL and Other Subversive Stratagems

1. Joel Best, *Threatened Children: Rhetoric and Concern about Child-Victims* (Chicago: University of Chicago Press, 1990).

2. Michel Foucault, *The History of Sexuality,* vol. 1 (New York: Pantheon, 1978).

3. See Bruno Latour, *The Pasteurization of France* (Cambridge: Harvard University Press, 1988), pp. 84–93; and Ian Hacking, "The Sociology of Knowledge and Child Abuse," *Noûs* 22 (1988): 53–63.

4. See Serena Nanda, *Neither Man nor Woman: The Hijras of India* (Belmont, Calif.: Wadsworth, 1990).

5. Anne Fausto-Sterling, "How Many Sexes Are There?" *New York Times,* March 12, 1993, p. A29(L).

6. Susan McClary, *Feminine Endings: Music, Gender, and Sexuality* (Minneapolis: University of Minnesota Press, 1991).

7. Ibid., p. 4.

8. Ibid., p. 69.

9. Ibid., pp. 128–29.

10. Ibid., p. 69.

11. These examples are taken from, respectively, Irving M. Copi, *Symbolic Logic* (New York: Macmillan, 1954), p. 89; Donald Kalish and Richard Montague, *Logic: Techniques of Formal Reasoning* (New York: Harcourt, Brace & World, 1964), p. 98; and Patrick Suppes, *Introduction to Logic* (Princeton, N.J.: Nostrand, 1957), p. 18. A spirited defense of the importance of logic and reason for feminism is made by Janet Radcliffe Richards in *The Sceptical Feminist: A Philosophical Enquiry* (London: Routledge & Kegan Paul, 1981).

12. Andrea Nye, *Words of Power: A Feminist Reading of the History of Logic* (New York: Routledge, 1990).

13. Ibid., p. 2.

14. Ibid., p. 169.

15. Ibid., p. 171.

16. Katharine Bement Davis, *Factors in the Sex Life of Twenty-two Hundred Women* (New York: Harper & Row, 1929).

7. "Mirror, Mirror on the Wall": Feminist Self-Scrutiny

1. Caryn McTighe Musil, ed., *The Courage to Question: Women's Studies and Student Learning* (Washington, D.C.: Association of American Colleges, 1992); and Musil, ed., *Students at the Center: Feminist Assessment* (Washington, D.C.: Association of American Colleges, 1992).

2. *Students at the Center,* p. 35.

3. Ibid., p. 43.

4. Ibid., pp. 33 (emphasis in original); 35.

5. Ibid., p. 35.

6. Mary Field Belenky, Blythe McVicker Clinchy, Nancy Rule Goldberger, and Jill Mattuck Tarule, *Women's Ways of Knowing: The Development of Self, Voice, and Mind* (New York: Basic Books, 1986). Although this book was slow to gain recognition, it is now a standard feminist text. It began to be cited frequently in 1990. The Arts and Humanities Citation Index lists 29 citations for 1990, 27 for 1991, and

40 for 1992. The Social Science Citations Index provides even more impressive figures, with 88 citations in 1991 and another 88 in 1992. Dozens of reviews also began to appear in 1991.

7. Nel Noddings, *Caring: A Feminine Approach to Ethics and Moral Education* (Berkeley: University of California Press, 1984); Sara Ruddick, *Maternal Thinking: Towards a Politics of Peace* (Boston: Beacon Press, 1989); Carol Gilligan, *In a Different Voice: Psychological Theory and Women's Development* (Cambridge: Harvard University Press, 1982).

8. *Women's Ways of Knowing,* p. ix.

9. Ibid., p. 229.

10. Ibid., pp. 24; 40; 41.

11. Ibid., pp. 55; 52–53; 69; 55.

12. Ibid., pp. 87; 93–94.

13. Ibid., p. 105.

14. Ibid. (emphasis in original).

15. Ibid., pp. 115–17; 118; 118 (emphasis added); 119; 120.

16. Ibid., pp. 114; 116.

17. Ibid., pp. 133 (emphasis in original); 140.

18. Ibid., pp. 141; 143, 146; 152.

19. *Students at the Center,* p. 51.

20. Ibid., p. 8.

21. Ibid., pp. 152; 182.

22. Ibid., p. 101.

23. *The Courage to Question,* p. 165.

24. *Students at the Center,* pp. 98; 92; 94.

25. Ibid., p. 101.

26. *The Courage to Question,* pp. 191; 119.

27. Ibid., pp. 172; 120; 128.

28. See *The Courage to Question,* p. 77, and *Students at the Center,* pp. 88–89.

29. See table entitled "Characteristics of Connected and Separate Knowing" in *Students at the Center,* p. 88.

30. Ibid., p. 89.

31. For a brief discussion of these dichotomies, see Noretta Koertge, "Analysis as a Method of Discovery During the Scientific Revolution," in *Scientific Discovery, Logic, and Rationality*, ed. Thomas Nickles (Dordrecht: D. Reidel, 1980), pp. 139–57.

32. *Students at the Center*, pp. 88–89.

33. *The Courage to Question,* pp. 53; 89.

34. Ibid., p. 1.

35. Ibid., p. 165.

36. Ibid., p. 1.

37. Lynne Goodstein, "When Is a Women's Studies Course a 'Women's Studies' Course?: Issues of 'Quality Control' of Cross-listed Courses," in *Re-Visioning Knowledge and the Curriculum: Feminist Perspectives,* ed. J. R. Ladenson, K. Geissler, L. Fine, and M. Anderson (East Lansing: Michigan State University Press, forthcoming). We appreciate Professor Goodstein's willingness to share this essay with us before its publication. Page numbers refer to the typescript.

38. Ibid., pp. 13; 10.

39. Ibid., pp. 13–15.

40. Ibid., pp. 16–17; 17.

41. Ibid., p. 21.

8. Cults, Communes, and Clicks

1. Our thanks to Kathleen Lowney, associate professor of sociology at Valdosta State University, for her informative comments on cults and sects.

2. Rosabeth Moss Kanter, *Commitment and Community: Communes and Utopias in Sociological Perspective* (Cambridge, Mass.: Harvard University Press, 1972), p. 57. For a trenchant critique of communitarian arguments recently advanced by philosophers and sociologists such as Alasdair MacIntyre, Charles Taylor, and Robert N. Bellah, see Derek L. Phillips, *Looking Backward: A Critical Appraisal of Communitarian Thought* (Princeton: Princeton University Press, 1993).

3. Kanter, *Commitment and Community,* pp. 82–91.

4. Ibid., p. 103.

5. Ibid., p. 222.

6. The following outline is based on a lecture by Audrey Murrell, "The Many Faces of Group Identification," at the University of Massachusetts at Amherst, March 10, 1993. Murrell draws on such work as: William E. Cross, "Negro-to-Black Conversion Experience: Toward a Psychology of Black Liberation," *Black World* 20 (1971): 13–27; William S. Hall, William E. Cross, Jr., and Roy Freedle, "Stages in the Development of Black Awareness: An Exploratory Investigation," in *Black Psychology*, ed. Reginald L. Jones (New York: Harper & Row,

1972), pp. 156–65; and William E. Cross, "The Thomas and Cross Models of Psychological Nigrescence: A Review," *Journal of Black Psychology* 5 (1978): 13–31.

7. Adena Bargad and Janet Shibley Hyde, "Women's Studies: A Study of Feminist Identity Development in Women," *Psychology of Women Quarterly* 15 (1991): 181–201.

8. Ellen Carol DuBois et al., *Feminist Scholarship: Kindling in the Groves of Academe* (Urbana: University of Illinois Press, 1985), p. 202.

9. From Dogma to Dialogue:
The Importance of Liberal Values

1. The Women's Freedom Network is a 1500-member, Washington-based organization of which Rita Simon, a sociologist at American University, is president. Their address is Women's Freedom Network, Suite 179, 4410 Massachusetts Ave. NW, Washington, D.C. 20016.

INDEX

Abortion, 24, 60, 92, 109, 110, 166
Accordion Concepts, 126–31
Achilles, 95
Adam (biblical figure), 131–32
Administrators, 42, 208. *See also* Governance, traditional
Aesthetics, musical, 149–51
Affirmative action, 5, 67, 75–76, 208
African-Americans, 19–21, 23–24, 31–32, 34, 42; and the Combahee River Collective's "Black Feminist Statement," 59–60; and fears of confrontation, 37; and IDPOL, 59–73, 77, 79–80; and language use, 133; and political purity, 19; and scholarly publishing, 61; and "Take Back the Night" marches, 73; and Western political thought, 30; and "white feminism," 59–72; and "womanist" theory, 125. *See also* Racism
AIDS, 58
Alcoholics Anonymous, 77
Amazons, 52–56
"Amazon's Brother: Testimony of a Committed Coed Feminist, The" (Hunter), 52–53
American Association of Women in Psychology, 162
American Philosophical Association, 153
American Sociological Association, 145–146
Anderson, Laurie, 151
Anger, 37, 94–97
ANGERCULT, 95
Another Mother Tongue (Grahn), 132
Anthrax bacillus, 137
Anti-scholarly viewpoints, 198
Anti-science, 191. *See also* Science
Anti-Semitism, 23
Appearance, physical, discussions of, 88
Aristotle, 50, 95, 111, 143, 153; Bacon's attack on, 123–24; theory of reproduction, 148
Armenia, 129
Assessment methods, 158–82; and "connected learning," 161, 168, 170, 172–75; and critical thinking, 175–76; and empowerment, 168, 170, 171, 179–80, 181; and the mission of Women's Studies, 168–71; and modes of knowledge, 161–68, 172–75, 185; and objectivity, 160, 173; and quality control, 177–82; and racism, 160, 169, 171, 175, 179

Association of American Colleges, 159
Atwood, Margaret, 129
Authoritarianism, 22
Author Meets Critics Symposium, 153

"Baby Jessica" custody case, 132
"Backlash," against feminism, *xiii,* 47, 140
Bacon, Francis, 123–24
Baldwin, James, 80
Balkans, 37, 72
Battered-baby problem, 137
Beethoven, Ludwig van, 150–51
Belenky, Mary Field, 161
Belloc, Hillaire, 197
Berdache, 140
Best, Joel, 136, 137
Bible, 5, 96, 131–132
BIODENIAL, 136–57
Biology, 136–57, 155, 174–75. *See also* Science
Birth control, 129
Bisexuality, 58, 59, 73, 87–88
"Black English," 125
"Black Feminist Statement" (Combahee River Collective), 59–60
"Born lesbian," 58
Bourgeois class, 29, 120

Calvinism, 195
Campbell, Norman, 155
Canadian Public Interest Project, 109
Capitalism, 68, 116
Caring: A Feminine Approach to Ethics and Moral Education *(Noddings),* 91
Case study individuals: Angela, 197–206, 214; Anna, 12–15, 17–18, 21–22, 26-30, 40–42, 212; Caroline, 83–85, 89; Jeanne, 12, 16–19, 22–23, 30–32, 36, 38–40,

213–14; Laura, 82, 86–91; Linda, 53–56, 67; Margaret, 12, 15–16, 19–20, 24–25, 32–38, 42–43, 94, 97; Marilyn, 68; Silvia, 57–59, 62–63, 78–79
Catholics, 73, 122, 188
Caucuses, political, based on identity, 60, 209
Child abuse, 92, 95, 104–5, 137
Childbearing, 129, 139, 143
China, 100–101
Chronicle of Higher Education, 104
Class: and assessment methods, 160, 171, 169; bourgeois class, 29, 120; and childbearing, 139; and IDPOL, 68, 76; and language use, 132
"Click" experiences, 96, 193
Clinchy, Blythe McVicker, 161
Clitoridectomies, 77, 95
Combahee River Collective, 59–60
"Coming out," 56
Communes, 183, 190–93
Communism, 30. *See also* Marxism
Community service, 92
"Compensatory education," 147, 167
Competence, 105–8
"Compulsory Heterosexuality and Lesbian Existence" (Rich), 57
Confession, rituals of, 81, 99, 100–104, 191
Connected knowing, 163–64, 165–66, 172–75, 176
Consciousness-raising, 3, 96, 102–3, 195–96
Constructed knowing, 164–66, 173
Constructionism, social, 135–47, 166–67
Conversion experiences, 96–97
Courage to Question (National Women's Studies Association), 159–61, 166, 167, 168–69, 171, 173–76
Creationists, 184
Critical thinking: feminist interpreta-

tion of, 110; feminist style, 175–76
Cross-listing, criteria for, 178–80
Cults, 183, 196
Cultural Revolution, 100–101

Daly, Mary, 77, 122
Darwin, Charles, 117
Davis, Katherine Bement, 154
"Dead white male," 17
Death of Nature, The (Merchant), 122
Debates, 82, 106, 107, 188
Departmental status, 55
Department of Education (United States), 159
Determinism, biological, 143
Dewey, John, 170
Dialectic of Sex, The (Firestone), 13–14
Dichotomies, 154, 155, 179
Dickinson, Emily, 8, 122
Disciplinary standards, 39–40
Disciplines, idea of, 111
Dobkin, Alix, 126–127
Domestic violence, 1, 52, 92, 95
Double standards, 62–63
Douglass, Frederick, 116
Dream of a Common Language, The (Rich), 132
Drug use, 143
Dualism, 154, 155, 172, 179, 193
Duhem, Pierre, 155
Dworkin, Andrea, 129, 130, 208
Dykes, 14, 57, 58, 157. *See also* Lesbianism
Dykewomon, Elana, 96
Dysfunctional family, metaphor of, 31, 45

Ecology, 123
Education: "compensatory," 147, 167; "negative," 185
Edward II (king), 137

Einstein, Albert, 122, 155
Elgin, Suzette Haden, 132
E-mail list, Women's Studies, *xvi,* 79, 96, 98–101, 104–5, 107–9, 111, 117, 125, 128, 130–131
Empathy, 105, 164, 166
Empowerment, 35, 68, 105, 163, 186; and assessment methods, 168, 170, 171, 179–80, 181; and nurturing atmospheres, 110
England, 123, 124
Epistemology, 120, 161, 167; and IDPOL, 51, 60; and social constructionism, 141–42. *See also* Knowledge
Equality, as ideology, 101
Equal Rights Amendment, 116
Essentialism, biological, 144
Ethnicity, 3, 68, 184; and IDPOL, 51, 55–56, 62; and racism, 66–67
Etymology, 121–22
Eurocentrism, 64, 115
Evaluation methods. *See* Assessment methods
Exclusion, problem of, 56, 69–70
Exiles, from feminism, 4, 11–43, 206
Experience, as knowledge, 112

FACT (Feminist Anti-Censorship Taskforce), 208
Factionalization, 188
Fausto-Sterling, Anne, 140
Feminine Endings: Music, Gender, and Sexuality (McClary), 149–51
Feminine Mystique (Friedan), 60
"Feminist process," 22
Firestone, Shulamith, 13–14
Fossey, Dian, 41
Foucault, Michel, 136–137
Freeman, Jo, 112–113
Frege, Gottlob, 153
Freire, Paulo, 100
Freud, Sigmund, 16, 117, 183
Friedan, Betty, 57

Fundamentalism, 183, 188, 215
Fund for the Improvement of Postsecondary Education, 159

Galileo, 124
Game(s), 49–50, 82, 97, 158; Accor-
dion Concepts, 126; "Believing
Games," 172, 173; BIODENIAL,
136–57; IDPOL as a, 52, 80; lan-
guage, 120–34; TOTAL REJ,
115–20, 135, 148; WORD-
MAGIC, 120–21, 135, 148
Gender: calls for an "integrated
analysis" of, 68; and GENDER-
AGENDA, 148-157; and musical
aesthetics, 149–51; and opposition
to exact science, 154–57; and
social constructionism, 138–42.
See also Sexuality
GENDERAGENDA, 148–157
Genesis, book of, 131–32
Genocide, 129
Gilligan, Carol, 40–41, 161, 166
Goals, of feminism, 207
Goethe, Johann Wolfgang von, 148
Goffman, Erving, 56
Goldberger, Nancy Rule, 161
Goodall, Jane, 41
Goodstein, Lynne, 177–82
Governance, traditional, 32–36. *See
also* Administrators
Grading, 111
Grahn, Judy, 132
Grammar, 111, 132
Great Books, 97
Group identity, model of, 193
"Group think," 29
Guilt, 24, 51, 77, 80
Guinier, Lani, 79

Hacking, Ian, 137
Harvey, William, 124

Helplessness, "learned," 107
Hermaphrodites, 140
Hijras, 140
Hippocratic oath, 157
Hispanics, 31, 42, 75
History, study of, 38–40, 73
History of Sexuality (Foucault),
136–137
Hitler, Adolf, 16, 153
Holocaust, 129
Homer, 95
Homophobia, 64, 139
Homosexuality, 76, 136–137; and psy-
choanalysis, 56, 136. *See also* Les-
bianism; Sexual preference
Hooks, Bell, 102
"Horizontal hostility," 46, 97
Hunter, Allan, 52–53
Hunter College, 169
Hygiene, personal, 88

Identity, 3, 56–59, 87–88, 160; and
communes, 191; development
models, 193-97; group, movement
from negative to positive, 193; and
knowledge, nature of, 141–42; politics, use of the term, 50; and social
constructionism, 137. *See also* Ideological policing; IDPOL
Ideological policing, *xii,* 2, 50, 208
Ideology, 10, 81, 184; and assessment
methods, 177, 182; and feminist
discontents, 45–49; and opposition
to quantitative analysis, 157; and
propaganda, 38–43; and religion,
187, 189; use of the term, 48–49.
See also Ideological policing;
IDPOL
IDPOL (identity politics and ideological policing), 50–76, 82, 208; and
creating of new categories of
oppression, 72; and the price of
oppressive privilege, 76–80; and

racism, 59–72; and sexual identity politics, 56–59, 74; and stating one's identity, 74
Imperialism, 68
Incest. *See* Sexual abuse
India, 140
Indoctrination, reverse, 82
"Inner flight," *xiv*
Integrated analysis, 68
"Intellectual Stalinism," 157
Internships, 7, 92

Jealousy, professional, 28
Jesuits, 195
Johnson, Samuel, 120
Journals, misuse of, 102
Judaism, 23, 73. *See also* Holocaust

Kanter, Rosabeth Moss, 191–92
Kidnapping, 136
Kimball, Roger, 26
Kinsey reports, 154
Knowledge: affirmation of students' "experience" as, 112; Aristotle's theory of, 123–24; and assessment methods, 161–68, 172–75; connected, 163–64, 165–66, 172–75, 176; constructed, 164–66, 173; "procedural," 163–66; "received," 162, 164; separate, 163–64, 165; and social constructionism, 141–42; subjective, 162–63, 164; and TOTAL REJ, 116–20; women's modes of, 161–68, 185. *See also* Epistemology
Korenman, Joan, *xvi*
Ku Klux Klan, 131

Language: enforcement of the rules of, 111; English as a second, 75; games, 49, 120–34; and Linguistic

Litmus Tests, 124-26; and Metaphor Madness, 122–24, 126; nonsexist, 125–26; and Phony Philology, 121–22, 126; and the power of naming, 131–34; preserving the "purity" of, 46; and the Sapir-Whorf hypothesis, 133–34
Latin America, 66–67
Latina women, 66–67
Latour, Bruno, 137
"Lavender Jane Loves Women" (record album), 126–127
Learning, "connected," 161, 168, 170, 172–75
Lesbianism, 15–16, 47; and IDPOL, 56–59, 60, 72–73, 74; and a lesbian continuum, concept of, 57, 58, 127, 129; and music, 126–27; and racism, 60; and views of nature, 123. *See also* Dykes; Sexual preference
"Leveling," effort at, 35, 192
Levi, Don, 153
Lewis and Clark College, 172, 174
Liberal education, *xv*, 25, 207–15
Life, philosophy of, concept of, 48–49
Litmus tests, linguistic, 124–26
Littlebear, Naomi, 94
Lobbyists, 50, 75
Logic, 152–55, 156–57, 172–73. *See also* Objectivity; Rationality
Lorde, Audre, 116–17
Lying, 46

McCarthyism, 215
McClary, Susan, 149–51
McClintock, Barbara, 108, 155
MacKinnon, Catharine, 127, 129, 130, 208
Male chivalry, 98
"Male-identified" individuals, 51, 89, 106–7
Male students, 86–87, 104–5, 128

Mantra, of race, class, gender, and so on, 68
Maoism, 214
Marx, Karl, 117, 132. *See also* Marxism
Marxism, 7, 13, 29–30, 48, 119, 183, 197, 214, 215. *See also* Marx, Karl
Masson, Jeffrey, 127
"Master's tools," 116
Maternalism, 22
"Maternal thinking," 166
Men: blaming, habit of, 89–90; male students, 86–87, 104–5, 128
Merchant, Carolyn, 122
Merrill, Daniel, 153
Metaphor Madness, 122–24
Michigan Women's Music Festival, 72
Middle Ages, 123
Middleway House, 131
Misogyny, 150, 151, 211
Modern Language Association, 122
Monty Python, 83
Morality, 2, 26, 46, 95, 166; and identity politics, 50–51, 67, 76, 80; and "negative education," 185; and racism, 67; and TOTAL REJ, 117
Morgan, Robin, 128–129
Morning sickness, 143
Moss, Cynthia, 41
Mothers, resentment against, 46
Motivational malnutrition, 113
Murrell, Audrey, 193
Music, 72, 126–27, 149–52
Musil, Caryn, 160

Naming, power of, 131–34
Nationalism, 37, 68
National Organization for Women, 57, 145
National Public Radio, 127
National Women's Studies Association. *See* NWSA (National Women's Studies Association)

Native Americans, 67, 75, 140
Nature, 123–24; vs. nurture debates, 138, 144
Nazism, 214. *See also* Hitler, Adolf; Holocaust
Near-sightedness, 142
"Negative education," 185
New Organon *(Bacon),* 122
New York Times, 125, 140
Noddings, Nel, 91, 161, 166
NOW (National Organization for Women), 57, 145
NWSA (National Women's Studies Association), 8, 12, 23–24, 60, 142, 210; constitution of, 4; *The Courage to Question,* 159–61, 166, 167, 168–69, 171, 173–76; *Students at the Center,* 159–61, 168, 169–70, 173, 176
Nye, Andrea, 152–54

Oakgrove, Artemis, 96
Oberlin College, 169, 171, 175
Objectivity, 105, 111, 116, 149; and assessment methods, 160, 166, 173
Ontario Institute for Studies in Education, 108–9
Oppression, 50–51, 185; and demanding special privileges, 76–80; positive response to, 78; "sweepstakes," 44. *See also* Patriarchy; Sexism
Other, concept of, 37, 68, 180

Pappus, 172
Parthenogenesis, 140, 144
Pasteur, Louis, 137
Patriarchy, 4, 45–46, 48, 184, 185; and assessment methods, 178, 179; and childbirth, 139; effort to transform, and male students, 53; and feminist conversion experiences,

97; and feminist pedagogy, 97, 111–16, 129, 133; hetero-, 57, 68; and "horizontal hostility," 46; and a "humanistic feminism," 210; and IDPOL, 53, 57, 68, 72–76, 78; and language use, 133; and lesbian separatism, 16; and logic, 154; and musical aesthetics, 150, 151; and opposition to exact science, 156; and political purity, 19; and rape, 129; and social constructionism, 141–142, 143; and TOTAL REJ, 115–16; and traditional academic practices, 111–12

Patrons, of scientific research, 131
Pennsylvania State University, 177–82
Phallocentrism, 68
Philology, 121–22, 126
Plato, 95
Pluralism, 47
Political correctness, 2, 18–19, 94, 171
"Political lesbians," 58
Pornography, 23, 24, 208
Postmodernism, 47, 78, 119
Practicums, 7, 92–93
Pregnancy, 139, 143
Procedural knowing, 163–66
Progressive education movements, 170, 197
Propaganda, 38–43, 97–100, 145, 175, 208
Prostitution, 95
Protestants, 188
Psychoanalysis, 26, 36, 47, 183; French versions of, 119; and homosexuality, 56, 136. *See also* Freud, Sigmund; Psychotherapy, methods of
Psychotherapy, methods of, 99, 101, 105–8. *See also* Psychoanalysis
Public and private, boundaries between, 112
Publishing, scholarly, and racism, 61
Puritans, 54

Quakers, 188
Quality control, 177–82

Racism, 3, 31–32, 99, 102, 139, 184; and assessment methods, 160, 169, 171, 175, 179; and feminist pedagogy, 103–4, 125, 131; and IDPOL, 55–56, 77–80; and language use, 131; and scholarly publishing, 61; "structural," 63, 68; and student "resistance," 99; and "white feminism," 59–72; and "womanist" theory, 125. *See also* African-Americans
Rape, 1, 24, 52, 60, 80; and feminist pedagogy, 84, 92, 95, 98, 110, 123, 126, 129–31; and heterosexual intercourse, association of, 129, 144; and language use, 127–31; legal definition of, 129–30; and views of nature, 123
Rationality, 105, 111, 149. *See also* Logic; Reasoning abilities
Reasoning abilities, 154–55, 166, 167. *See also* Knowledge; Logic; Rationality
Relativity theory, 122
Religion, 186–90; and critical thinking, 176; and feminist conversion experiences, 96–97; and homosexuality, 56; and identity development, 195; and IDPOL, 55–56; and original sin, doctrine of, 183–84; and separatism, 190. *See also* Bible; Calvinism; Catholics; Jesuits; Judaism; Protestants
Reproductive rights, 92, 129. *See also* Abortion
Resistance, "student," 97–101
Respect, lack of, 37–38, 71
Responsibility, 80, 85
Rich, Adrienne, 46, 57, 58, 127, 132
Rossi, Alice, 145–147, 157

Royal Society, 122
Ruddick, Sara, 161, 166

SAF (Society for Analytic Feminism),
    209
Sapir-Whorf hypothesis, 133–34
Sappho, 136
Saul (biblical figure), 96
Schliemann, Heinrich, 140
Schubert, Franz, 150–51
Science, 92, 117, 122–24; exact, oppo-
    sition to, 154–57. *See also* Biology;
    Logic
Scrabble, 129
Sellars, Wilfrid, 126
Separate knowing, 163–64, 165
Separatism, 5–6, 9, 15–16; and the gay
    male liberation movement, 56–57;
    and IDPOL, 54–57, 68, 72–73;
    and religious movements, 190; and
    social constructionism, 141
Sexism, 5, 150–51, 210; and assess-
    ment methods, 160, 175, 179; and
    biology, 139, 140; and the "click"
    phenomenon, 193; and IDPOL,
    52, 77; and language use, 125–26,
    131; and male students, 52;
    "reverse," 83, 88
Sexual abuse, 92, 95, 104–5
Sexual assaults. *See* Rape; Sexual
    abuse
Sexual harassment, 78, 80, 92, 129,
    130
Sexuality, 3, 56–59, 68, 169; Davis's
    1926 study of, 154; and social con-
    structionism, 136–47. *See also*
    Gender; Homosexuality; Lesbian-
    ism; Sexual preference
Sexual preference: declaring, 56, 87;
    and IDPOL, 55–56. *See also* Homo-
    sexuality; Lesbianism; Sexuality
Shakespeare, William, 91
Signs, 161

Silence, 11, 38, 77, 162
Sin, original, 183–84
Sisterhood, 20, 44, 45
Slavery, 116
Smith, Adam, 16
Social constructionism, 135–47,
    166–67
Social identity theory, 193
Socialism, 47. *See also* Marxism
Social sorting, 46
Sontag, Susan, 62
Splitting, concept of, 37–38
Stalinism, 157, 214
State University of New York at Stony
    Brook, 53
Stein, Gertrude, 137
Stepford Wives, 22
Stereotypes, 3, 120, 140, 152, 154–55
"Stigmatized identity," 56
Students at the Center (National
    Women's Studies Association),
    159–61, 168, 169–70, 173, 176
Substance abuse, 143
Suicide, 45
Support groups, 107–8
Surveillance, 177–181, 191, 198, 205
Survivor, use of the term, 130
SWIP (Society for Women in Philos-
    ophy), 209
Syndrome, use of the term, 137

Tailhook scandal, 131
"Take Back the Night" marches,
    72–73
Tarule, Jill Mattuck, 161
"Therapeutic classrooms," *xiv,* 104,
    107
Threatened Children (Best), 136
Thumos, concept of, 95
Tolerance, absence of, 54–55, 187,
    188, 212
"Totalizing tendencies," 180, 183
TOTAL REJ, 115–20, 135, 148

Transsexuals, 144
Tribal strategies, 46, 72
Truth, 80, 163, 166, 215
Twelve-step programs, *xiv*

Unitarians, 188
University administrators. *See* Administrators; Governance, traditional
University of Chicago, 112
University of Maryland, 126, 127
University of Missouri–Columbia, 169
University of Pittsburgh, 193
Utopianism, 144, 191–92

Vanderwelde, Janika, 151
Victims: of feminism rhetoric, 126; and "negative education," 185; rape, 127–28, 130; representation of women as, 84–85
Victorian era, 46, 120
Vidal, Gore, 76
Voice, finding one's, *xiv,* 11, 108, 163, 170

Walker, Alice, 68–71
Wars, complicity of women in, 145
Wellesley College, 170, 171

"When Is a Women's Studies Course a 'Women's Studies' Course?" (Goodstein), 177–82
Whewell, William, 140
White-skin privilege, 67, 70
White women, "complicity of," 69–70
Wickedary (Daly), 122
Wilde, Oscar, 137
Winnicott, D. W., 46
Wittgenstein, Ludwig, 48
Wittig, Monique, 37
"Womanist" theory, 47, 68, 125
"Women and Honor: Some Notes on Lying" (Rich), 46
"Women-identified women," 57
Women's Freedom Network, 209
Women's Ways of Knowing (Belenky, Clinchy, Goldberger, and Tarule), 107, 161–67, 173
WORDMAGIC, 120–21, 135, 148
Words of Power: A Feminist Reading of the History of Logic (Nye), 152–54
Worldviews, 48, 131, 135, 183

Xenophobia, 142–43

Yugoslavia, 72, 215